Excel

YEAR 12

Mathematics Standard 2 Revision & Exam Workbook

ESSENTIAL skills

Get the Results You Want!

Allyn Jones & AS Kalra

PASCAL PRESS

Updated for HSC syllabus changes 2022

ISBN 978 1 74125 686 4

Pascal Press
PO Box 250
Glebe NSW 2037
(02) 8585 4050
www.pascalpress.com.au

Publisher: Vivienne Joannou
Project editor: Rosemary Peers
Edited by Rosemary Peers
Answers checked by Peter Little
Additional material written by Jim Stamell and Chelsea Smithies
Page design and typesetting by Replika Press, Precision Typesetting (Barbara Nilsson), DiZign Pty Ltd and lj Design (Julianne Billington)
Printed by Vivar Printing/Green Giant Press

Students
All care has been taken in the preparation of this study guide, but please check with your teacher or the NSW Education Standards Authority about the exact requirements of the course you are studying as these can change from year to year.

Contents

Chapter 7—Measurement: Rates and ratio

Chapter 8—Statistical analysis: Bivariate data analysis

Chapter 9—Statistical analysis: The normal distribution

Chapter 10—Networks: Introduction to networks

Chapter 11—Networks: Critical path analysis

Chapter 12—Sample HSC Examinations

Answers

Introduction

This workbook has been written for the Year 12 Mathematics Standard 2 course.

For students to successfully complete this course they must undertake assessment tasks in each year of Stage 6 and sit for the HSC Examination—this workbook will support them in the revision for the course.

This workbook, combined with the *Excel Year 11 Mathematics Standard Revision & Exam Workbook*, will provide an excellent resource for students to use to maximise their marks in the HSC Examination.

Features of this book include:

- **graded exercises** that follow the topics of the syllabus—students can practise the skills they need to complete the course
- **space for students to write their answers** in a workbook format—there should be sufficient space to answer each question, setting out clearly and working down each page
- **answers at the back of the book** to check students' work
- **timed topic tests at the end of each chapter** that have been designed to completely cover the content of each topic and to test the understanding of all skills needed, with HSC-styled questions and marks allocated for every question
- **page references to the *Excel Year 12 Mathematics Standard 2* study guide**—students can refer to the guide if they need help with any of the work
- **three HSC-style Sample Examinations**. The HSC Mathematics Standard 2 Examination consists of topics studied throughout Stage 6. This means the majority of questions will be based on Year 12 topics but some questions will be on topics students have studied in Year 11.

Remember

The best way to study Mathematics is by working through examples.

Using this workbook for revision will allow you to have all the questions, working and answers together in one book.

You can write notes in the margins and have a complete personalised review book.

You can also use this book as a diagnostic tool to quickly assess areas of concern and determine any weaknesses in your revision.

Any student who has worked through all these questions and understands the content should feel confident of doing well in the Year 12 Mathematics Standard 2 course.

Some useful hints for the HSC Examination

Know what to expect

- Find out from your teacher exactly what topics will be assessed in the examination.
- Determine what format is being used for the exam. Are there multiple-choice questions?

Show all working

- Read the instructions on the examination paper—marks may be allocated for working.
- Even when marks are not allocated, working is important and it is rewarded, even though your answer may be incorrect.
- Never use correction fluid—just put a line through any incorrect working. Let the examiner see all your work.

Allocate your time

- Ensure you are working through the paper efficiently and not spending too much time on each question, only to find you have run out of time at the end of the exam.

Understand mark allocations

- The questions worth the most marks are often the most complex and difficult. Showing working is crucial for these types of questions.

Re-read and check

- Once you have completed the question, rather than moving to the next, re-read that question to make sure you have in fact answered the correct question. This will only take a second or two.
- If you finish the examination with time still remaining, check your answers—often mistakes are found and can be corrected.

Use quality diagrams

- Diagrams should be of good quality, large and drawn with a lead pencil. Use an eraser for deleting mistakes, not correction fluid.

Be ready

- Finally, you need to be prepared for the examination.
- Always study Mathematics actively. Active study means using pen and paper to make notes, writing down difficult questions and their solutions, and recording rules to learn.

Excel ESSENTIAL SKILLS Year 12 Mathematics Standard 2 Revision & Exam Workbook

NSW Education Standards Authority

2020 | **HIGHER SCHOOL CERTIFICATE EXAMINATION**

Mathematics Standard 1
Mathematics Standard 2

REFERENCE SHEET

Measurement

Limits of accuracy

Absolute error $= \dfrac{1}{2} \times$ precision

Upper bound = measurement + absolute error

Lower bound = measurement − absolute error

Length

$$l = \dfrac{\theta}{360} \times 2\pi r$$

Area

$$A = \dfrac{\theta}{360} \times \pi r^2$$

$$A = \dfrac{h}{2}(a + b)$$

$$A \approx \dfrac{h}{2}\left(d_f + d_l\right)$$

Surface area

$$A = 2\pi r^2 + 2\pi rh$$

$$A = 4\pi r^2$$

Volume

$$V = \dfrac{1}{3}Ah$$

$$V = \dfrac{4}{3}\pi r^3$$

Trigonometry

$$\sin A = \dfrac{\text{opp}}{\text{hyp}}, \quad \cos A = \dfrac{\text{adj}}{\text{hyp}}, \quad \tan A = \dfrac{\text{opp}}{\text{adj}}$$

$$A = \dfrac{1}{2}ab \sin C$$

$$\dfrac{a}{\sin A} = \dfrac{b}{\sin B} = \dfrac{c}{\sin C}$$

$$c^2 = a^2 + b^2 - 2ab \cos C$$

$$\cos C = \dfrac{a^2 + b^2 - c^2}{2ab}$$

Financial Mathematics

$$FV = PV(1 + r)^n$$

Straight-line method of depreciation

$$S = V_0 - Dn$$

Declining-balance method of depreciation

$$S = V_0(1 - r)^n$$

Statistical Analysis

An outlier is a score

  less than $Q_1 - 1.5 \times IQR$
  or
  more than $Q_3 + 1.5 \times IQR$

$$z = \dfrac{x - \mu}{\sigma}$$

Normal distribution

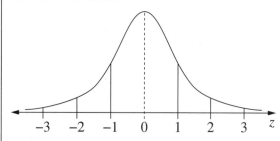

- approximately 68% of scores have z-scores between −1 and 1
- approximately 95% of scores have z-scores between −2 and 2
- approximately 99.7% of scores have z-scores between −3 and 3

CHAPTER **1**
Financial mathematics: Investments

Excel MATHEMATICS STANDARD 2
Ch. 4, p. 97

Interest rates

QUESTION **1**   An interest rate of 6% p.a. is what rate:

a monthly?

b quarterly?

c six-monthly?

d four-monthly?

QUESTION **2**   Find the monthly interest rate if the annual rate is:

a 9%

b 7.5%

QUESTION **3**   Find the quarterly interest rate if the annual rate is:

a 8%

b 5%

QUESTION **4**   Find the number of:

a months in 5 years

b quarters in 3 years

c six-monthly periods in 8 years

d four-monthly periods in 2 years

QUESTION **5**   Interest on an investment is to be paid quarterly. If the principal is invested for 4 years and the annual interest rate is 9% find:

a the number of quarters

b the quarterly interest rate

QUESTION **6**   Find the annual interest rate when it is:

a 2.5% per quarter

b 0.9% per month

c 6.5% per six-monthly period

d 0.046% per day

Financial mathematics: Investments

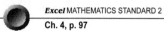
Simple interest 1

QUESTION **1**   Find the simple interest for each of the following:

a $4500 at 8% p.a. for 2 years

b $8000 at 7% p.a. for 6 years

c $20 000 at 9% p.a. for 8 years

d $5900 at 12% p.a. for 6 months

e $20 500 at $7\frac{1}{2}$% p.a. for 3 months

f $36 000 at 10.25% p.a. for 4 years

g $65 000 for 5 years at 6.5% p.a.

h $82 000 for 2 years at 8.25% p.a.

QUESTION **2** $3000 is invested at 5% p.a. simple interest for 4 years. Find:

a the total amount of interest earned

b the total value of the investment at the end of the 4 years

QUESTION **3**   Find the length of time for:

a $500 to be the interest on $1800 at 6% p.a.

b $850 to be the interest on $2400 at 8% p.a.

QUESTION **4**   Find the rate per cent per annum for:

a $1500 to be the interest on $5400 for 5 years

b $900 to be the interest on $2700 for 2 years

Financial mathematics: Investments

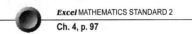

Simple interest 2

QUESTION **1**   Find the principal required for the simple interest to be:

a $900 on an amount invested for 2 years
at 10% p.a.

_____

_____

_____

b $250 on an amount invested for 1 year
at 9% p.a.

_____

_____

_____

QUESTION **2**

a   Complete the table to show the amount of simple interest earned (I) if $500 is invested for n years at each of the given rates.

	n	0	1	2	3	4	5	6	7	8	9	10
4% p.a.	I											
7% p.a.	I											
9% p.a.	I											

b   Draw the graph of I against n for each of the above interest rates.

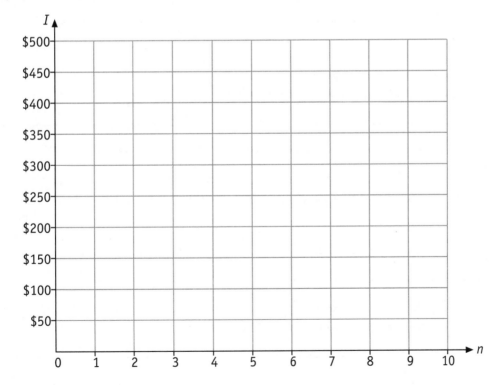

Financial mathematics: Investments

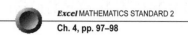
Compound interest

QUESTION **1** $8000 is invested for 5 years at 6.5% p.a. interest, compounded annually. Find:

a the future value

b the compound interest earned

QUESTION **2**   Find the amount of compound interest earned from the following investments:

a $6000 at 9% p.a. for 4 years, compounded annually

b $18 000 at 14% p.a. for 2 years, compounded 6-monthly

c $48 000 at 10% p.a., compounded quarterly for 5 years

d $32 000 for 3 years at 7.25% p.a., compounded monthly

e $120 000 for 25 years at 4% p.a. interest, compounded monthly

f $3650 for 5 years at 6.5% p.a., compounded quarterly

Financial mathematics: Investments

Excel MATHEMATICS STANDARD 2
Ch. 4, p. 98

Future value 1

QUESTION **1**   Find *FV* when:

a PV = $4000, r = 6%, n = 3

b PV = $9500, r = 2%, n = 24

QUESTION **2**   Find the future value if the following amounts are invested for the given time at the given interest rate, compounded annually:

a $5000 at 8% p.a. for 2 years

b $8500 at $9\frac{1}{2}$% p.a. for 5 years

c $15 000 at 10% p.a. for 3 years

d $6000 at 8% p.a. for 12 years

QUESTION **3**   Find the final balance if the given amount is invested for the given number of years at the given interest rate, compounded monthly:

a $4000 at 12% p.a. for 3 years

b $18 000 at 9% p.a. for 6 years

Financial mathematics: Investments

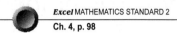

Future value 2

QUESTION **1**   Find the future value if:

a $6000 is invested for 4 years at 8% p.a., compounded quarterly

_____

_____

_____

_____

b $2500 is invested for 3 years at 10% p.a., compounded six-monthly

_____

_____

_____

_____

c $20 000 is invested for 5 years at 7.5% p.a., compounded monthly

_____

_____

_____

_____

d $32 000 is invested for 7 years at 9% p.a., compounded quarterly

_____

_____

_____

_____

QUESTION **2**   Mia's grandparents deposited $10 000 into a savings account when she was born. The interest rate was fixed at 6% per annum compounded monthly. Calculate the future value of the investment if Mia withdraws all the money on her:

a 21st birthday

b 32nd birthday, as a deposit for her home

Financial mathematics: Investments

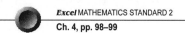

Present value

QUESTION **1**   Find the present value to the nearest dollar if:

a future value is $3345.56 with an interest rate of 6% p.a., compounded annually for 5 years

_____

_____

_____

b future value is $8531.14 with an interest rate of 4.8% p.a., compounded monthly for 6 years

_____

_____

_____

c future value is $18 223.59 with an interest rate of 4.2% p.a., compounded quarterly for 10 years

_____

_____

_____

QUESTION **2**   What sum of money would need to be invested to be worth $5000 at the end of 7 years at the given interest rate?

a 6% p.a., compounded annually   **b** 8% p.a., compounded quarterly

_____   _____

_____   _____

_____   _____

_____   _____

_____   _____

QUESTION **3**   What will be their initial deposits if Bill and Ben each want to withdraw $20 000 from their own savings account in 8 years if:

a Bill's account pays interest of 5.4% p.a., compounded quarterly?

_____

_____

_____

b Ben's account pays compound interest of 5.4% p.a., compounded monthly?

_____

_____

_____

Financial mathematics: Investments

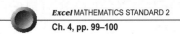

Tables of future values

QUESTION **1**   The table shows the future value of $1 if invested at the given interest rate for the given number of periods, interest compounded per period.

	Interest rate per period							
Period	**1%**	**2%**	**2.5%**	**4%**	**5%**	**6%**	**10%**	**12%**
1	1.0100	1.0200	1.0250	1.0400	1.0500	1.0600	1.1000	1.1200
2	1.0201	1.0404	1.0506	1.0816	1.1025	1.1236	1.2100	1.2544
3	1.0303	1.0612	1.0769	1.1249	1.1576	1.1910	1.3310	1.4049
4	1.0406	1.0824	1.1038	1.1699	1.2155	1.2625	1.4641	1.5735
5	1.0510	1.1041	1.1314	1.2167	1.2763	1.3382	1.6105	1.7623
6	1.0615	1.1262	1.1597	1.2653	1.3401	1.4185	1.7716	1.9738
7	1.0721	1.1487	1.1887	1.3159	1.4071	1.5036	1.9487	2.2107
8	1.0829	1.1717	1.2184	1.3686	1.4775	1.5938	2.1436	2.4760

Use the table to find the future value of:

a $2000 invested for 7 years at 5% p.a., compounded annually

_____

_____

b $5500 invested for 2 years at 10% p.a., compounded quarterly

_____

_____

c $14 400 invested for 3 years at 12% p.a., compounded six-monthly

_____

_____

d $9750 invested for 5 months at 12% p.a., compounded monthly

_____

_____

QUESTION **2**   Use the above table to find the amount of money which could be invested now to give:

a $10 000 at the end of 8 years, at 4% p.a. interest, compounded annually

_____

_____

_____

b $15 000 at the end of 18 months, at 8% p.a. interest, compounded quarterly

_____

_____

Financial mathematics: Investments

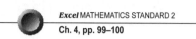

Graphs of future values

QUESTION **1**   The graph shows the future value of $1000 if invested at 18% p.a., compounded monthly. Use this graph to answer the following questions.

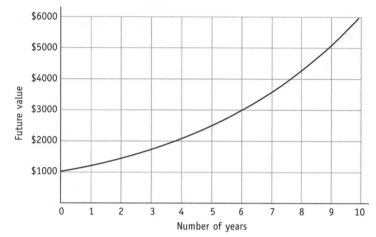

a What is the approximate value of the investment after 3 years? _____

b After approximately how many years is the value $5000? _____

c If $600 was invested at 18% p.a., compounded monthly, what would be its approximate value after 4 years?

_____

_____

d Give a brief description of what will happen to the future value over the next few years.

_____

_____

_____

QUESTION **2** $1000 is invested at 18% p.a., compounded six-monthly.

a Briefly explain why the future value, A, after n six-monthly periods, will be given by $A = 1000(1.09)^n$.

_____

_____

b Complete the table of values giving A to the nearest whole number.

n	2	4	6	8	10	12	14	16	18	20
A										

c Draw another graph on the axes in Question 1 to show the future value of this investment.

d Briefly comment on the expected difference between the two investments over the next few years.

_____

_____

_____

Financial mathematics: Investments

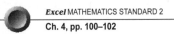
Modelling future value and present value

QUESTION **1**   Carmen uses a spreadsheet to predict the future value of investments at different interest rates and number of years and compounded at different intervals.

Calculation of *FV* given various interest rates/periods/compounding intervals					
Present value (*PV*):		$10000.00	$20000.00	$20000.00	$20000.00
Interest rate p.a.:		3.00	3.00	6.00	6.00
No. of years:		8	8	8	16
Future value (*FV*) compounded	annually:	$12667.70	$25335.40	$31876.96	$50807.03
	quarterly:	*A*	$25402.22	$32206.49	$51862.89
	monthly:	$12708.68	$25417.37	$32282.85	$52109.13
	fortnightly:	$12710.73	$25421.47	$32303.62	$52176.19
	weekly:	$12711.61	$25423.22	*B*	$52205.03

a What is the difference between investing $20 000 for 8 years at 3% p.a., compounded quarterly and compounded monthly?

_____

b What is the value in the following cells?

i *A*?

ii *B*?

_____   _____

c What is the amount of interest earned on an investment of $20000 invested for:

i 8 years at 3% p.a., compounded quarterly?   **ii** 16 years at 6% p.a., compounded fortnightly?

_____   _____

QUESTION **2**   The spreadsheet is used to show the amounts to be invested (present value) that provide various amounts (future value) of investments at different interest rates and number of years and compounded at different intervals.

Calculation of *PV* given various interest rates/periods/compounding intervals					
Future value (*FV*):		$50000.00	$100000.00	$250000.00	*D*
Interest rate p.a.:		6.00	8.00	10.00	12.00
No. of years:		8	15	20	35
Present value (*PV*) compounded	annually:	*A*	$31524.17	$37160.91	$5681.86
	quarterly:	$31049.65	*B*	$34676.14	$4785.31
	monthly:	$30976.20	$30239.61	*C*	$4593.51

a What amount will need to be invested by Joseph in a savings account today offering 10% p.a. interest, compounded quarterly, if he wants $250000 available to his grandson in 20 years?

_____

b What is the value in the following cells?

i *A*   **ii** *B*   **iii** *C*   **iv** *D*

_____   _____   _____   _____

_____   _____   _____   _____

Financial mathematics: Investments

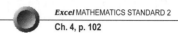

Appreciation and inflation

QUESTION **1**   A house appreciates at 4.5% per annum. If it costs $350 000 now, what will it be worth in 3 years time?

_____

_____

QUESTION **2**   The price of a car now is $38 000. If the inflation rate is 2.75% p.a., what would you expect to pay for the car in 2 years time?

_____

_____

QUESTION **3**   The current price of a table is $650. Calculate its price 5 years ago, if the inflation rate during this time was 2.25% p.a.

_____

_____

QUESTION **4**   A block of land increased in value this year from $460 000 to $520 880. What is the rate of appreciation?

_____

_____

_____

QUESTION **5**   What was the price of a home unit 12 years ago, if its current value is $380 000 and it has appreciated at 5% p.a.?

_____

_____

_____

QUESTION **6**   The cost of a television is $6500. If the average inflation rate is 3%, what will be the price of the television in 3 years?

_____

_____

_____

QUESTION **7**   For the following, calculate the cost of the item after one year.

a   a lawnmower costing $750 with an inflation rate of 2.5% p.a.

_____   _____

_____   _____

b   a bottle of milk costing $2.40 with inflation at 6% p.a.

_____   _____

_____   _____

Financial mathematics: Investments

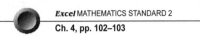

Shares 1

QUESTION **1**

a Amy wishes to buy 7000 shares in an oil company. The market price of the shares is $4.38 each. Calculate the total cost of the shares.

b Amy has to pay various fees. The stockbroker charges a basic order fee of $10 plus a commission of 1.5% of the cost of the shares. Find the total fee the stockbroker will charge.

c The State Government levies stamp duty on the cost of the shares. The rate is 30 cents per $100 or part thereof. Calculate the stamp duty on the shares.

QUESTION **2**   A company has an after-tax profit of $73.2 million. There are 120 million shares in the company. What dividend per share will the company declare if all the profits are distributed to the shareholders?

QUESTION **3**   Sandra bought 12 000 shares at $5.00 each. The face value of the shares was $3.75.

a Stamp duty is charged at 60 cents for every $100 of the price of the shares. How much does Sandra pay in stamp duty?

b Sandra also paid a brokerage fee of 4.5 cents per share. What is the total cost of the shares Sandra bought?

c A few weeks later a dividend of 17.5 cents per share was paid. What was the total dividend Sandra received?

QUESTION **4**   A company's prospectus predicts that the dividend yield for the next year will be 8.9%. Its share price is $24.50. Calculate the dividend per share if the dividend yield in the prospectus is paid.

Financial mathematics: Investments

Shares 2

QUESTION 1   Find the dividend yield when the:

a dividend per share is $0.23 and the price is $4.60   **b** dividend per share is $1.32 and the price is $24

_____   _____

_____   _____

QUESTION 2   A company with a share price of $6.80 declares a dividend of 36 cents. Calculate the dividend yield correct to two decimal places.

_____

_____

_____

QUESTION 3   An after-tax profit of $969 500 is to be distributed. If the company has 387 800 shares issued:

a what dividend per share will be paid?

_____

_____

b what is the dividend yield if the market price of the share is $50?

_____

_____

QUESTION 4   A company pays a dividend of 19 cents per share. The dividend yield was 4%. What was the market price of the shares?

_____

_____

_____

QUESTION 5   The graph shows the performance of certain shares over 6 months.

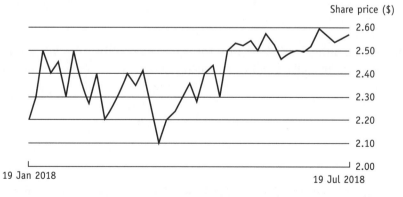

Briefly comment on the expected future price movement.

_____

_____

_____

Financial mathematics: Investments

TOPIC TEST

Instructions
- This section consists of 5 multiple-choice questions.
- Each question is worth 1 mark.
- Fill in only ONE CIRCLE for each question.

Time allowed: 7 minutes   **Total marks: 5**

1 Tyrone invests $3200 for a term of 15 months. Simple interest is paid at a flat rate of 4.25% p.a. How much will Tyrone's investment be worth at the end of the term?

Ⓐ $3370

Ⓑ $3376.80

Ⓒ $3404

Ⓓ $4170

2 Florence invests $16 000 at an interest rate of 3.6% p.a., compounded monthly. What is the future value of the investment after 2 years?

Ⓐ $16 115.41

Ⓑ $17 048.69

Ⓒ $17 172.74

Ⓓ $17 192.63

3 Which of these shares has the best dividend yield?

Ⓐ share price = $4.20, dividend per share = $0.28

Ⓑ share price = $13.90, dividend per share = $0.85

Ⓒ share price = $63.80, dividend per share = $4.09

Ⓓ share price = $147.20, dividend per share = $8.53

4 Over a 5-year period the annual inflation rate for a basket of groceries was an average of 2.6%. If the price of the groceries was initially $230, how much has the price increased at the end of the 5 years?

Ⓐ $30.45

Ⓑ $31.20

Ⓒ $31.50

Ⓓ $32.70

5 Neil has $10 000 to invest with each of two different financial institutions for a period of 5 years. One institution offers 4.8% p.a., while another 5.4% p.a., both compounded monthly. What is the difference between the two future values of the investments?

Ⓐ $300

Ⓑ $348.20

Ⓒ $385.31

Ⓓ $1867.92

Instructions • This section consists of 6 questions.
         • Show all working.

Time allowed: 53 minutes   **Total marks: 35**

6

	Compounded values of $1					
	Interest rate per period					
Period	**0.50%**	**1.00%**	**2.00%**	**5.00%**	**10.00%**	**12.00%**
1	1.005	1.010	1.020	1.050	1.100	1.120
2	1.010	1.020	1.040	1.103	1.210	1.254
3	1.015	1.030	1.061	1.158	1.331	1.405
4	1.020	1.041	1.082	1.216	1.464	1.574
5	1.025	1.051	1.104	1.276	1.611	1.762
6	1.030	1.062	1.126	1.340	1.772	1.974
7	1.036	1.072	1.149	1.407	1.949	2.211
8	1.041	1.083	1.172	1.477	2.144	2.476
9	1.046	1.094	1.195	1.551	2.358	2.773
10	1.051	1.105	1.219	1.629	2.594	3.106
11	1.056	1.116	1.243	1.710	2.853	3.479
12	1.062	1.127	1.268	1.796	3.138	3.896

a Use the table of compounded values of $1 to find the value of an investment of:

  i $5000, compounded annually at 5% per annum over 7 years   **1 mark**

_____

_____

  ii $3400, compounded monthly at 0.5% per month over 1 year   **1 mark**

_____

_____

b Use the table to find the amount of interest earned on an investment of:

  i $12 000, compounded annually at 10% per annum over 8 years   **2 marks**

_____

_____

_____

  ii $9600, compounded monthly at 6% per annum over 10 months   **2 marks**

_____

_____

_____

7 Find the future value, to the nearest cent, of an investment of:

a $16 000 over 7 years at 4% per annum, compounded annually   **2 marks**

_____

_____

b $24 000 over 5 years at 6% per annum, compounded monthly   **2 marks**

_____

_____

c $8000 over 4 years at 8% per annum, compounded quarterly   **2 marks**

_____

_____

d $11 400 over 3 years at 9% per annum, compounded monthly   **2 marks**

_____

_____

_____

8 Find the present value, to the nearest cent, of an investment worth:

a $6000 over 12 years at 5% per annum, compounded annually   **2 marks**

_____

_____

b $15 000 over 20 years at 4% per annum, compounded quarterly   **2 marks**

_____

_____

c $9500 over 10 years at 6% per annum, compounded monthly   **2 marks**

_____

_____

d $32 000 over 25 years at 4.8% per annum, compounded monthly   **2 marks**

_____

_____

9 Theo's father invested $5000 in a savings account when his son was born. The interest rate was fixed at 4% per annum, compounded annually. Calculate the future value, to the nearest dollar, of the investment if Theo withdraws his money on his:

a 18th birthday to buy a car   **2 marks**

_____

_____

_____

_____

b 65th birthday to help with his retirement   **2 marks**

_____

_____

_____

_____

10 A financial institution guarantees 6% per annum interest, compounded monthly, on any investment for any number of years. What sum of money, to the nearest dollar, will have to be invested today to accumulate an amount of:

a $120 000 after 15 years?   **2 marks**

_____

_____

_____

_____

b $500 000 after 30 years?   **2 marks**

_____

_____

_____

_____

11 Tomislav bought 5000 shares in a company.

a Find the total cost of the shares if the price was $6.80 per share, stamp duty was charged at 60 cents per $100 and brokerage fees were 2.5% of the value of the shares.   **2 marks**

_____

_____

_____

_____

b A month after Tomislav bought the shares, dividends were paid. The dividend yield was 4.5% and the market price was $7.20 per share. Find the total dividend Tomislav received.   **1 mark**

_____

_____

_____

_____

c Tomislav sold all his shares two months later. He received $6.75 per share after costs. Did he make a profit or loss? Justify your answer.   **2 marks**

_____

_____

_____

_____

CHAPTER 2

Financial mathematics: Depreciation and loans

Excel MATHEMATICS STANDARD 2
Ch. 4, pp. 103–107

Declining-balance depreciation 1

QUESTION **1**   Convert the following percentages to decimals:

a   22% = _____   b   16.5% = _____   c $18\frac{3}{4}$% = _____

QUESTION **2**   Convert the following decimals to percentages:

a   0.15 = _____   b   0.235 = _____   c   0.098 = _____

QUESTION **3**   Use the declining-balance method of depreciation to calculate the following.

a   Benedict buys a car for $28 500. It depreciates at the rate of 20% p.a. What is the value of the car after:

   i   2 years?   ii   5 years?

b   Majeda purchased her car 6 years ago and it is now worth $12 600. Given it is depreciating at 12% p.a., what was the value of the car when she bought it? _____

c   Geoff bought a van for $37 800, 4 years ago. It is now worth $19 500. What annual rate of depreciation did he use? _____

d   Ming's vehicle is depreciating at 15% p.a. It was bought for $45 000 and is now worth $14 400. How long ago did she buy it? _____

QUESTION **4**   Complete the following table showing the declining-balance depreciation of a vehicle purchased for $30 000 and depreciating at an annual rate of 12% p.a. (Round all depreciated values to the nearest dollar.)

Year	Net book value ($)	Depreciation ($)	Final value ($)
1	30 000	0.12 × 30 000 = 3600	30 000 − 3600 = 26 400
2	26 400		
3			
4			
5			
6			
7			
8			

a   What do you notice about the depreciation amount from year to year? _____

b   How is this different from the depreciation amount using the straight-line method? _____

Financial mathematics: Depreciation and loans

Declining-balance depreciation 2

QUESTION **1**   The graph shows the declining-balance depreciation for a vehicle over a given period.

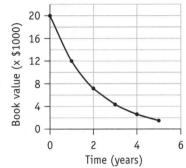

Depreciation of a vehicle

a   What was the initial cost of the vehicle? _____

b   By how much had the vehicle depreciated in the first year? _____

c   Using the graph, and the declining-balance formula, calculate the annual rate of depreciation, r, as a percentage.

_____

_____

d   Use the formula to calculate the salvage value of the vehicle after 6 years.

_____

_____

e   Compare your calculated value to the one obtained by extrapolating (extending) the graph.

_____

_____

QUESTION **2**   Bella and her brother Ryan each buy a car in the same year. The car Bella buys is depreciating at a rate of 23% p.a. while the one Ryan buys is depreciating at a rate of 18% p.a. Use the graph showing the value of their respective cars over the next 5 years to answer the following questions.

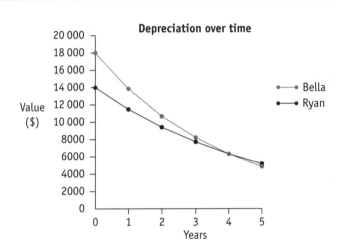

Depreciation over time

a   How much did Bella pay for her car? _____

b   How much did Ryan pay for his car? _____

c   After how many years is the value of each of their cars approximately equal? _____

_____

d   In the long run, Ryan's car was the better purchase because it is worth more than Bella's car. Is this statement correct? Justify your answer.

_____

_____

_____

Financial mathematics: Depreciation and loans

Loans involving flat-rate interest 1

QUESTION **1**   James wanted to buy a car and approached a bank for a personal loan of $20 000. The manager approved the loan at an 8% p.a. flat rate of interest. He has to repay the loan in 5 years.

a What interest will James pay during that period?

_____

_____

_____

b What will be his monthly repayment?

_____

_____

_____

QUESTION **2**   John bought a TV marked at $3000. He paid 20% deposit and the balance over 3 years, with interest charged at a flat rate of 15% on the balance.

a Find the deposit paid.

_____

_____

_____

b Calculate the balance owing.

_____

_____

_____

c Calculate the interest paid.

_____

_____

_____

d Find the total amount that was repaid on the loan.

_____

_____

_____

e What was the monthly repayment?

_____

_____

_____

QUESTION **3**   Chris wants to buy a boat and takes out a loan of $10 000 on which the interest rate charged is 9.5% flat. There is also a loan protection fee of 30 cents for each $100 borrowed. The loan is to be repaid over 5 years in equal monthly instalments.

a Calculate the total amount which will be repaid.

_____

_____

_____

_____

b Find the amount of each monthly repayment.

_____

_____

_____

_____

Financial mathematics: Depreciation and loans

Loans involving flat-rate interest 2

QUESTION **1**   Lachlan borrowed $12 900 at 15% p.a. simple interest for 5 years so that he could furnish his home unit. At the end of 5 years both the interest and the principal had been repaid.

a Calculate the amount of interest charged. _____

_____

_____

b How much did he pay back altogether? _____

_____

_____

c If Lachlan repaid the loan in equal monthly instalments, how much was each instalment?

_____

_____

_____

QUESTION **2**   Nana borrows $150 000 at a flat rate of 10.5% p.a. The rate is fixed for 5 years. She is to pay back the interest only during this period.

a How much interest is to be paid in the 5 years? _____

_____

_____

b After paying the fixed rate of interest for 4 years, Nana finds that the bank will drop her interest rate to 6.25% if she pays a penalty of $1600. How much will she save by changing to the lower interest rate for the last year?

_____

_____

_____

_____

QUESTION **3**   Alex takes a loan of $10 000 over 48 months. The repayment rate is $262.50 per month.

a How much will Alex pay back altogether? _____

_____

_____

b What is the flat interest rate for the loan? _____

_____

_____

_____

_____

Loans involving reducible interest 1

QUESTION **1** Kate's bank agrees to lend her $300 000 towards the purchase of an apartment. The interest rate for the loan is 6.5% p.a. monthly reducible and Kate will repay the loan in monthly instalments of $1860 over 30 years. A table shows the amount ($P + I - R$) Kate still owes on the loan after repayments.

Month	Principal (P)	Interest (I)	$P + I$	$P + I - R$
1	$300 000.00	$1625.00	$301 625.00	$299 765.00
2	$299 765.00	$1623.73	$301 388.73	$299 528.73
3	$299 528.73	$1622.45	$301 151.17	$299 291.17
4	$299 291.17	$1621.16	$300 912.33	$299 052.33
5	*A*	*B*	*C*	*D*
6	*D*	$1618.57	$300 430.77	$298 570.77

a How much does Kate still owe on the loan after 6 months? _____

b What are the values of:

  i *A*? _____   **ii** *B*? _____

  iii *C*? _____   **iv** *D*? _____

c After 6 months:

  i how much has Kate paid in repayments?   **ii** by what amount has the principal been reduced?

_____   _____

QUESTION **2** Mia takes out a loan of $20 000 and is charged a reducible interest rate of 3.2% p.a. At the end of each month she is charged interest and then she makes a repayment of $1500. Mia uses a spreadsheet to calculate the balance owing after each monthly repayment.

a What is the balance owing after the first repayment? _____

b Calculate the values in the following cells:

  i *E* _____

  ii *F* _____

  iii *G* _____

c What is the total interest charged by the financial institution in the first 3 months?

_____

d What is the meaning of the negative numbers in the last two rows of the spreadsheet?

_____

e How much does Mia actually pay as her final repayment? _____

Loan table			
	Amount:	$20 000	
	Annual interest rate:	3.20%	
	Monthly repayment:	$1500	
n	Principal (P)	Interest (I)	$P + I$	$P + I - R$
1	$20 000.00	$53.33	$20 053.33	$18 553.33
2	$18 553.33	$49.48	$18 602.81	*E*
3	$17 102.81	$45.61	$17 148.42	$15 648.42
4	$15 648.42	$41.73	$15 690.15	$14 190.15
5	$14 190.15	$37.84	$14 227.99	$12 727.99
6	$12 727.99	$33.94	$12 761.93	$11 261.93
7	$11 261.93	$30.03	$11 291.96	$9791.96
8	$9791.96	*F*	$9818.07	$8318.07
9	$8318.07	$22.18	$8340.25	$6840.25
10	$6840.25	$18.24	$6858.49	$5358.49
11	$5358.49	$14.29	*G*	$3872.78
12	$3872.78	$10.33	$3883.11	$2383.11
13	$2383.11	$6.35	$2389.46	$889.46
14	$889.46	$2.37	$891.83	−$608.17
15	−$608.17	−$1.62	−$609.79	−$2109.79

Financial mathematics: Depreciation and loans

Loans involving reducible interest 2

QUESTION **1** The table below shows the monthly repayments per $1000 on a bank loan for various annual interest rates.

Term	5.5%	6.0%	6.5%	7.0%	7.5%	8.0%
20 years	$6.8684	$7.1643	$7.4581	$7.7506	$8.0560	$8.3669
30 years	$5.6754	$5.9955	$6.3233	$6.6503	$6.9921	$7.3404

a Calculate the monthly repayment on the following loans, to the nearest cent:

i $260 000 at 6.5% p.a. for 20 years _____

ii $312 000 at 8.0% p.a. for 20 years _____

iii $435 000 at 5.5% p.a. for 30 years _____

b To the nearest dollar, what is the total amount of interest paid over the period of the loan of:

i $385 000 for 20 years at 6.0% p.a.?   **ii** $482 500 for 30 years at 7.5% p.a.?

c What is the interest rate on a loan of:

i $270 000 over 20 years if the monthly repayment is $2175.12? _____

ii $340 000 over 30 years if the monthly repayment is $1929.64? _____

d Andrew is borrowing $327 000 for 30 years at 7.5% p.a. Find:

i his monthly repayment _____

ii the total of his repayments _____

iii the amount of interest he pays _____

e Last year Ava was given a loan of $245 000 to be paid off over 20 years at a fixed interest rate of 6.5% p.a. Now, her brother Simon wants to borrow the same amount over 20 years but the interest rate has been increased by 1.5% p.a. By how much will Simon's monthly repayment be more than his sister's repayment?

QUESTION **2** Alessandro intends to borrow $460 000 over 30 years at a reducible interest rate of 6.5%. Use the table in question 1 for the following calculations.

a What will be his monthly repayment? _____

b Find the amount of interest Alessandro will have to pay, to the nearest dollar? _____

c If the monthly repayment increased by $307.65 per month, what is the new interest rate on the loan?

Financial mathematics: Depreciation and loans

Excel MATHEMATICS STANDARD 2
Ch. 4, pp. 108–114

Loans involving reducible interest 3

QUESTION **1**   Todd borrows $400 000 from a bank at 6% p.a. reducible interest for 30 years. He makes monthly repayments of $2398. The graph represented as **Scenario 1** shows the balance owing throughout the life of the loan.

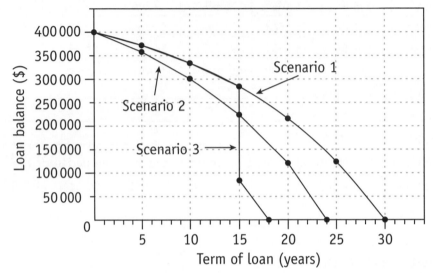

a How much money is still owed on the loan after 15 years? Estimate to the nearest $10 000.

_____

b After how many years will half the loan be repaid? _____

c Calculate the total:

  i repayments _____   **ii** amount of interest _____

QUESTION **2**   Suppose instead, Todd was to make fortnightly repayments of $1199. The balance owing throughout this loan is shown on the graph above as **Scenario 2**.

a Approximately how many years earlier will the loan be paid? Give your answer to the nearest year.

_____

_____

b Calculate, to the nearest $10 000, the new total:

  i repayments   **ii** amount of interest

  _____   _____

QUESTION **3**   Assuming Todd chooses the monthly payment but after 15 years uses an inheritance to pay off some of the balance of his loan as a lump sum. This is shown on the graph as **Scenario 3**.

a Estimate the lump sum amount. _____

b If he pays the loan out after 18 years:

  i find the total amount paid by Todd _____

  ii what is the amount of interest saved by Todd between Scenario 3 and Scenario 1?

_____

_____

Financial mathematics: Depreciation and loans

Credit cards 1

QUESTION **1**   The credit card statement is used to answer the questions below.

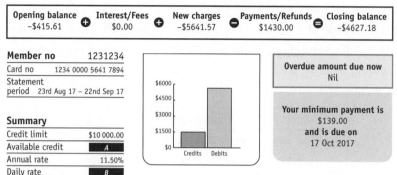

| Opening balance −$415.61 | ⊕ | Interest/Fees $0.00 | ⊕ | New charges −$5641.57 | ⊖ | Payments/Refunds $1430.00 | ⊜ | Closing balance −$4627.18 |

Member no   1231234

Card no   1234 0000 5641 7894

Statement period   23rd Aug 17 – 22nd Sep 17

Summary

Credit limit	$10 000.00
Available credit	*A*
Annual rate	11.50%
Daily rate	*B*

Overdue amount due now
Nil

Your minimum payment is
$139.00
and is due on
17 Oct 2017

a What is the credit limit on the card?_____

b Find the values of the:

   i available credit, *A* _____

   ii daily interest rate, *B*. Answer correct to five decimal places _____

c What percentage of the closing balance is the minimum payment, correct to one decimal place?

_____

QUESTION **2**   Heidi used her credit card to pay her electricity bill valued at $960 on 7 November. She made no other purchases on her credit card account in November. She paid the account in full on 3 December. The credit card has no interest-free period. Compound interest is charged at the rate of 18% per annum, including the date of purchase and the date the account is paid.

a What is the daily interest rate, correct to six decimal places? _____

b For how many days will Heidi be charged interest?

_____

c What is the total amount owed?

d What is the total amount of interest paid?

QUESTION **3**   Jack uses a credit card which has no interest-free period and a compound interest rate of 13.2% p.a. from the day of purchase. His credit-card payment is due on the 28th of each month. During May, Jack made the following purchases.

Date	Retailer	Amount
7 May	Supermarket 1	$186.70
15 May	Supermarket 2	$216.80
21 May	Supermarket 3	$187.20
24 May	Supermarket 4	$104.90

a What is the daily interest rate, correct to five decimal places?

_____

b How much interest will Jack pay on the transaction from:

   i Supermarket 2?

   ii Supermarket 4?

c What is the total amount due on 28 May? _____

d Rather than having to pay the total amount, the credit card company allows cardholders to only pay a 'Minimum Payment' which is set at 4% of the balance owing. If Jack only pays the minimum amount how much will Jack still owe on the card?

_____

Financial mathematics: Depreciation and loans

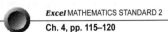

Credit cards 2

QUESTION **1** A credit card company has the following conditions. There is no charge if the account is paid in full by the due date.

- An initial charge of 2.25% on any outstanding balance beyond the due date must be paid.
- An additional continuing charge of 0.075 75% compound interest per day accrues on the outstanding balance until it is paid in full.

Shown is a copy of Amy's monthly statement.

Date	Transaction	$
	Opening balance	0.00
6.8.18	M Cotton & Co.	42.95
7.8.18	J Electronics	57.60
8.8.18	Recent Fashions	235.65
25.8.18	The Corner	80.20
	Closing balance	

a Calculate the closing balance.

_____

_____

_____

b Calculate the interest charged if Amy repays $200 by the due date and the remainder 18 days later, to the nearest dollar.

_____

_____

QUESTION **2** Steve and Linda each use their credit cards to buy holiday packages to Singapore. The cost of each package is $1900.

a The charge on Steve's credit card is 1.5% interest per month on the unpaid balance. Steve pays $900 after one month and another $900 after the next month. After his second payment, how much does he still owe for his holiday?

_____

_____

_____

b Linda's credit card company charges no interest in the first month and 2% interest per month on the unpaid balance from then on. She pays $900 after one month and another $900 after the next month. How much does she still owe for her holiday after this second payment?

_____

_____

_____

TOPIC TEST

SECTION I

Instructions
- This section consists of 5 multiple-choice questions.
- Each question is worth 1 mark.
- Fill in only ONE CIRCLE for each question.

Time allowed: 7 minutes

Total marks: 5

1 A car is purchased for $26990. It will depreciate at the rate of 16% per annum. Using the declining-balance method, which of these is closest to the salvage value of the car after 4 years?

Ⓐ $4528

Ⓑ $13438

Ⓒ $13552

Ⓓ $21879

2 A car is purchased but over time its value drops. Which graph best represents the salvage value of the car using the declining-balance method of depreciation over 12 years?

 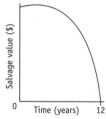

 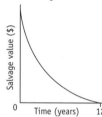

 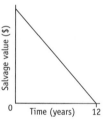

Ⓓ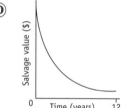

3 Leila used her credit card to purchase a washing machine for $1250 on 18 April. Simple interest is charged at a rate of 16.2% p.a. for purchases on her credit card. There were no other purchases on the credit card account and there was no interest-free period. The period for which interest is charged includes the date of purchase and the date of payment. The account was paid in full on 3 May. Which of these is closest to the amount paid?

Ⓐ $1258.19

Ⓑ $1258.22

Ⓒ $1258.88

Ⓓ $1452.50

4 The price of a new car is $41250. Rod buys this car on terms of 20% deposit and monthly repayments of $910 over 4 years. How much more does Rod pay by buying the car on terms?

Ⓐ $2430   Ⓑ $8250   Ⓒ $9208   Ⓓ $10680

5 Ingrid borrows $18000 to buy a boat and is charged 8% p.a. flat-rate interest over 10 years. Which of these will be her monthly repayment?

Ⓐ $260   Ⓑ $270   Ⓒ $280   Ⓓ $290

TOPIC TEST

SECTION II

Instructions • This section consists of 4 questions.
• Show all working.

Time allowed: 53 minutes

Total marks: 35

6 A spreadsheet is used to present key features of a credit card statement.

Credit card statement						
Credit limit:	$10 000.00			**Date of issue:**	**12/08/19**	
Opening balance:	$1435.00					
Statement duration				Payment summary		
From date:	10/07/19			Due date:	24/08/19	
To date:	10/08/19			Balance owing:	$2305.38	
Total number of days:	32			Minimum monthly payment:		
Transaction details				Remaining credit available:	$7694.62	
Date	Description	Amount	Balance			
29/07/19	Purchase – POS	$125.00	$1560.00	**Interest rates***	**Annual**	**Daily**
1/08/19	Purchase – POS	$340.00	$1900.00	**Purchases:**	**19.99%**	**0.054 767%**
4/08/19	Cash advance	$400.00	**A**	**Cash advances:**	**21.49%**	**B**
	Total interest	$5.38	$2305.38	*** Flat interest rates apply**		
Total interest charges				**This credit card has no interest-free period.**		
	Purchases:					
	Cash advances:					
	Total:	**$5.38**				

a What is the value in:

  i cell **A**?   1 mark

  _____

  ii cell **B**? Give the answer correct to six decimal places.   1 mark

  _____

b Calculate the interest charged on the two purchases.   2 marks

  _____

  _____

  _____

c What is the amount of credit available for the following month?   1 mark

  _____

d The minimum monthly payment is calculated as 1% of the balance owing plus the total interest charged. Calculate the minimum monthly payment.   3 marks

  _____

  _____

  _____

7 Mike takes out a loan of $35 000 and is charged a reducible interest rate of 3.3% p.a. At the end of each month he is charged interest and then makes a repayment of $2140. Mike uses a spreadsheet to calculate the balance owing after each monthly repayment.

Loan table				
	Amount:	$35 000.00		
	Annual interest rate:	3.30%		
	Monthly repayment:	$2140.00		
n	Principal (*P*)	Interest (*I*)	*P* + *I*	*P* + *I* − *R*
1	$35 000.00	$96.25		*A*
2	*A*	$90.63	$33 046.88	$30 906.88
3	$30 906.88	$84.99	$30 991.87	$28 851.87
4	$28 851.87	$79.34	$28 931.22	$26 791.22
5	$26 791.22	$73.68	$26 864.89	$24 724.89
6	$24 724.89	$67.99	$24 792.89	$22 652.89
7	$22 652.89	$62.30	$22 715.18	$20 575.18
8	$20 575.18	*B*		
9	$18 491.76	$50.85	$18 542.62	$16 402.62
10	$16 402.62	$45.11	$16 447.72	$14 307.72
11	$14 307.72	$39.35	$14 347.07	$12 207.07
12	$12 207.07	$33.57	$12 240.64	$10 100.64
13	$10 100.64	$27.78	$10 128.41	$7988.41
14	$7988.41	$21.97	$8010.38	$5870.38
15	$5870.38	$16.14	$5886.53	$3746.53
16	$3746.53	$10.30	$3756.83	$1616.83
17	$1616.83	$4.45		−$518.72

a Calculate the values in the following cells:

i *A*   **1 mark**

_____

ii *B*   **1 mark**

_____

b Calculate the total interest charged by the financial institution in the first 4 months, writing your answer to the nearest dollar.   **2 marks**

_____

_____

c What is the meaning of the negative number in the last row of the spreadsheet?   **2 marks**

_____

_____

d How much does Mike actually pay as his final repayment?   **1 mark**

_____

8 The table below shows the monthly repayments per $1000 on a bank loan for various annual interest rates.

Term (years)	Monthly repayments per $1000							
	Interest rate (%)							
	4.5	5	5.5	6	6.5	7	7.5	8
20	$6.326	$6.600	$6.879	$7.164	$7.456	$7.753	$8.056	$8.364
25	$5.558	$5.846	$6.141	$6.443	$6.752	$7.068	$7.390	$7.718
30	$5.067	$5.368	$5.678	$5.996	$6.321	$6.653	$6.992	$7.338

a Calculate the monthly repayment, to the nearest cent, on a loan of $310000 at 7% p.a. for 25 years. **2 marks**

_____

b What is the interest rate on a loan of $360000 over 20 years if the monthly repayment is $2476.44? **2 marks**

_____

c Nigel borrows a sum of money and his monthly repayments over 25 years are $2278.78. If he is paying interest of 4.5% p.a., what is the amount Nigel has borrowed? **2 marks**

_____

d Olaf is borrowing $340000 for 30 years at 6.5% p.a. Find the total amount of monthly repayments made over the life of the loan. **2 marks**

_____

e To the nearest dollar, what is the total amount of interest paid using monthly repayments over the period of the loan of $400000 for 20 years at 7.5% p.a.? **3 marks**

_____

_____

f Pedro intends to borrow $460000 over 30 years at a reducible interest rate of 5.5%. How much interest would be saved if his loan had been taken over 20 years at the same interest rate? **3 marks**

_____

_____

g Many years ago Thor borrowed $280000 for a term of 30 years at an interest rate of 5% p.a. Today, Thor still owes $200000 and decides to repay the balance with a new loan from a different financial institution which offers Thor 6% p.a. interest for 20 years. What is the difference in the two monthly repayments? **3 marks**

_____

_____

9 For the first 5 years after Cecile's purchase of a new car for $42500, the annual rate of depreciation is 18%. For the following 5 years the rate is 12%.

Using the declining-balance method of depreciation, what is the value of Cecile's car after:

a 3 years? _____ **1 mark**

b 10 years? _____ **2 marks**

_____

CHAPTER **3**
Financial mathematics: Annuities

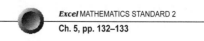

Excel MATHEMATICS STANDARD 2
Ch. 5, pp. 132–133

Annuities

QUESTION **1**   **a** Find the final balance if $600 is invested into an account earning 5% p.a. interest, compounded annually, for:

i 1 year

_____

_____

ii 2 years

_____

_____

iii 3 years

_____

_____

iv 4 years

_____

_____

b If four separate amounts of $600 had been invested at 5% p.a. interest, compounded annually, over 4 years so that one amount earned interest for 1 year, one earned interest for 2 years, one for 3 years and one for 4 years, find:

i the total of all these investments

_____

_____

ii how much interest is earned in total

_____

_____

QUESTION **2**   Kurt invests $100 at the end of each month into an account earning 0.75% per month compound interest. At the end of 6 months, just after the last investment has been made, Kurt suddenly finds he needs the money and withdraws the whole amount.

a How much money does Kurt invest altogether?

_____

b Briefly explain why the last amount invested earns no interest.

_____

_____

c For how many months does the first amount earn interest?

_____

_____

d Find the final value of the first amount invested.

_____

_____

e Explain why the total value of the investment is given by
$[100(1.0075)^5 + 100(1.0075)^4 + 100(1.0075)^3 + 100(1.0075)^2 + 100(1.0075) + 100]$.

_____

_____

f Find the amount Kurt withdrew.

_____

_____

Financial mathematics: Annuities

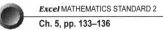

Using a table of future-value interest factors of annuities

QUESTION **1**   The following table shows the future values of an ordinary annuity of $1.

Interest rate per period								
Period	1%	2%	3%	4%	5%	6%	7%	8%
1	1.0000	1.0000	1.0000	1.0000	1.0000	1.0000	1.0000	1.0000
2	2.0100	2.0200	2.0300	2.0400	2.0500	2.0600	2.0700	2.0800
3	3.0301	3.0604	3.0909	3.1216	3.1525	3.1836	3.2149	3.2464
4	4.0604	4.1216	4.1836	4.2465	4.3101	4.3746	4.4399	4.5061
5	5.1010	5.2040	5.3091	5.4163	5.5256	5.6371	5.7507	5.8666
6	6.1520	6.3081	6.4684	6.6330	6.8019	6.9753	7.1533	7.3359
7	7.2135	7.4343	7.6625	7.8983	8.1420	8.3938	8.6540	8.9228
8	8.2857	8.5830	8.8923	9.2142	9.5491	9.8975	10.260	10.637

Use the table to find the future value of an annuity of:

a $5000 per year at 7% p.a. for 6 years

_____

_____

b $400 per quarter at 3% per quarter for 2 years

_____

_____

c $250 per month at 2% per month for 5 months

_____

_____

d $3000 every 6 months at 8% p.a. interest compounded half-yearly for 4 years

_____

_____

QUESTION **2**   Sonia wants to take a holiday in 6 months time and needs $8000. She has been advised to deposit $1250 each month into an account earning 12% p.a. interest, compounded monthly. Use the above table to answer the following questions.

a Will Sonia have enough money for the trip? _____

_____

b By how much will she fall short or overshoot her goal?

_____

_____

c What amount do you suggest she should deposit each month into that account?

_____

_____

Financial mathematics: Annuities

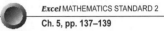
Excel MATHEMATICS STANDARD 2
Ch. 5, pp. 137–139

Using a table of present-value interest factors of annuities

QUESTION **1**   The following table shows the present values of an ordinary annuity of $1.

	Interest rate per period							
Period	**1%**	**2%**	**3%**	**4%**	**5%**	**6%**	**7%**	**8%**
1	0.9901	0.9804	0.9709	0.9615	0.9524	0.9434	0.9346	0.9259
2	1.9704	1.9416	1.9135	1.8861	1.8594	1.8334	1.8080	1.7833
3	2.9410	2.8839	2.8286	2.7751	2.7233	2.6730	2.6243	2.5771
4	3.9020	3.8077	3.7171	3.6299	3.5460	3.4651	3.3872	3.3121
5	4.8534	4.7135	4.5797	4.4518	4.3295	4.2124	4.1002	3.9927
6	5.7955	5.6014	5.4172	5.2421	5.0757	4.9173	4.7665	4.6229
7	6.7282	6.4720	6.2303	6.0021	5.7864	5.5824	5.3893	5.2064
8	7.6517	7.3255	7.0197	6.7327	6.4632	6.2098	5.9713	5.7466

Use the table to find the present value of an annuity of:

a $4000 per year at 5% p.a. for 7 years

_____

_____

b $750 per quarter at 1% per quarter interest for $1\frac{1}{2}$ years

_____

_____

_____

c $1400 per month at 12% p.a., compounded monthly, for 4 months

_____

_____

QUESTION **2**   Use the above table to find what sum of money invested today at 7% p.a. for 8 years would give the same result as an annuity of $3750 invested at the same rate.

_____

_____

_____

QUESTION **3** $60 000 is borrowed over 5 years at 8% p.a. compound interest.

a Use the table (above) to find the amount of each yearly instalment.

_____

_____

b What is the total interest paid?

_____

_____

_____

Financial mathematics: Annuities

Formulae for the future and present values of an annuity

QUESTION **1**   The values in a table of future-value interest factors can be obtained using the formula for the future value of an annuity, $FVA = a\left\{\dfrac{(1 + r)^n - 1}{r}\right\}$ where FVA is the future value, a is the contribution per period, r is the rate as a decimal and n is the number of time periods.

a Using the formula above, complete the missing values in this table:

Future value of $1					
Interest rate per period					
Period	3%	4%	5%	6%	10%
1	1.0000		1.0000	1.0000	
2	2.0300	2.0400		2.0600	
3		3.1216		3.1836	3.3100
4	4.1836		4.3101		4.6410
5	5.3091	5.4163	5.5256		6.1051
10		12.0061		13.1808	
20	26.8704		33.0660		57.2750

b Use the table to calculate the future value of an annuity where $a = 300$, $r = 5\%$ and $n = 4$. Give your answer correct to two decimal places.

QUESTION **2**   The values in a table of present-value interest factors can be obtained using the formula for the present value of an annuity, $PVA = a\left\{\dfrac{(1 + r)^n - 1}{r(1 + r)^n}\right\}$ where PVA is the present value, a is the contribution per period, r is the rate as a decimal and n is the number of time periods.

a Using the formula above, complete the missing values in this table:

Present value of $1					
Interest rate per period					
Period	3%	4%	5%	6%	10%
1		0.9615		0.9434	0.9091
2	1.9135		1.8594	1.8334	
3		2.7751	2.7233		2.4869
4	3.7171	3.6299		3.4651	
5	4.5797		4.3295	4.2124	
10		8.1109	7.7217		6.1446
20	14.8775		12.4622	11.4699	

b Use the table to calculate the present value of an annuity where $a = 5000$, $r = 6\%$ and $n = 4$. Give your answer correct to two decimal places.

Financial mathematics: Annuities

Excel MATHEMATICS STANDARD 2
Ch. 5, pp. 141–145

Calculating loan instalments 1

Use the table of interest factors below to answer the following questions

Present value of $1				
Interest rate per period				
Period	3%	4%	5%	6%
5	4.5797	4.4518	4.3295	4.2124
10	8.5302	8.1109	7.7217	7.3601
15	11.9300	11.1184	10.3797	9.7122
20	14.8775	13.5903	12.4622	11.4699
25	17.4131	15.6221	14.0939	12.7834

QUESTION **1**   Tim borrows $400 000 to purchase his first home. The bank offers him a 20-year loan with an interest rate of 5%.

a Calculate the amount of each yearly instalment needed to repay the loan.

_____

_____

b What is the total amount Tim repays over the 20 years?

_____

_____

c What is the total amount of interest paid?

_____

_____

_____

QUESTION **2**   Jenn is considering buying an apartment. She requires a loan of $280 000 and is comparing loan offers. Bank A offers her a loan of 4% p.a. over 25 years while Bank B offers her 6% p.a. over 15 years.

a Calculate the yearly repayment and total paid for Bank A's loan.

_____

_____

b Calculate the yearly repayment and total paid for Bank B's loan.

_____

_____

c Which loan would you recommend Jenn take? Justify your answer.

_____

_____

_____

Financial mathematics: Annuities

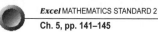

Calculating loan instalments 2

QUESTION **1** Paul wants to buy a car and takes out a personal loan of $10 000 at 1.5% per month compound interest. He repays the loan (including interest) by equal monthly instalments over 5 years. Find the amount of each instalment if the interest factor is 39.3803.

QUESTION **2** Amy borrows $25 000 at a reducible interest rate of 16% p.a. and pays it off over a period of 15 years. If the interest factor is 5.5755, find:

a the amount of each yearly instalment

b the total amount paid for the loan

QUESTION **3** Melissa borrows $150 000 in order to buy a house. She agrees to repay the loan in equal quarterly instalments over 10 years. What is the amount of each instalment, if interest is charged at 12% p.a. on any money owing? (Use an interest factor of 23.1148.)

QUESTION **4** Colin is looking at purchasing an investment property and has been offered a loan of $450 000 at 6% p.a. interest. The loan is to be repaid in equal fortnightly instalments over 15 years.

a Using an interest factor of 256.9704, calculate the amount of each fortnightly instalment.

b What is the total amount of interest Colin will pay?

Financial mathematics: Annuities

Excel MATHEMATICS STANDARD 2
Ch. 5, pp. 141–145

Calculating loan instalments 3

			Present value of $1			
			Interest rate per month			
r	0.0038	0.0042	0.0046	0.0050	0.0054	0.0058
N						
24	22.8966	22.7846	22.6734	22.5629	22.4531	22.3441
36	33.5866	33.3457	33.1072	32.8710	32.6372	32.4057
48	43.8010	43.3888	42.9819	42.5803	42.1839	41.7926
60	53.5610	52.9393	52.3275	51.7256	51.1332	50.5502
72	62.8866	62.0213	61.1724	60.3395	59.5224	58.7206

QUESTION **1**   Rob and Tasha are refinancing their home loan to find a wiser repayment option. They currently owe $275 000 on their home. Use the table above to calculate:

a their monthly repayment if they take a 5-year loan at 5.5% p.a.

_____

_____

_____

b how much they will save if they instead take a 3-year loan at 7% p.a.

_____

_____

_____

QUESTION **2**   Jason is considering renovating his property. iBank offers him a loan of $150 000 to be repaid monthly over 5 years at 5% p.a. They charge a $250 loan application fee and a $75 annual fee.

a Calculate the monthly repayment Jason would need to make for the loan only.

_____

_____

_____

b What is the total he would repay including fees and charges?

_____

_____

_____

c If Jason repays the loan over 6 years instead, iBank will waive all fees and charges.
Is Jason better off with the 5-year or the 6-year loan? Justify your answer.

_____

_____

_____

Financial mathematics: Annuities

TOPIC TEST

Instructions
- This section consists of 5 multiple-choice questions.
- Each question is worth 1 mark.
- Fill in only ONE CIRCLE for each question.

Time allowed: 7 minutes   **Total marks: 5**

The table below is used to find the future value of an annuity per $1 invested regularly and compounded at the end of each time period. Use the table to answer Questions 1 and 2.

Table of future-value interest factors					
Period	**Interest rate per period**				
	1.00%	**2.00%**	**3.00%**	**4.00%**	**5.00%**
1	1.0000	1.0000	1.0000	1.0000	1.0000
2	2.0100	2.0200	2.0300	2.0400	2.0500
3	3.0301	3.0604	3.0909	3.1216	3.1525
4	4.0604	4.1216	4.1836	4.2465	4.3101
5	5.1010	5.2040	5.3091	5.4163	5.5256
6	6.1520	6.3081	6.4684	6.6330	6.8019

1 Pete invests $2000 at the end of every year for 3 years at 4% p.a., compounded annually. Which of these is the future value of the annuity?

   (A) $2249.73

   (B) $6229.70

   (C) $6243.20

   (D) $6249.73

2 Liana wants to have $10 000 in an annuity after contributing an equal amount at the end of every year for 6 years at an interest rate of 3% p.a., compounded annually. What amount, to the nearest dollar, will she need to contribute each month?

   (A) $1546

   (B) $1610

   (C) $1658

   (D) $1667

The table below is used to find the present value of an annuity per $1 invested regularly and compounded at the end of each time period. Use the table to answer Questions 3 and 4.

Table of present-value interest factors						
	Interest rate per period					
Period	0.50%	1.00%	2.00%	4.00%	6.00%	8.00%
4	3.9505	3.9020	3.8077	3.6299	3.4651	3.3121
8	7.8230	7.6517	7.3255	6.7327	6.2098	5.7466
12	11.6189	11.2551	10.5753	9.3851	8.3838	7.5361
16	15.3399	14.7179	13.5777	11.6523	10.1059	8.8514
20	18.9874	18.0456	16.3514	13.5903	11.4699	9.8181
24	22.5629	21.2434	18.9139	15.2470	12.5504	10.5288
36	32.8710	30.1075	25.4888	18.9083	14.6210	11.7172
48	42.5803	37.9740	30.6731	21.1951	15.6500	12.1891

3 Margot wants to generate an income of $25 000 every year for 8 years by investing into an account at an interest rate of 6% p.a., compounding annually. What amount will she need to invest now?

Ⓐ $96 000

Ⓑ $155 245

Ⓒ $164 460

Ⓓ $182 528

4 For the next 4 years Tom is living on campus while completing his university degree. He has estimated that he will need $2000 per month. He plans to borrow a lump sum from his grandmother and invest it at 6% p.a., compounding monthly. What amount will he need to borrow, to the nearest dollar?

Ⓐ $69 302

Ⓑ $84 288

Ⓒ $85 161

Ⓓ $96 000

5 The formula $FV = a\left\{\dfrac{(1+r)^n - 1}{r}\right\}$ can be used to find the future value (FV) of an annuity where

a = contribution per period, r = rate as a decimal and n = number of time periods. Which of these is used to find the future value of an annuity at the end of 3 years if $500 is invested each month at an interest rate of 6% p.a., compounded monthly?

Ⓐ $FV = 500\left\{\dfrac{(1.06)^{36} - 1}{0.06}\right\}$

Ⓑ $FV = 500\left\{\dfrac{(1.06)^3 - 1}{0.06}\right\}$

Ⓒ $FV = 500\left\{\dfrac{(1.005)^3 - 1}{0.005}\right\}$

Ⓓ $FV = 500\left\{\dfrac{(1.005)^{36} - 1}{0.005}\right\}$

TOPIC TEST

SECTION II

Instructions
- This section consists of 3 questions.
- Show all working.

Time allowed: 53 minutes

Total marks: 35

6 A table of future values for an annuity of $1 is shown.

Table of future-value interest factors								
	Interest rate per period							
Period	0.50%	1.00%	1.50%	2.00%	3.00%	4.00%	5.00%	6.00%
1	1.0000	1.0000	1.0000	1.0000	1.0000	1.0000	1.0000	1.0000
2	2.0050	2.0100	2.0150	2.0200	2.0300	2.0400	2.0500	2.0600
3	3.0150	3.0301	3.0452	3.0604	3.0909	3.1216	3.1525	3.1836
4	4.0301	4.0604	4.0909	4.1216	4.1836	4.2465	4.3101	4.3746
5	5.0503	5.1010	5.1523	5.2040	5.3091	5.4163	5.5256	5.6371
6	6.0755	6.1520	6.2296	6.3081	6.4684	6.6330	6.8019	6.9753
7	7.1059	7.2135	7.3230	7.4343	7.6625	7.8983	8.1420	8.3938
8	8.1414	8.2857	8.4328	8.5830	8.8923	9.2142	9.5491	9.8975

a Olivia contributes $5000 at the end of each quarter into her superannuation account which gains interest at 6% p.a., compounded quarterly for 2 years.

    i What is the total amount of Olivia's contributions?   **1 mark**

    ii Find the future value of the annuity.   **1 mark**

    iii What is the amount of interest earned?   **1 mark**

b What is the value of the:

    i annual contribution to an annuity that would provide a future value of $198 990 after 6 years at 4% p.a. compound interest?   **1 mark**

    ii 6-monthly contribution that would provide a future value of $44 212.35 after 3 years at 10% p.a. with interest compounded 6-monthly?   **1 mark**

c Florence needs to save $4800 for an overseas holiday in 8 months. How much will she have to contribute each month into an account offering 6% p.a., compounded monthly, for her to have enough money to pay for her holiday? Give your answer to the nearest dollar.   **1 mark**

d Justin is paid an annual salary of $106 500 and he contributes 9.5% of his salary into a superannuation account at the end of each year. At the contribution stage his fund manager charges $2400 each year for fees. If the remainder of the money earns interest of 5% p.a. what will be the balance in his fund after 8 years?　　　　　　　　　　　　　**2 marks**

_____

_____

_____

7 The table below details the present-value interest factors to compare annuities of $1.

	Table of present-value interest factors							
	Interest rate per period							
Period	**0.45%**	**0.50%**	**0.75%**	**1.00%**	**1.25%**	**1.50%**	**1.75%**	**2.00%**
60	52.4796	51.7256	48.1734	44.9550	42.0346	39.3803	36.9640	34.7609
120	92.5656	90.0735	78.9417	69.7005	61.9828	55.4985	50.0171	45.3554
180	123.1851	118.5035	98.5934	83.3217	71.4496	62.0956	54.6265	48.5844
240	146.5735	139.5808	111.1450	90.8194	75.9423	64.7957	56.2543	49.5686
300	164.4385	155.2069	119.1616	94.9466	78.0743	65.9009	56.8291	49.8685
360	178.0846	166.7916	124.2819	97.2183	79.0861	66.3532	57.0320	49.9599

a What amount of money needs to be invested today to provide for the following annuities:

i $5000 per month for the next 25 years, earning interest of 6% p.a., compounded monthly?　　　　　　　　　　　　　　　　　　　　　**1 mark**

_____

_____

ii $32 000 every 6 months for the next 30 years, earning interest of 4% p.a., compounded 6-monthly?　　　　　　　　　　　　　　　　　　　**2 marks**

_____

_____

iii $25 000 every 3 months for the next 60 years, earning interest of 7% p.a., compounded quarterly?　　　　　　　　　　　　　　　　　　　**2 marks**

_____

_____

b Gary has two choices for a loan of $80 000. Loan A can be taken over a period of 20 years at 6% p.a., compounded monthly, or Loan B is for a period of 25 years at 5.4% p.a., compounded monthly. What is the:

i amount of each monthly instalment?　　　　　　　　　　　　**3 marks**

_____

_____

ii difference in the interest paid on each of the loans?　　　　　**2 marks**

_____

_____

_____

c Marcos has a loan of $380 000 which is to be paid off in monthly instalments over 30 years. His bank charges interest of 9% p.a., compounded monthly, but Marcos decides to make monthly repayments as if the interest was 12% p.a., compounded monthly, so that he pays the loan out faster. How much extra does Marcos pay each month?   **3 marks**

_____

_____

8 A table of future-value interest factors is used to compare annuities of $1.

Table of future-value interest factors						
	Interest rate per period					
Period	**0.50%**	**1.50%**	**2.00%**	**3.00%**	**4.00%**	**6.00%**
4	4.0301	4.0909	4.1216	4.1836	4.2465	4.3746
8	8.1414	8.4328	8.5830	8.8923	9.2142	9.8975
16	16.6142	17.9324	18.6393	20.1569	21.8245	25.6725
32	34.6086	40.6883	44.2270	52.5028	62.7015	90.8898
48	54.0978	69.5652	79.3535	104.4084	139.2632	256.5645
96	122.8285	211.7202	284.6467	535.8502	1054.2960	4462.6505

a The Federal Bank offered 6% p.a. compound interest for a term of 8 years. Find the amount of interest earned if Yvette invested:

i $18 000 every year, compounded annually   **2 marks**

_____

_____

ii $9000 every 6 months, compounded 6-monthly   **2 marks**

_____

_____

iii $4500 every quarter, compounded quarterly   **2 marks**

_____

_____

iv $1500 every month, compounded monthly   **2 marks**

_____

_____

b Evan and Solomon were offered interest of 6% p.a. for 4 years. Evan invested $1500 each quarter, compounded quarterly. Solomon invested $500 every month, compounded monthly. Calculate the difference in the interest earned by the two men.   **3 marks**

_____

_____

c Melita invests $5000 every year for 8 years at a rate of 6% p.a. interest, compounded annually. What single investment amount, to the nearest dollar, would provide the same return of interest for 8 years at 6% p.a., compounded annually?   **3 marks**

_____

_____

CHAPTER **4**

Algebra: Simultaneous linear equations

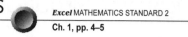

Excel MATHEMATICS STANDARD 2
Ch. 1, pp. 4–5

Graphing linear equations

QUESTION **1**   Complete the table of values for each equation.

a $y = 2x$

x	−1	0	1	2
y				

b $y = x + 1$

x	−1	0	1	2
y				

c $y = 2x - 1$

x	−1	0	1	2
y				

d $y = 5 - x$

x	−1	0	1	2
y				

e $y = -2x + 2$

x	−1	0	1	2
y				

f $y = 3x + 3$

x	−2	−1	0	1
y				

QUESTION **2**   Sketch the graph of each of the above lines on the number plane below. Clearly label each line.

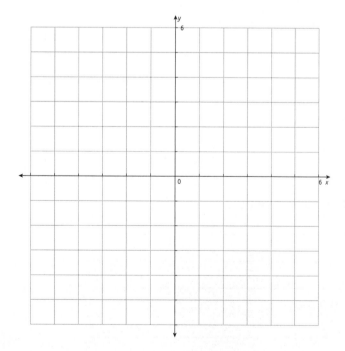

Algebra: Simultaneous linear equations

Meaning for gradient and y-intercept

QUESTION **1**   Liam receives a fixed amount of pocket money each week. In addition, if Liam chooses to help his mother she gives him an extra amount per hour for the time spent. The graph shows the amount of money Liam might receive in pocket money each week.

a What is the intercept on the vertical axis?

_____

b What does the intercept on the vertical axis represent?

_____

_____

c What is the gradient of this line?

_____

_____

d What does the gradient represent?

_____

_____

_____

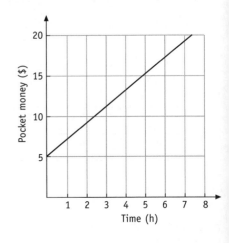

QUESTION **2**   Dorian intends to ride a bicycle from Aden to Barton to raise money for the local hospital. The graph shows his expected distance from Barton in kilometres over time (in hours).

a What is the intercept on the vertical axis?

_____

_____

b What information does this intercept tell us?

_____

_____

_____

c What is the gradient of the line?

_____

_____

d What information does the gradient tell us?

_____

_____

_____

e What is the equation of the line?

_____

_____

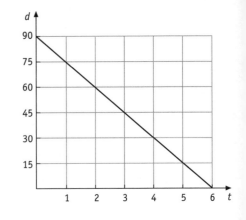

Algebra: Simultaneous linear equations

Solving graphically a pair of simultaneous equations

QUESTION **1**

a Complete the tables of values for:

i $y = 20x$

x	0	10	20	30	40
y					

ii $y = 600 - 10x$

x	0	10	20	30	40
y					

b Use the completed tables in part **a** to graph the lines $y = 20x$ and $y = 600 - 10x$ on the number plane.

c What is the point of intersection of the two graphs?

_____

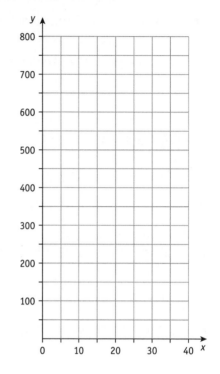

QUESTION **2**   Using the values from $x = 0$ to $x = 7$, find the point of intersection of the lines $y = 60 + 20x$ and $y = 300 - 40x$.

$y = 60 + 20x$

x	0	1	2	3	4	5	6	7
y								

$y = 300 - 40x$

x	0	1	2	3	4	5	6	7
y								

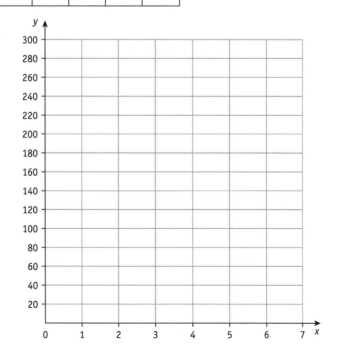

Algebra: Simultaneous linear equations

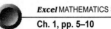
Linear functions and physical phenomena

QUESTION **1**   Part of the school oval needs to be returfed. A quote is given from Top Turf stating the cost of the turf as being $50 for delivery and $6 per metre.

a Write an equation for the cost of the turf, C.

_____

_____

b Draw a graph of the cost on the axes provided.

c What is the cost of returfing 100 m of the school oval?

_____

_____

d Explain why the model cannot be used to calculate the **total** cost of returfing part of the school oval.

_____

_____

QUESTION **2**   A group of Year 12 students are going on an excursion to a chocolate factory. The cost of hiring a bus licensed to seat 54 people involves a $200 booking fee plus $5 per person.

a Write an equation to calculate the cost, C, of hiring a bus for n people.

_____

_____

b Draw a graph for the cost of hiring a bus on the axes provided.

c 45 students and 5 teachers are going on the excursion. What is the cost of hiring the bus?

_____

_____

d Why is the model not accurate for $n > 54$?

_____

_____

_____

Algebra: Simultaneous linear equations

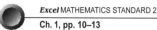

Developing a pair of simultaneous equations

QUESTION **1**   Develop an equation to represent the cost (C) of:

a n apples at 60 cents each

b x litres at \$7 per litre

QUESTION **2**   A taxi driver charges \$4 plus \$2 per kilometre of each fare.

a Write an equation where C = cost, in dollars, and n = number of kilometres.

b Use the equation to find the cost of a journey of 12 km. _____

QUESTION **3**   The cost of an electrician is a \$70 callout fee plus \$50 for every half hour or part thereof. If P = price, in dollars, and n = number of half hours, write an equation linking P and n.

QUESTION **4**   Over the course of a trip, a train has an average speed of 70 km/h. If d = distance, in kilometres, and t = time in hours:

a write an equation for d in terms of t

b use the equation to find the distance travelled by the train in 6 hours

QUESTION **5**   Tom is driving 280 km from his home to his holiday unit. His average speed is 80 km/h.

a Given d = distance (in kilometres) yet to travel and n = number of hours travelled, explain why the formula $d = 280 - 80n$ represents the distance Tom is from his holiday unit.

b After travelling for 2.5 hours, how far does Tom need to travel to reach his destination?

QUESTION **6**   It costs Annika \$120 plus \$8 for every T-shirt she makes and then she sells them for \$16 each. Using cost = C, in dollars, sales = S, in dollars, and the number of T-shirts sold = n, write equations for:

a C in terms of n _____

b S in terms of n _____

QUESTION **7**   Carrie makes small containers of slime for her friends at school, selling them for \$2 each. She spent \$10 on a box of containers and she estimates that the amount of slime in each container cost her 30 cents to produce. If C = cost in cents, S = sales in cents, P = profit in cents and n = number of containers sold, write equations for:

a C in terms of n

b S in terms of n

c P in terms of n

QUESTION **8**   Two women are driving towards each other between Hillcrest and Parklea which are 240 km apart. Keira leaves Hillcrest and drives at an average speed of 60 km/h towards Parklea. Indi leaves Parklea and averages 80 km/h as she drives towards Hillcrest. Find the equation for the distance d, in kilometres:

a Keira is from Hillcrest after time t, in hours

b Indi is from Hillcrest after time t, in hours

Algebra: Simultaneous linear equations

Break-even analysis 1

QUESTION **1**   Hayley bakes and decorates incredible cakes and plans to sell them via an online sales page. She works out that her costs (in $) can be represented by the equation $C = 40x + 250$, where x is the number of cakes produced.

a Graph Hayley's costs on the axes provided.

b What is the gradient of the line?

_____

_____

c What does it represent?

_____

_____

d If Hayley wants to break even after 20 cakes, how much does she need to charge per cake?

_____

_____

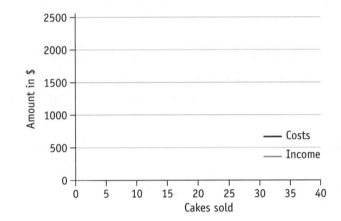

e Graph the line $I = 52.5x$ on the same axes.

f Shade the profit zone indicating where Hayley's income from cake sales exceeds her costs of producing the cakes.

QUESTION **2**   Jason plans to sell screen-printed T-shirts at the local markets. He conducts a break-even analysis to evaluate the plan's financial viability, shown to the right.

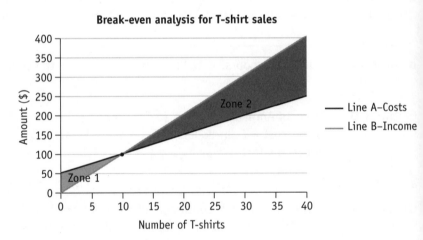

a How many T-shirts sold represent the break-even point for Jason's plan? _____

b Which is the profit zone? _____

c Which is the loss zone? _____

d For Line A, what is represented by **i** the gradient? **ii** the y-intercept? _____

e For Line B, what is represented by **i** the gradient? **ii** the y-intercept? _____

f What is the income equation? (Use the form $I = mx$.) _____

g What is the cost equation? (Use the form $C = mx + c$.) _____

Algebra: Simultaneous linear equations

Break-even analysis 2

QUESTION **1** Jonny hires a function centre for an MND fundraising dinner, where tickets are sold at $120 per person. He pays $2400 to hire the facility and the cost of the meal and drinks will be $40 per person. The function centre has a capacity of 100 people.

a Given C = total cost of the dinner and n = number of tickets, explain why $C = 2400 + 40n$.

_____

b Given I = income from the dinner and n = number of tickets, explain why $I = 120n$.

_____

c Draw a graph displaying both equations.

d How many tickets will need to be sold for Jonny to break even?

_____

e If 70 tickets were sold, what is the profit made from the dinner?

_____

f Is it possible to make a profit of $6000?

_____

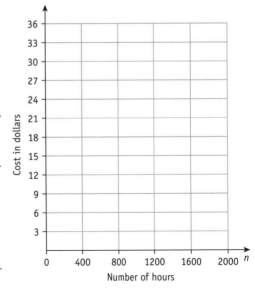

QUESTION **2** The costs of buying and running two types of light globes are recorded in the tables below, where n = number of hours, H = the total cost of buying and running a halogen globe, and L = the total cost of buying and running an LED globe.

Halogen:

n	0	400	800	1200	1600	2000
H	3	9	15	21	27	33

LED:

n	0	400	800	1200	1600	2000
L	13	15	17	19	21	23

a What is the purchase price of an LED globe?

_____

b What is the hourly cost of using a halogen globe?

_____

c Represent the cost of both globes on the number plane opposite.

d After how many hours is the total cost of the globes identical?

_____

e The life of a halogen globe is 2000 hours while an LED globe lasts 40 000 hours. If the light is turned on for 4000 hours, how much cheaper would it be to use an LED globe compared to a halogen globe (including the cost of the globes)?

_____

Algebra: Simultaneous linear equations

TOPIC TEST

SECTION I

Instructions
- This section consists of 5 multiple-choice questions.
- Each question is worth 1 mark.
- Fill in only ONE CIRCLE for each question.

Time allowed: 7 minutes **Total marks: 5**

1 A company manufactures widgets. The company's cost equation and income equation are drawn on the same graph. Which region of the graph represents the profit zone?

ⓐ P   ⓑ Q

ⓒ R   ⓓ S

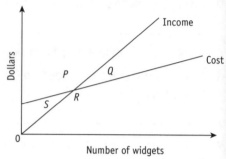

2 What is the equation of the line k?

ⓐ $y = \dfrac{x}{3} - 1$ ⓑ $y = 3x - 1$

ⓒ $y = -\dfrac{x}{3} - 1$ ⓓ $y = -3x - 1$

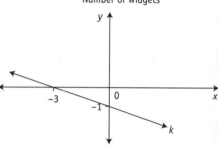

3 Paul and Lauren are working out the cost of hiring tradespeople to build a granny flat on their property. They are told that employing a team of tradespeople will involve a fixed cost of \$650 and then an additional \$450 per day. What is the correct equation connecting the cost in dollars, C, with the number of days, d, worked by the team of tradespeople?

ⓐ $C = 650 + 450d$ ⓑ $C = \dfrac{450d}{650}$ ⓒ $C = 650 - 450d$ ⓓ $C = \dfrac{650d}{450}$

4 According to the graph, at what value for units produced will production break even?

ⓐ 0   ⓑ 15

ⓒ 15 000   ⓓ none of these

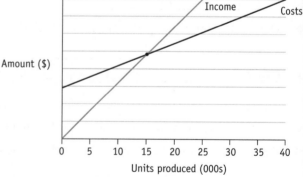

5 Sean drew the graphs of $y = 2x$ and $y = x + 5$ on the same number plane. What are the coordinates of the point of intersection of the two lines?

ⓐ (2, 4)   ⓑ (3, 8)   ⓒ (4, 9)   ⓓ (5, 10)

SECTION II

Instructions • This section consists of 5 questions.
• Show all working.

Time allowed: 53 minutes   **Total marks: 35**

6 **a** Complete the table of values and graph each line on the number plane below.

  i $y = 3x - 1$

x	−1	0	1	2
y				

  ii $y = x + 5$

x	−1	0	1	2
y				

2 marks each

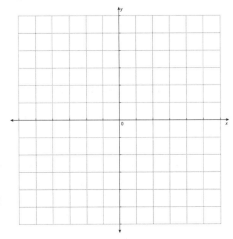

  b At what value of x do the two lines intersect?   **1 mark**

7 Match each equation with a table of values.   **1 mark each**

  a

x	−2	−1	0	1
y	−5	−3	−1	1

  b

x	−2	−1	0	1
y	−2	1	4	7

  c

x	−2	−1	0	1
y	−4	−2	0	2

  d

x	−2	−1	0	1
y	9	7	5	3

  i $y = 2x$ **ii** $y = 2x - 1$

  iii $y = 5 - 2x$ **iv** $y = 3x + 4$

8 Grace makes batches of homemade lemonade which she sells to her friends by the jug. Grace has calculated that the cost of producing the jugs of lemonade is $8 plus $3 for every jug.

  a Complete the table of values   **2 marks**

Number of jugs	0	4	8	12	16	20
Cost ($)						

b Draw a graph of the cost on the number plane provided. **2 marks**

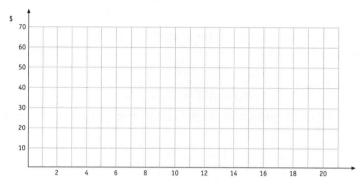

c What is the intercept on the vertical axis? Briefly explain what this represents. **2 marks**

_____

_____

_____

d What is the gradient of the line? Briefly explain what it represents. **2 marks**

_____

_____

_____

e What is the cost of producing 14 jugs of lemonade? **1 mark**

_____

f The total cost of a batch Grace made was $56. How many jugs did this batch contain? **1 mark**

_____

g If Grace sells the lemonade for $4 per jug, draw the graph of her return from sales on the same number plane. **1 mark**

_____

h Where do the two lines intersect? Briefly explain what this means. **2 marks**

_____

_____

_____

_____

9 Samone runs a small business of selling birthday cakes. The graph shows the cost of producing the cakes and the income received from their sale each week.

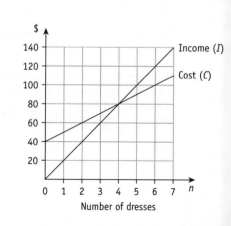

a How many cakes need to be sold to break even? **1 mark**

_____

b How much is the profit or loss when Samone sells:

i 2 cakes? **1 mark**

_____

ii 7 cakes? **1 mark**

_____

c By finding the gradient and vertical intercept, write an equation, in terms of cakes sold (n), for the:

i income (I) **1 mark**

_____

ii cost (C) **2 marks**

_____

_____

10 Harry-Rose makes dresses and sells them at a weekend market. It costs her $100 plus $15 for every dress she makes and she sells them for $40 each.

a Using cost = C, in dollars, sales = S, in dollars, and the number of dresses sold = n, write equations for:

i C in terms of n **1 mark**

_____

ii S in terms of n **1 mark**

_____

b Use the grid below to draw the graphs of C and S in terms of n. **2 marks**

c How many dresses does Harry-Rose need to sell to break even? **1 mark**

_____

_____

_____

d What is the difference in the profit between Harry-Rose selling 8 dresses and 10 dresses? **2 marks**

_____

_____

_____

_____

Number of dresses

CHAPTER **5**

Algebra: Non-linear relationships

 Excel MATHEMATICS STANDARD 2
Ch. 1, pp. 15–20

Exponential function 1: $y = ka^x$

QUESTION **1**   Complete the table of values and sketch the graph of each curve on the given number plane. Clearly label each curve.

a $y = 2^x$

x	0	0.5	1	2	3	4	5	6
y								

b $y = 3^x$

x	0	0.5	1	1.5	2	2.5	3	3.5	4
y									

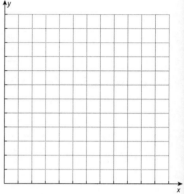

QUESTION **2**   Complete the table of values and sketch the graph of the curve.

a $y = 5(1.2)^x$

x	0	1	2	3	4	5	6	7	8
y									

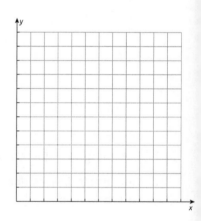

b $y = 2(1.7)^x$

x	0	1	2	3	4	5	6	7
y								

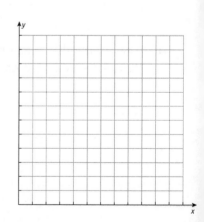

Algebra: Non-linear relationships

Exponential function 2: $y = ka^x$

QUESTION **1**   If $2000 is invested at 8% p.a. compound interest, then the value of the investment, A, after x years is given by the formula $A = 2000(1.08)^x$. The graph of $A = 2000(1.08)^x$ is given below.

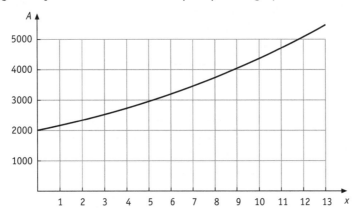

a What is the value of the investment after 7 years?

_____

b After how many years does the amount double?

_____

c By how much did the value of the investment increase in the second year?

_____

QUESTION **2**   A large motor vehicle dealership has determined that the salvage value, S, of a car can be found by the formula $S = V(0.7)^n$ where V is the original value and n the number of years. The graph of $y = 0.7^n$ is shown below. Use the graph to answer the following questions.

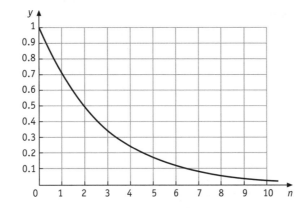

a What is the salvage value of a car, originally worth $20 000, at the end of 5 years?

_____

b After how many years does the dealership determine that the cars have halved in value?

_____

_____

Algebra: Non-linear relationships

Quadratic function 1: $y = ax^2 + bx + c$

QUESTION **1**   Complete the table of values for each equation.

a $y = x^2$

x	0	0.5	1	1.5	2	2.5	3	3.5	4
y									

b $y = x^2 + 2x - 3$

x	0	0.5	1	1.5	2	2.5	3	3.5	4
y									

c $y = 2x^2 - 5$

x	0	0.5	1	1.5	2	2.5	3	3.5	4
y									

d $y = 3x^2 - 7x - 4$

x	0	0.5	1	1.5	2	2.5	3	3.5	4
y									

QUESTION **2**   Sketch the graph of each of the above quadratic functions on the number plane below. Clearly label each graph.

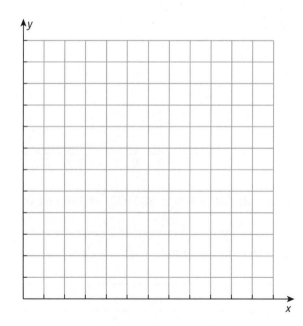

Algebra: Non-linear relationships

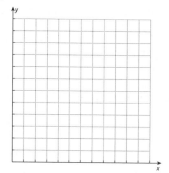

Quadratic function 2: $y = ax^2 + bx + c$

QUESTION 1

a Complete each table of values and sketch the graph on the number plane provided.

$y = (x - 1)^2 - 2$

x	0	0.5	1	1.5	2	2.5	3	3.5	4
y									

$y = x^2 - 2x - 1$

x	0	0.5	1	1.5	2	2.5	3	3.5	4
y									

b What did you notice about the two graphs? What does this mean about the two equations? Briefly comment.

_____

_____

_____

_____

QUESTION 2

The graph below shows the height above the ground of a ball t seconds after it was thrown into the air from the top of a building.

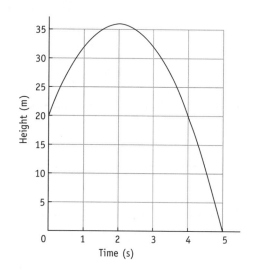

a What was the maximum height reached by the ball above the ground?

_____

b How high was the building?

_____

c How long was it before the ball hit the ground?

_____

Algebra: Non-linear relationships

Quadratic function 3: $y = ax^2 + bx + c$

QUESTION **1**   If a stockyard is to be rectangular and have a perimeter of 72 m then the area (A m^2) of the yard is given by the formula $A = 36l - l^2$ where l is the length of one side.

a Complete the table of values.

l	0	4	8	12	16	20	24	28	32
A									

b Sketch the graph of $A = 36l - l^2$.

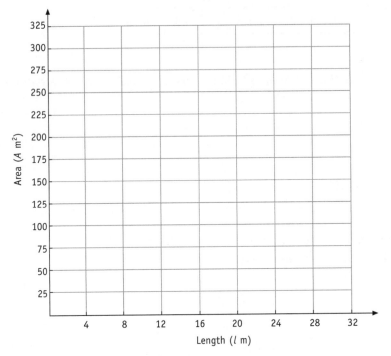

c What will be the length of the stockyard if it is to have maximum area?

_____

_____

d What is the maximum possible area?

_____

_____

_____

e Can the graph be used to find the area if $l = 40$? Justify your answer.

_____

_____

_____

_____

_____

Algebra: Non-linear relationships

Excel MATHEMATICS STANDARD 2

Ch. 1, pp. 27–29

Hyperbolic function 1: $y = \dfrac{a}{x}$

QUESTION **1**   Complete the table of values and sketch the graph of each hyperbola.

a $y = \dfrac{8}{x}$

x	0.25	0.5	1	2	4	8	16	32
y								

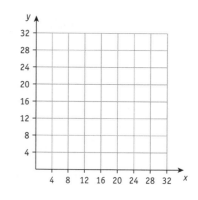

b $y = \dfrac{24}{x}$

x	1	2	3	4	6	8	12	16	20	24
y										

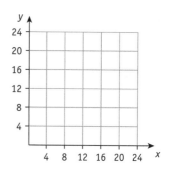

c $y = \dfrac{6}{x}$

x	1	2	3	4	5	6	8	10	12
y									

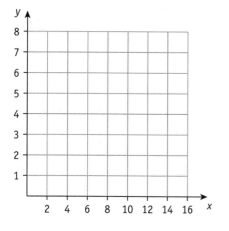

d $y = \dfrac{4}{x}$

x	0.25	0.5	1	2	4	8	16
y							

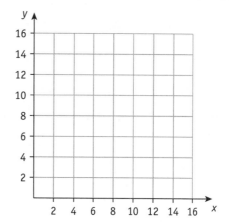

Algebra: Non-linear relationships

Hyperbolic function 2: $y = \dfrac{a}{x}$

QUESTION **1** Greg wants to borrow $600 from his sister. She agrees to lend him the money, interest free, provided he repays a fixed amount each month. The graph shows the amount of each repayment for different numbers of months.

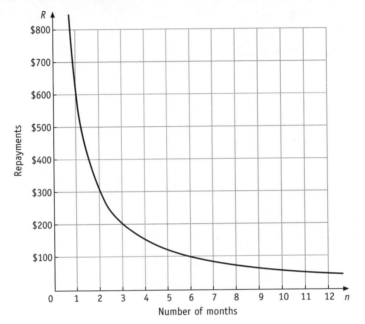

a How much will the monthly repayments be if Greg agrees to repay the loan over 8 months?

_____

b Over how many months will Greg repay the loan if he pays $120 per month?

_____

c If Greg wanted to pay $90 per month, how many months would it take to repay the loan? Briefly comment on the sense of your answer.

_____

d Could the graph be used to find the amount of each repayment if the loan was repaid over 4 years? Comment.

_____

e Greg finds he needs to borrow $840 and his sister agrees to the same terms.

  i Complete the table of values given $R = \dfrac{840}{n}$, when n is the number of months and R the amount of each repayment.

n	1	2	3	4	5	6	7	8	10	12
R										

  ii Draw the graph of $R = \dfrac{840}{n}$ on the diagram above.

  iii Use the graphs to find approximately how much extra Greg would need each month to repay $840 rather than $600 over 9 months.

_____

Algebra: Non-linear relationships

Inverse variation

QUESTION **1**   Given $h = \dfrac{a}{t}$:

a first find a if $h = 24$ when $t = 3$

b then find h if $t = 8$

QUESTION **2**   If y is inversely proportional to x, and $y = 24$ when $x = 4$, find:

a the equation connecting y and x

b the value of y when $x = 8$

c the value of x when $y = 72$

QUESTION **3** y varies inversely with x. If $y = 12$ when $x = 4$, find y when $x = 8$.

QUESTION **4**   Time varies inversely with speed for a journey. If it takes 6 hours to complete the journey when travelling at 60 km/h, how long would the same journey take if the speed were to be increased to 90 km/h?

QUESTION **5**   The number of tables in a revolving restaurant varies inversely with the distance between them. When they are 10 m apart, the restaurant can accommodate 48 tables. For a distance between the tables of 16 m, how many tables can be arranged?

Algebra: Non-linear relationships

TOPIC TEST

SECTION I

Instructions
- This section consists of 5 multiple-choice questions.
- Each question is worth 1 mark.
- Fill in only ONE CIRCLE for each question.

Time allowed: 7 minutes   **Total marks: 5**

1 $y = 2(1.5)^x$. When $x = 0$, $y =$
    Ⓐ 0   Ⓑ 1

    Ⓒ 1.5   Ⓓ 2

2 If $T = \dfrac{k}{n}$, and $T = 12$ when $n = 4$, then $k =$
    Ⓐ 3   Ⓑ 6   Ⓒ 8   Ⓓ 48

3 Sophie wants to build a chicken enclosure in her backyard. She has 16 m of fencing and will use an existing wall as one side of the enclosure. The plan for her enclosure is shown, where x m is the width of her enclosure. Which of these equations shows the area A, in m², of her chicken enclosure?

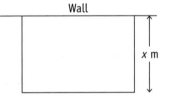

    Ⓐ $A = 16x - 2x^2$ Ⓑ $A = 16x - x^2$

    Ⓒ $A = 8x - x^2$ Ⓓ $A = 8x - 2x^2$

4 Which graph best represents $y = 2^x$?

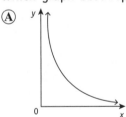

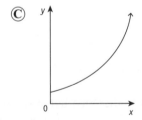

5 Time varies inversely with speed for a journey. If it takes 8 hours to complete the journey when travelling at 80 km/h, how long will the same journey take if the speed is increased to 100 km/h?
    Ⓐ 2.3 h   Ⓑ 5 h

    Ⓒ 6.4 h   Ⓓ 5.8 h

TOPIC TEST

SECTION II

Instructions • This section consists of 8 questions.
• Show all working.

Time allowed: 53 minutes
Total marks: 35

6 The number of penguins, N, after t years in a colony can be found using the formula $N = k.2^t$.

a If there are 28 penguins after 3 years, find the value of k.
2 marks

b How many penguins are in the colony after 5 years?
1 mark

c How many years will it take until the population of the colony first exceeds 3584?
2 marks

7 Joel makes water tanks. All the tanks he makes are cylindrical with the same height, but different radii. Joel knows that the volume of each of his tanks is directly proportional to the square of the radius. A tank of radius 1.2 m has volume 10.8 m³. What would be the radius of a tank with volume 24.3 m³?
3 marks

8 The table of values has been drawn to show the distance (d m) an object will fall in t seconds.

t	0	1	2	3	4	5	6	7	8	9	10
d	0	5	20	45	80	125	180	245	320	405	500

a Use the table of values to draw a graph on the number plane provided.
2 marks

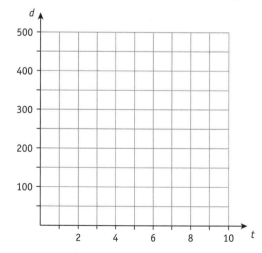

b How far would you expect an object to fall in 7.5 seconds? **1 mark**

_____

c How many seconds would you expect an object to take to fall 100 m? **1 mark**

_____

9 The diagram shows the population growth of a city over several years.

1 mark each

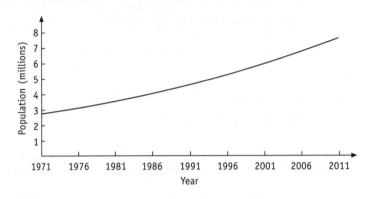

a The population growth is an example of what type of growth?

_____

b What was the population of the city in 2001?

_____

c When did the population reach 5 million?

_____

d Give an estimate of the expected population in 2021.

_____

10 The cost per person for a bus trip is inversely proportional to the number of people taking the trip. When 16 people go on the trip, the cost per person is $12.

a Show that $C = \dfrac{192}{n}$ where $\$C$ is the cost per person and n the number of people taking the trip.

1 mark

_____

b Complete the table of values for $C = \dfrac{192}{n}$.

2 marks

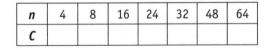

n	4	8	16	24	32	48	64
C							

c Draw the graph of $C = \dfrac{192}{n}$ on the number plane.

2 marks

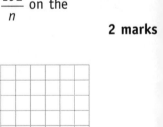

11 The frequency of a vibrating guitar string varies inversely as its length changes. Suppose a guitar string 0.6 m long vibrates 4.2 times per second. What would be the frequency of vibrations of a 0.5 m length of string? **2 marks**

_____

_____

_____

12 A rock is catapulted into the air and falls back to ground. The height, h in metres, that the rock is above the ground is given by the formula $h = 4t - t^2$, where t is the time expressed in seconds.

a Complete the table. **2 marks**

t	0	1	2	3	4
h					

b Draw the graph of $h = 4t - t^2$. **2 marks**

c When was the maximum height reached by the rock? **1 mark**

_____

d What percentage of the time of flight was the rock at least 3 m above the ground? **2 marks**

_____

_____

_____

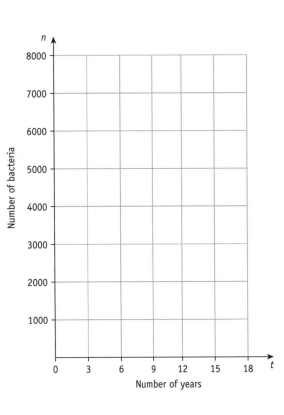

13 The number of bacteria (n) grows according to the formula $n = 2000(1.08)^t$, where t is the number of hours.

a How many bacteria were initially in the culture? **1 mark**

_____

_____

b Complete the table, expressing n as whole numbers.

t	0	3	6	9	12	15	18
n		2519		3999		6344	

2 marks

c Use the table to draw the graph of $n = 2000(1.08)^t$. **2 marks**

CHAPTER 6

Measurement: Non-right-angled trigonometry

Excel MATHEMATICS STANDARD 2
Ch. 2, p. 42

Review of right-angled triangles

QUESTION 1   Evaluate correct to three decimal places.

a   sin 65° = _____

b   tan 56°18′ = _____

c   cos 88°36′ = _____

QUESTION 2   If 0° ≤ θ ≤ 90°, find θ to the nearest minute.

a   sin θ = 0.7

b   cos θ = 0.625

c   tan θ = 2.681

_____

_____

_____

QUESTION 3   Find the length of the unknown side, correct to one decimal place.

a

b

c

d

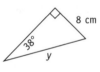

e

f

QUESTION 4   Find the size of angle θ to the nearest minute.

a

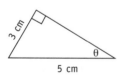

b

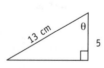

c

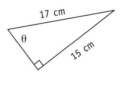

Measurement: Non-right-angled trigonometry

Solving problems with right-angled triangles 1

QUESTION **1**

a Find the length of *DC*.

_____

_____

b Find the length of *CB*.

_____

_____

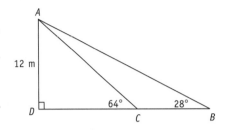

QUESTION **2**

a The angle of elevation of the top of a tower *AB* is 65° from a point *C* on the ground at a distance of 30 m from the base of the tower. Calculate the height of the tower to the nearest metre.

_____

_____

_____

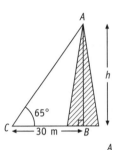

b A man 1.65 m tall is 28 m away from a tower 38 m high. What is the angle of elevation of the top of the tower from his eyes?

_____

_____

c From the top of a building 90 m high, the angle of depression of a car parked on the ground is 63°. Find the distance of the car from the base of the building. (Answer correct to two decimal places.)

_____

_____

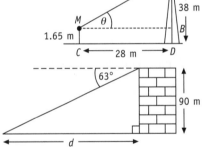

QUESTION **3**   Give each answer to the nearest centimetre.

a

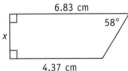

Find *x*.

_____

_____

_____

_____

b

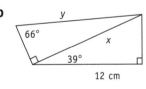

i Find *x*.

_____

_____

ii Find *y*.

_____

_____

Measurement: Non-right-angled trigonometry

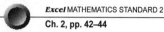

Solving problems with right-angled triangles 2

QUESTION **1**   An 18-m ladder standing on level ground reaches 14 m up a vertical wall. The angle that the ladder makes with the ground is θ.

a Draw a diagram to represent this information.   **b** Find θ to the nearest degree.

QUESTION **2**   *ABCD* is a rectangle with sides *AD* = 5 cm and *AB* = 12 cm.

a Draw a diagram to represent this information.   **b** Find the length of *AC*, the diagonal, using Pythagoras' theorem.

c Find angle *ACD* correct to the nearest minute.

QUESTION **3**   A pole 15 m tall casts a shadow 20 m long. The angle of elevation of the top of the pole from the tip of the shadow is θ.

a Draw a diagram to represent this information.   **b** Find θ, the angle of elevation (to the nearest degree).

c Find the distance from the tip of the shadow to the top of the pole.

Trig ratios and obtuse angles

QUESTION 1   Use your calculator to evaluate the following correct to two decimal places.

a sin 120° = _____

b cos 150° = _____

c tan 130° = _____

d cos 141°53′ = _____

e sin 165°37′ = _____

f sin 145° = _____

QUESTION 2   Use your calculator to find the sin, cos and tan of the following angles correct to four decimal places.

a 120°;   sin 120° = _____   cos 120° = _____   tan 120° = _____

b 135°;   sin 135° = _____   cos 135° = _____   tan 135° = _____

c 98°;   sin 98° = _____   cos 98° = _____   tan 98° = _____

d 164°;   sin 164° = _____   cos 164° = _____   tan 164° = _____

e 175°;   sin 175° = _____   cos 175° = _____   tan 175° = _____

f 130°;   sin 130° = _____   cos 130° = _____   tan 130° = _____

QUESTION 3   Determine whether the trig ratios of the following angles are positive or negative.

a sin 160°   **b** cos 160°   **c** tan 160°   **d** sin 99°

_____   _____   _____   _____

e tan 35°   **f** sin 145°   **g** cos 10°   **h** tan 95°

_____   _____   _____   _____

i sin 175°   **j** cos 121°   **k** tan 104°   **l** sin 111°

_____   _____   _____   _____

m sin 24°   **n** cos 100°   **o** tan 135°   **p** cos 86°

_____   _____   _____   _____

QUESTION 4   Choose positive or negative to complete each sentence.

a If θ is an obtuse angle then sin θ is _____

b If θ is an obtuse angle then cos θ is _____

c If θ is an obtuse angle then tan θ is _____

QUESTION 5   Find correct to two decimal places:

a $\dfrac{8}{\sin 120°} \times \sin 35°$

b $\dfrac{15 \times \sin 135°}{21.25}$

c $\dfrac{\tan 120°}{15.8}$

d $7^2 + 8^2 - 2 \times 7 \times 8 \times \cos 127°$

Measurement: Non-right-angled trigonometry

Using the sine rule to find a side

QUESTION **1**   Use the sine rule to find the value of the unknown side correct to two decimal places.

a

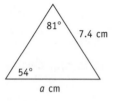

b

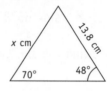

_____

_____

_____

_____

c

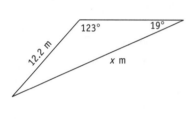

d

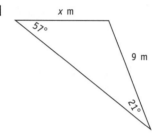

_____

_____

_____

QUESTION **2**   Find:

a

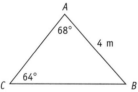

i the size of ∠*ABC*

_____

_____

ii the length of side *AC*

_____

_____

_____

b

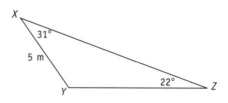

i the size of ∠*XYZ*

_____

_____

ii the length of side *XZ*

_____

_____

Measurement: Non-right-angled trigonometry

Excel MATHEMATICS STANDARD 2
Ch. 3, pp. 47–49

Using the sine rule to find an angle

QUESTION **1**   In the following triangles, find angle θ to the nearest degree.

a

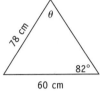

b

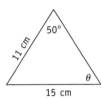

_____

_____

_____

_____

_____

_____

_____

_____

c

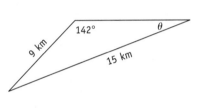

d

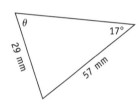

_____

_____

_____

_____

_____

_____

_____

_____

QUESTION **2**

a Use the sine rule to find the size of $\angle ABC$ to the nearest whole degree.

_____

_____

_____

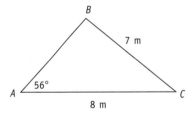

b What is the size of $\angle ACB$?

_____

_____

QUESTION **3**   Find the size of $\angle PQR$ to the nearest minute.

_____

_____

_____

_____

_____

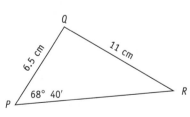

Measurement: Non-right-angled trigonometry

Using the cosine rule to find a side

QUESTION **1**   Use the cosine rule to find the value of the unknown side correct to two decimal places.

a

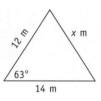

b

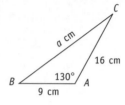

c

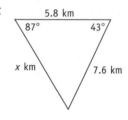

d

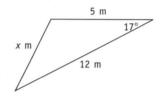

QUESTION **2**   In the given diagram:

a use Pythagoras' theorem to find the length *AC*

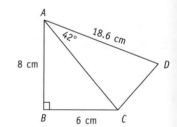

b use the cosine rule to calculate the length of *CD* correct to two decimal places

Measurement: Non-right-angled trigonometry

Using the cosine rule to find an angle

QUESTION **1**   In the following triangles, find θ to the nearest degree.

a

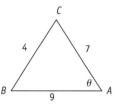

b

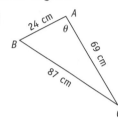

_____

_____

_____

_____

_____

_____

_____

_____

_____

_____

c

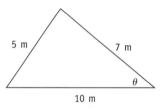

d

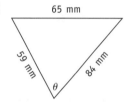

_____

_____

_____

_____

_____

_____

_____

_____

QUESTION **2**   Using the diagram shown:

a find $\angle ABC$ to the nearest degree

_____

_____

_____

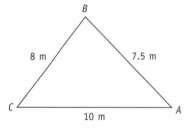

b find $\angle CAB$ to the nearest degree

_____

_____

_____

c what is the size of $\angle ACB$?

_____

_____

_____

Area of a triangle

QUESTION **1**   Find the area of each of the following triangles to the nearest square centimetre.

a

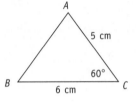

b

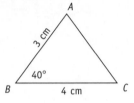

_____

_____

_____

_____

c

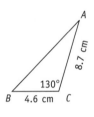

d

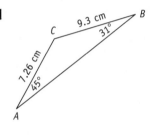

_____

_____

_____

_____

QUESTION **2**   Find the area of the parallelograms.

a

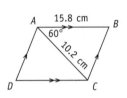

b

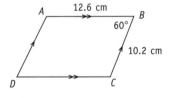

_____

_____

_____

_____

QUESTION **3**   The area of this triangle is 52.5 cm². What is the length of side *AC*?

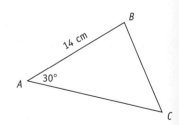

_____

_____

_____

_____

Excel MATHEMATICS STANDARD 2

Ch. 3, pp. 54–55

Miscellaneous problems 1

QUESTION **1**

a In $\triangle ABC$, $a = 2.5$ cm, $b = 3$ cm and $c = 4$ cm. Find $\angle A$ correct to the nearest degree.

b In $\triangle ABC$, $\angle A = 75°$, $\angle B = 38°$ and $a = 14.7$ cm. Find b.

_____

_____

_____

_____

_____

_____

_____

_____

_____

_____

QUESTION **2**   In the figure below (not drawn to scale), $LM = 9$ m, $NR = 5$ m, $\angle RLM = 63°$, $\angle RML = 30°$, $\angle NRM = 36°$, $RM = a$ metres and $MN = b$ metres. Use the sine rule to find a and the cosine rule to find b (correct to one decimal place).

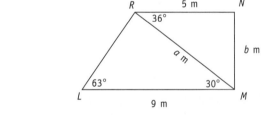

_____

_____

_____

_____

_____

_____

_____

_____

_____

_____

_____

_____

Measurement: Non-right-angled trigonometry

Miscellaneous problems 2

QUESTION **1**

a Using the information given in the diagram and the sine rule in $\triangle ABC$, show that $b = \dfrac{120 \sin 38°}{\sin 32°}$.

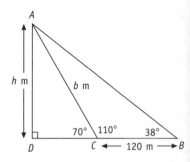

_____

_____

_____

_____

_____

b Hence find the value of b correct to two decimal places.

_____

_____

_____

_____

c Use the right-angled $\triangle ADC$ to find the value of h correct to two decimal places.

_____

_____

_____

_____

_____

QUESTION **2**   In the diagram P, Q and R represent three towns. Town P is 25 km due west of town Q. The bearing of P from R is 018° and of Q from R is 048°.

a Find the size of $\angle PRQ$.

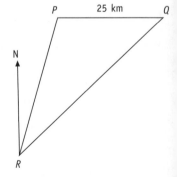

_____

_____

_____

b Find the size of $\angle PQR$.

_____

_____

_____

c Find the distance from P to R.

_____

_____

_____

Measurement: Non-right-angled trigonometry

Bearings 1

QUESTION **1**   For each diagram, write down the true bearing of Q from P.

a

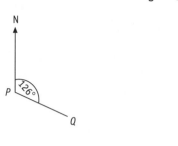

_____

_____

b

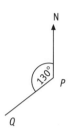

_____

_____

c

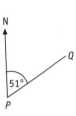

_____

_____

d

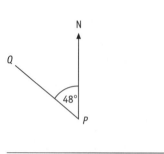

_____

_____

e

_____

_____

f

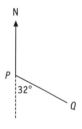

_____

_____

QUESTION **2**   A ship sets out from a point A and sails due north to a point B, a distance of 150 km. It then sails due east to a point C. If the bearing of C from A is 048°, find:

a   the distance BC

_____

_____

_____

_____

b   the distance AC

_____

_____

_____

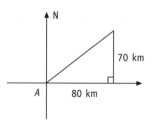

QUESTION **3**   A ship leaves port for a destination 80 km east and 70 km north. On what compass bearing should it sail?

_____

_____

_____

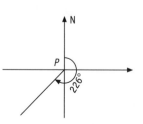

QUESTION **4**   A ship starts from a port P, sails 226°T for a distance of 120 km. Find:

a   how far south of P it is

_____

_____

_____

b   how far west of P it is

_____

_____

_____

Measurement: Non-right-angled trigonometry

Bearings 2

QUESTION 1   What is the size of the angle between each pair of directions?

a N and E _____

b N and S _____

c S and SW _____

d S and SE _____

e N and NE _____

f N and SW _____

QUESTION 2   Show each bearing:

a 035°

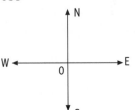

b N 64° E

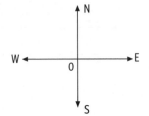

c 260°

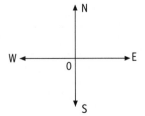

QUESTION 3   Write the true bearing and the compass bearing of *P* from 0:

a

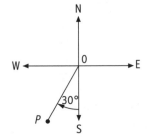

b

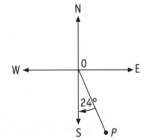

c

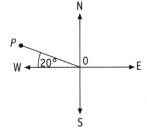

QUESTION 4   A ship sailed 12 km north and then 20 km west. Find its bearing (to the nearest degree) from the starting point.

_____

_____

_____

QUESTION 5   A man walked due south and then turned and walked due east. He was then 3 km S 50° E from his starting point. How far (to the nearest metre) was he south of his initial position?

_____

_____

_____

QUESTION 6   A lighthouse is 10 km north-east of a ship. How far is the ship west of the lighthouse (correct to two decimal places)?

_____

_____

_____

Measurement: Non-right-angled trigonometry

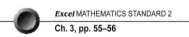

Excel MATHEMATICS STANDARD 2

Ch. 3, pp. 55–56

Compass radial survey

QUESTION **1**   The diagram shows the result of a compass radial survey conducted on an area of land.

a Find the magnitude of angles *BPC* and *APC*.

_____

_____

_____

_____

b Use the cosine rule to find the length in metres of *BC*, correct to one decimal place.

_____

_____

_____

_____

_____

_____

_____

_____

_____

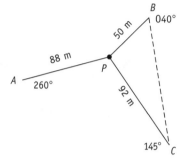

(Figure not to scale)

QUESTION **2**   The diagram shows the results of a compass radial survey of a triangular area of land.

a Find the size of angle *ROQ*.

_____

_____

_____

_____

b Find the area of the triangle *ROQ*.

_____

_____

_____

_____

_____

_____

_____

_____

Measurement: Non-right-angled trigonometry

TOPIC TEST

SECTION I

Instructions • This section consists of 5 multiple-choice questions.
• Each question is worth 1 mark.
• Fill in only ONE CIRCLE for each question.

Time allowed: 7 minutes   **Total marks: 5**

1 If A is an acute angle, find A to the nearest degree in the expression $\sin A = \dfrac{25 \sin 65°}{36}$.

ⓐ 30°   ⓑ 39°

ⓒ 47°   ⓓ 63°

2 Determine the value of a correct to one decimal place if $a^2 = 8^2 + 9^2 - 2 \times 8 \times 9 \cos 85°$.

ⓐ 11.5   ⓑ 6.3

ⓒ 7.8   ⓓ 12.3

3 Find the size of angle A correct to the nearest degree if $\cos A = \dfrac{5^2 + 6^2 - 7^2}{2 \times 5 \times 6}$.

ⓐ 89°   ⓑ 38°

ⓒ 49°   ⓓ 78°

4 The area of the triangle is 220 cm².

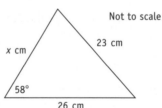

Which of these is closest to the value of x?

ⓐ 19   ⓑ 20

ⓒ 21   ⓓ 22

5 In the diagram P is due west of Q and R is due north of Q. $\angle RPQ = 38°$. The bearing of P from R is:

ⓐ 038°   ⓑ 052°

ⓒ 218°   ⓓ 232°

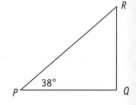

Instructions
- This section consists of 9 questions.
- Show all working.

Time allowed: 53 minutes

Total marks: 35

6 Find the length of the side marked x. Give the answer to the nearest metre.

3 marks each

a

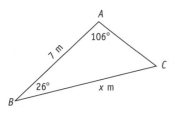

b

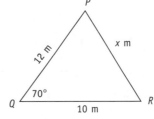

_____
_____
_____
_____
_____

_____
_____
_____
_____
_____

7 Find the size of the angle θ to the nearest degree.

3 marks each

a

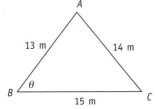

b

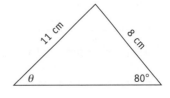

_____
_____
_____
_____

_____
_____
_____
_____

8 In the diagram Y is 15 km due east of X and 25 km due north of Z.
Find the true bearing of X from Z.

3 marks

_____
_____
_____
_____
_____
_____

9 In the diagram drawn, *ABCD* is a quadrilateral in which *AB* = 14 m, *BC* = 10 m, *AD* = 17.5 m, ∠*A* = 50°, ∠*C* = 55°.

2 marks each

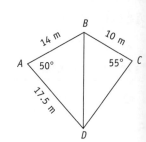

a Use the cosine rule to find the length of *BD* correct to one decimal place.

_____

_____

_____

_____

_____

b Use the sine rule to find the size of ∠*BDC* correct to the nearest degree.

_____

_____

_____

_____

_____

10 a Using the information given in the diagram and the sine rule in *ABC*, show that $b = \dfrac{135 \sin 46°}{\sin 34°}$.

2 marks

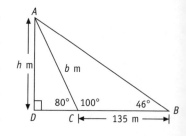

_____

_____

_____

_____

_____

b Hence find the value of *b* correct to one decimal place.

1 mark

_____

_____

c Use the right-angled triangle *ADC* to find the value of *h* correct to one decimal place.

2 marks

_____

_____

_____

11 *ABCD* is a parallelogram in which *AD* = *BC* = 11.2 cm, *AC* = 13.5 cm and ∠*DAC* = ∠*ACB* = 60°.

a Find the area of ∠*ABC* to one decimal place.

2 marks

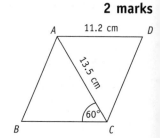

_____

_____

_____

_____

_____

b Hence find the area of the parallelogram to the nearest square centimetre.　　　　**1 mark**

_____

_____

12 A radial survey of a field is shown.

a Find the size of ∠POQ.　　　　**1 mark**

_____

b Calculate the area of △POQ.　　　　**2 marks**

_____

_____

_____

_____

c Find the size of ∠SOP.　　　　**1 mark**

_____

_____

_____

(Not to scale)

13 A surveyor's notebook contained the following radial survey. Calculate the distance between the tree and the tower to the nearest metre.　　　　**2 marks**

_____

_____

_____

_____

_____

_____

_____

_____

_____

_____

_____

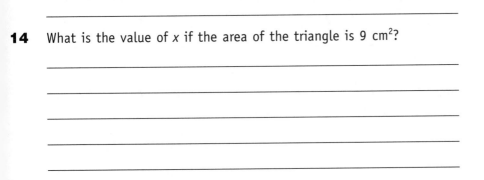

14 What is the value of x if the area of the triangle is 9 cm²?　　　　**2 marks**

_____

_____

_____

_____

_____

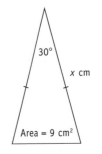

CHAPTER 7

Measurement: Rates and ratio

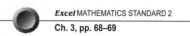

Using unit pricing

QUESTION 1   Find the cost per 100 g for the following products, correct to four decimal places if necessary:

a 440-g packet of spaghetti at $2.35

b 175-g packet of chocolate biscuits at $3.45

c 640-g box of cereal at $5.40

d 420-g can of crushed tomatoes at $1.60

QUESTION 2   Find the cost per 100 mL for the following products, correct to four decimal places:

a 600-mL container of thickened cream at $3.40

b 510-mL bottle of barbecue sauce at $2.80

c 390-mL bottle of shampoo at $6.80

d 1.25 L of soft drink at $2.18

QUESTION 3   Macca surveyed the price of vegemite available in different sized jars in different stores and recorded the results in the table below. Complete the table by calculating each price/100 g, correct to two decimal places.

Store	Size	Price	Price/100 g
A	560 g	$7.90	
B	453 g	$6.45	
C	380 g	$5.80	
D	280 g	$4.90	
E	220 g	$3.75	

QUESTION 4   Arrange these packets of toilet rolls from the most to least expensive: 6 rolls for $4.05, 12 rolls for $8.40, 8 rolls for $5.80 and 24 rolls for $14.60.

QUESTION 5   Arrange these nuts from the least to most expensive: brazil nuts at $5.49/100 g, cashews at $7.49/250 g, pecans at $2.35/50 g, hazelnuts at $9.29/300 g.

QUESTION 6   Kiwifruit is sold in different ways: 4 for $2.85, 6 for $4.40, 12 for $8.65 and 3 for $2.15. Which product gives the cheapest way to buy one dozen kiwifruit?

Measurement: Rates and ratio

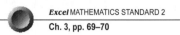

Speed

QUESTION 1 Express each of these speeds as m/s, correct to one decimal place:

a 60 km/h

b 45 km/h

c 110 km/h

_____ _____ _____

QUESTION 2 Write these speeds as km/h:

a 12 m/s

b 34 m/s

c 18 m/s

_____ _____ _____

QUESTION 3 A certain tortoise can walk at 60 m/h and a certain hare can run at 36 km/h.

a How far, in metres, can both animals travel in a minute?

_____

b The hare and the tortoise plan to have a race over a distance of 100 m. The hare is so confident he gives the tortoise a 99.5-m head start. Which animal is likely to win the race? Justify your answer with calculations.

_____

QUESTION 4 Daniel left Albay at 9:20 am and drove to Bichero averaging 90 km/h. He arrived at his destination at 11:10 am.

a What is the distance from Albay to Bichero?

_____

b Daniel drove the same route home. If he left Bichero at 4:25 pm and averaged 75 km/h at what time would he arrive in Albay?

_____

QUESTION 5 The Mecano highway has a 200-km straight section of road. The midpoint of the straight section is the town of Cronkers Creek. At 2:30 pm, Bill leaves Cronkers Creek and drives east at an average speed of 100 km/h. Jill leaves from the same spot and at the same time as Bill and drives west at an average speed of 90 km/h.

a How far are they apart at 3 pm? _____

b After what time will the distance between them exceed 114 km?

_____

QUESTION 6 The distance-time graph for two moving objects is shown.

a What is the speed of object *A*, in kilometres/hour?

_____

b How much further has object *A* travelled than object *B* after 2 hours?

_____

QUESTION 7 When Juliet is driving her car her reaction time before she brakes is 0.95 seconds. Find her reaction-time distance, to the nearest metre, if she is travelling at:

a 40 km/h _____

b 90 km/h _____ _____

c 110 km/h _____

Measurement: Rates and ratio

Heart rates

QUESTION **1**   Cedric measures his heart rate by counting his pulse for 30 seconds. What is his heart rate in beats per minute (bpm) if he counts:

a 32 beats?

b 38 beats?

QUESTION **2**   The table shows the resting heart rate (RHR) for women of different age ranges across four fitness levels.

Resting heart rate (RHR) for women (bpm)					
	Age range				
Fitness level	**18 to 25**	**26 to 35**	**36 to 45**	**46 to 55**	**56 to 65**
Athlete	54–60	54–59	54–59	54–59	54–59
Good	66–69	65–68	65–69	66–69	65–68
Average	74–78	73–76	74–78	74–77	73–76
Poor	85+	83+	85+	84+	84+

a Jessica is 42 years old and her resting heart rate is 76 bpm. What is her likely fitness level?

b Melissa is 27 years old and represents NSW in netball. What is a likely range of Melissa's resting heart rate?

c The resting heart rate for a man is about 3 beats per minute less than for a woman of a similar age and fitness level. Estimate the range of RHR for 59-year-old Bob with a 'good' fitness level.

QUESTION **3**   The suggested maximum heart rate is 220 bpm minus your age. What is the maximum heart rate for a person aged:

a 25? _____   **b** 45? _____   **c** 75? _____

QUESTION **4**   An alternative method to determine a person's maximum heart rate (MHR), in beats per minute (bpm), is to use the formula MHR = 208 − 0.7a, where a is the person's age in years. Use the formula to estimate the maximum heart rate, to the nearest bpm, of a person who is:

a 30 years old _____   **b** 60 years old _____   **c** 86 years old _____

QUESTION **5**

Generally, the target heart rate during moderate intensity activity is 50–70% of the maximum heart rate, while during vigorous physical activity the rate is 70–85% of the maximum heart rate. Use this information to complete the table.

	Heart rates after activity based on age		
	Target heart rate zone (bpm)		
	Moderate activity	**Intense activity**	**Maximum heart rate**
Age	**50-70% max.**	**70-85% max.**	**(bpm)**
20	100–140	140–170	200
30	95–133	133–162	190
40	90–126		180
50		119–145	170
60	80–112	112–136	160
70	75–105	105–127.5	150

Measurement: Rates and ratio

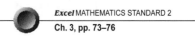

Watts and kilowatt hours

QUESTION **1** Complete:

a _____ W = 120 J for 3 seconds

b 60 W = _____ J for 2 seconds

c 100 W = 1 kJ for _____ seconds

QUESTION **2** Calculate the number of kilowatt hours for an appliance that uses:

a 600 W for 3 hours _____

b 450 W for 24 hours _____

c 60 W for 8 hours each day for 6 days _____

QUESTION **3** An electricity company published the price of electricity available to consumers.

Period of day	Time	Price per kWh
Peak	Weekdays: 2 pm – 8 pm	53.911 cents
Shoulder	Weekdays: 7 am – 2 pm and 8 pm – 10 pm Weekends: 7 am – 10 pm	22.594 cents
Off-peak	All other times	15.191 cents

a A clothes dryer uses 3000 W of electricity. What is the cost of running the dryer for 90 minutes starting at:

i 5:30 pm on a Wednesday?   **ii** 8:30 pm on a Monday?   **iii** 10:30 pm on a Sunday?

_____   _____   _____

b A dishwasher uses 1800 W. What is the cost of using the dishwasher for 40 minutes starting at:

i 11:50 pm on a Wednesday?   **ii** 8:30 am on a Friday?   **iii** 7:00 pm on a Tuesday?

_____   _____   _____

c Comment, using calculations, on the cost of using a 1500-W heater for 2 hours starting at 5:30 pm on a weekday compared to a weekend.

_____

d i Use the table to find the average cost of electricity per hour across the entire week.

_____

ii Hence, compare the cost of running a 12-W LED light globe to a 20-W halogen light globe all day (24 hours) for a week.

_____

QUESTION **4** Bridgett washes two loads of washing every Saturday morning from 7:30. For a cold water cycle she uses 0.3 kWh of electricity per load, but when Bridgett selects a warm water cycle she uses 4.5 kWh per load. How much money does Bridgett save by using cold water rather than warm water in one year if electricity costs 22.594 cents/kWh?

_____

QUESTION **5** An old-fashioned incandescent 100-W light globe converts 5% of its energy to light and 95% to heat. If electricity costs an average of 21.6 cents/kWh, how much money is wasted on heat, rather than light, if the globe is turned on for 24 hours for one week?

_____

Measurement: Rates and ratio

Fuel consumption

QUESTION **1**   Find the fuel consumption (in L/100 km) for a car, correct to one decimal place, that:

a uses 45 L of fuel on a journey of 650 km

b travels 586 km and uses 38 L of fuel

QUESTION **2**   On a trip Andrew's car has a fuel consumption rate of 7.6 L/100 km. How much fuel has been used on a trip of:

a 380 km?

b 515 km?

QUESTION **3**   If a car uses fuel at the rate of 8.3 L/100 km, how far will it travel, to the nearest kilometre, using:

a 45 litres of fuel?

b $60 of fuel if fuel costs 172.9 c/L?

QUESTION **4**   Luke buys fuel at 166.9 cents/L. If his car has a fuel consumption rate of 8.1 L/100 km, what is the cost of fuel, to the nearest cent, for a journey of:

a 180 km?

b 435 km?

QUESTION **5**   Michael and Jenny are both driving their own vehicles from Gloucester to Broadbeach, a distance of 605 km. Michael's car has a fuel consumption rate of 7.3 L/100 km while Jenny's car averages 5.9 L/100 km. If both drivers buy fuel at a price of 179.9 c/L, what is the difference in the amount of money they pay for fuel, correct to the nearest cent?

QUESTION **6**   The table shows the price per litre of three types of petrol.

a Connor spent $45 on 95-octane petrol. If his car averages 6.8 L/100 km, how far will he travel on his purchase, to the nearest kilometre?

Cost of petrol	
Fuel type	**Cost/L**
91-octane	143.9
95-octane	154.9
98-octane	161.9

b Eliana's car has an average fuel consumption rate of 7.9 L/100 km. What is the cost of a trip of 290 km, to the nearest cent, if she uses:

i 91-octane petrol?

ii 98-octane petrol?

c Ryan drove 480 km and his car averaged 6.9 L/100 km. How much would he have saved on petrol if he had used 91-octane petrol rather than 95-octane petrol, to the nearest cent?

d Lincoln and Sarah both paid $60 for their petrol. Lincoln used 91-octane petrol and his car averaged 8.3 L/100 km while Sarah used 98-octane and her car averaged 7.7 L/100 km. Which person drove the greater distance on the petrol purchase? Justify your answer with calculations.

Measurement: Rates and ratio

Simplifying ratio

QUESTION 1   Write these ratios in their simplest forms:

a   6:8

b   2.5:10

c   3 km:10 m

d   2 weeks:6 days

e $1.20:80c

f   2.7 mm:5.4 cm

QUESTION 2   Each week Mia is paid a net wage of $450. She saves $120 and spends the remainder. Express the following in simplest form:

a   the ratio of money saved to money spent

b   the ratio of money spent to money earned

QUESTION 3   A rectangle has its sides in the ratio of 2:3. Calculate the length of the:

a   shorter side if the longer side is 18 cm

b   perimeter if the shorter side is 24 cm

QUESTION 4   Eucalypts and acacias are planted along a roadside in the ratio of 3:7. If there are 210 acacias, how many eucalypts are there?

QUESTION 5   James and Merrill are employed at a restaurant to provide background music. James plays the piano and Merrill sings. They decide to split any tips they receive in their tip-jar in the ratio of 3:4.

a   If Merrill's share of the tips is $60, how much will James receive?

b   If James's share of the tips is $36, what was the total amount collected?

QUESTION 6   Find the value of n if the following ratios are simplified to the form 1:n:

a   6:24

b   4:6

c   5:13

QUESTION 7

a   Steve mixes petrol and oil in the ratio of 25:1 to make fuel for his brush cutter. How much oil does Steve add to a container of 4.75 L of petrol?

b   How much fuel does the container now hold? _____

c   If Steve wants the ratio to change to 60:1 how much petrol would he now need to add to the container?

Measurement: Rates and ratio

Dividing a quantity into a given ratio

QUESTION **1**   Divide the following amounts in the ratio given:

a $20 in the ratio of 3:5

b   1.2 kg in the ratio of 2:3:1

c   8 hours in the ratio of 3:5:2

_____

_____

_____

QUESTION **2**   A 2-L bottle of soft drink is to be shared between three boys in the ratio of 1:4:5. How many millilitres will each boy drink?

_____

_____

QUESTION **3**   Grandma gives $20000 to her three granddaughters in the ratio of their ages. If Olivia is 16, Ava is 14 and Sophia is 10 years old how much money will each girl receive?

_____

_____

QUESTION **4**   Concrete is mixed using cement, sand and gravel in the ratio of 1:3:6. If Davo wants to make 120 kg of concrete how much of each product will he need?

_____

_____

QUESTION **5**   Barb and Ernie together bought a $10 lottery ticket. Barb contributed $6 and Ernie the remainder. If they share in a win of $120000 in the ratio of their contributions, how much will Ernie receive?

_____

_____

QUESTION **6**   The side lengths of a triangle are in the ratio of 3:5:7. What is the length of the longest side if the perimeter is 75 cm?

_____

_____

QUESTION **7**   The ratio of the populations of town A and town B is 4:3, and the populations of town B to town C is 5:6.

a What is the ratio of the population of town A to town B to town C? _____

b If the total population of the three towns is 10600, what is the population of town C?

_____

QUESTION **8**   A rectangular paddock had a perimeter of 480 m. If the ratio of its length to width is 7:5, find the area of the paddock, in hectares.

_____

_____

Measurement: Rates and ratio

Capture-recapture

QUESTION **1** A ranger caught a random sample of 60 rabbits in a national park. She tagged them and then released them. She returned to the park later in the week and caught a random sample of 50 rabbits. In this sample four had been tagged. Using the capture/recapture technique, what is the estimated number of rabbits in the park?

QUESTION **2** A biologist used the following method to estimate the population of frogs in an ecosystem.
- 50 frogs were caught, tagged and released.
- Later, 140 frogs were caught at random.
- 30 of these 140 frogs had been tagged.

What was the estimated population of frogs in the ecosystem?

QUESTION **3** Melinda wishes to estimate the number of sunflower plants on a square paddock of land measuring 1 hectare. She counts the number of sunflower plants on a 2 m by 2 m section of the paddock and finds there are nine plants. Based on this, estimate the number of sunflower plants on the entire square block of land.

QUESTION **4** A station manager used the capture-recapture technique to estimate the number of feral camels he had on his property. He captured, tagged and released 32 of the camels. Later, he caught 54 camels at random and found that six had been tagged. What is the estimate for the total number of camels on his property?

QUESTION **5** The capture-recapture technique was used to estimate a population of seals in 2021.
- 80 seals were caught, tagged and released.
- Later, 160 seals were caught at random
- 12 of these 160 seals had been tagged.

The estimated population of seals in 2021 was 8% more than the estimated population for 2015. What was the estimated population for 2015?

QUESTION **6** A scientific study uses the 'capture-recapture' technique. In the first stage of the study, 36 crocodiles were caught, tagged and released. Later, in the second stage of the study, some crocodiles were captured from the same area. It was found that 45% of the captured crocodiles were tagged. Estimate the total population of crocodiles in this area.

Measurement: Rates and ratio

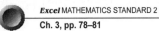

Converting map scales

QUESTION **1**   Write each of the following scales in simplest ratio form:

a 1 mm to 1 m

b 1 cm to 1 m

c 1 cm to 100 m

d 10 cm to 1 km

e 4 mm to 1 m

f 5 cm to 1 m

g 1 mm to 20 m

h 20 cm to 1 m

i 1 mm to 6 m

QUESTION **2**   Using a scale of 1:100, what length, in metres, is represented by:

a 1 cm?

b 3 cm?

c 5 cm?

d 8 mm?

e 6 mm?

f 12 m?

QUESTION **3**   Using a scale of 1:1000, what is the real length represented by each of the following?

a 8 mm

b 5 cm

c 6 m

d 9.5 cm

e 8.3 m

f 63.25 m

QUESTION **4**   The distance between two points in real life is given. What is this distance on a scale drawing with scale 1 cm to 100 m?

a 500 m

b 400 m

c 1260 m

d 80 m

e 3000 m

f 2835 m

QUESTION **5**   A map has a scale of 1:100 000.

a A distance of 1 cm on the map will represent a real distance of how many kilometres?

b The distance between two towns on the map is 8.4 cm. How far apart are the two towns?

c The real straight-line distance between *A* and *B* is 26 km. How long will this distance be on the map?

Measurement: Rates and ratio

Scale drawings 1

QUESTION **1**   A block of land, along with the proposed building, has been drawn using a scale of 1:500. By measurement and calculation find:

a   the width of the block

_____

b   the depth of the block

_____

c   the area of the block

_____

d   how far the proposed building is from the southern boundary

_____

_____

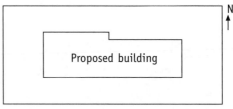

Scale 1 : 500

e   the area of the proposed building

_____   _____

_____   _____

_____   _____

QUESTION **2**   The diagram shows a scale drawing of a cross-section of a pipe. The outer diameter of the pipe is 1.44 m.

a   By measurement and calculation find the scale used for the drawing.

_____

_____

_____

_____

b   What is the inside diameter of the pipe?

_____

_____

_____

QUESTION **3**   Toby has made a rough sketch of a block of land he is considering buying.

a   Make a scale drawing of the block (below) using a scale of 1:400.

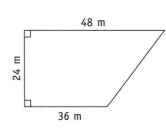

b   What is the perimeter of the block to the nearest metre? _____

Measurement: Rates and ratio

Scale drawings 2

QUESTION 1   Use the scale to determine the length and width of this swimming pool.

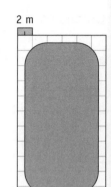

2 m

_____

QUESTION 2   *Edmontosaurus* was a large, duck-billed dinosaur of the late Cretaceous Period.

Assuming the man stands 1.8 m tall, how long is the dinosaur?

_____

_____

QUESTION 3   Calculate the perimeter of this land.

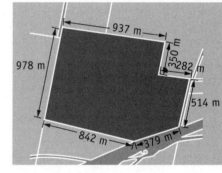

_____

_____

_____

QUESTION 4   The diagram shows some land area with a lake inside it. A scale is provided.

a   Use the scale to estimate the perimeter of the land.

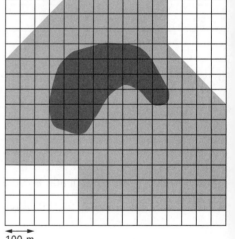

_____

b   Estimate the perimeter of the lake.

_____

c   What is the area of each of the small squares on the grid?

_____

d   By counting the number of these small squares, estimate the area of land (including lake). Write the answer both in square metres and hectares (1 ha = 10 000 m²).

_____

_____

100 m

e   Estimate the area of the lake.

_____

f   What percentage of the land area is taken up by the lake?

_____

Measurement: Rates and ratio

Interpreting floor plans

QUESTION **1**   The diagram shows a floor plan of a house.

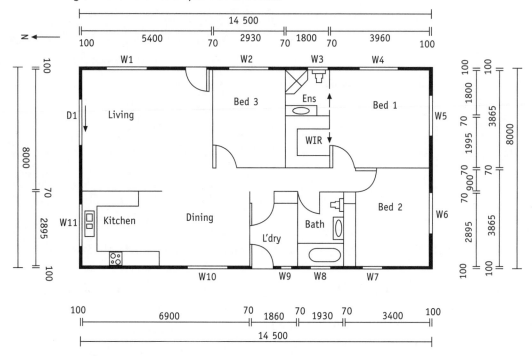

a What is the width of the house? _____

b What is the feature marked D1? _____

c What is the feature labelled WIR? _____

d What are the dimensions of bedroom 3? _____

e What is the width of each internal wall? _____

f What is the width of the external walls? _____

g In which elevation is there not a door? _____

h One of the measurements for the living room is missing. What should it be?

_____

i If building costs are $775 per square metre, how much will it cost to build this house?

_____

_____

_____

_____

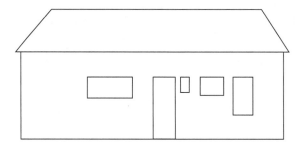

j Lisa has drawn a sketch, not to scale, of one side of the house. Which elevation did she sketch?

_____

Measurement: Rates and ratio

Land areas and lengths

QUESTION **1**   The island of Hispaniola is shared by Haiti and the Dominican Republic.

a Using North–South distances, how wide is the widest part of the island?

_____

b How far, in a straight line, is Port-au-Prince from Santo Domingo?

_____

c Calculate the closest distance from Haiti to Cuba.

_____

_____

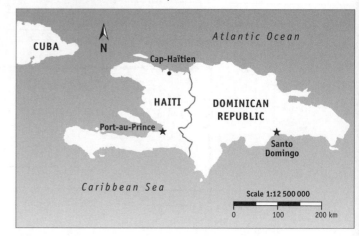

d Given that the area of Haiti is 27 750 km², which of the following is closest to the area of the Dominican Republic?

   Ⓐ 30 000 km²　　Ⓑ 40 000 km²　　Ⓒ 50 000 km²　　Ⓓ 60 000 km²

QUESTION **2**   A land area is being subdivided to build houses. The diagram is drawn to scale.

a Block number 2 has a 20-m frontage. Calculate the length of the dimension marked.

_____

b Calculate the area for block number 2.

_____

c What is the combined length of Blaise Road and Pascal Street (measured between points A and B) shown in the diagram?

_____

_____

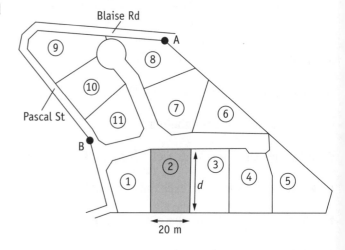

QUESTION **3**   The diagram shows the water catchment area for a river.

a Estimate the area of land covered by this catchment.

_____

b Suppose the average rainfall over this catchment area is 75 mm. Calculate the volume of water, in megalitres, that would flow into the river system.

_____

_____

_____

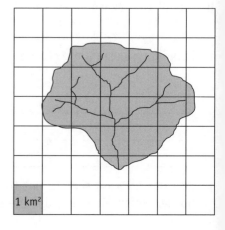

Measurement: Rates and ratio

Applying the trapezoidal rule

QUESTION **1**   Use the trapezoidal rule to calculate the approximate area of the shapes below:

a

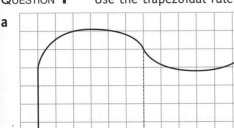

—30 m—

b

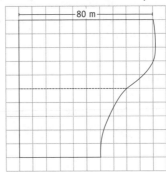

—80 m—

_____

_____

_____

_____

QUESTION **2**   The diagram, drawn to scale, shows a dam *PQRS* in the middle of a rectangular paddock *ABCD*. The distance *QS* is 60 m.

a Use your ruler to complete the scale

1 cm = _____ m.

b Express these lengths, to the nearest metre:

  i *AX* _____

  ii *AP* _____

  iii *XQ* _____

  iv *BR* _____

  v *PD* _____

  vi *SY* _____

  vii *RC* _____

c Using applications of the trapezoidal rule, find an approximation for the area of the dam.

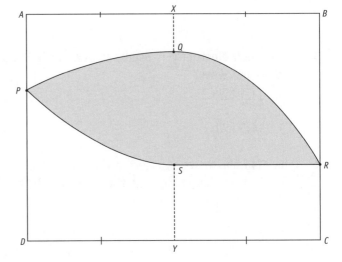

_____

d If the dam has an average depth of 2.4 m, find an approximation for the volume of water in the dam, to the nearest megalitre.

_____

_____

QUESTION **3**   The diagram shows a scale drawing of the roof of a building with *AE* = 25 m.

a Explain why *AP* = 15 m and *PE* = 20 m. _____

_____

b Find the area of the roof. _____

c All rain that falls on the roof is drained to a tank. If 40 mm of rain fell, how much water is added to the tank, in litres?

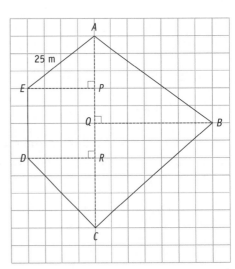

25 m

_____

Measurement: Rates and ratio

TOPIC TEST

Instructions
- This section consists of 5 multiple-choice questions.
- Each question is worth 1 mark.
- Fill in only ONE CIRCLE for each question.

Time allowed: 7 minutes   **Total marks: 5**

---

1 The concentration of a drug in a certain medication is 80 mg/5 mL. A patient is prescribed 280 mg of the drug. How many millilitres of the medication will the patient need to be given?

Ⓐ 7 mL   Ⓑ 16 mL

Ⓒ 17.5 mL   Ⓓ 22.5 mL

2 When Oriana is driving her car, her reaction time before she brakes is 0.92 seconds. What is her reaction-time distance, to the nearest metre, if she is travelling at 68 km/h?

Ⓐ 17 m   Ⓑ 18 m

Ⓒ 21 m   Ⓓ 23 m

3 How much electricity is used per week by a 3000-W clothes dryer if it is used for 90 minutes on each of 3 days per week?

Ⓐ 11.7 kWh   Ⓑ 13.5 kWh

Ⓒ 14.5 kWh   Ⓓ 31.5 kWh

4 The diagram shows a scale drawing of a paddock *ABCD* in the shape of a trapezium. A farmer is to use a chemical on the paddock at the rate of 3.2L/ha. Which of these is the amount of chemical used?

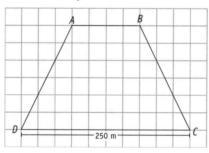

Ⓐ 3.9 L   Ⓑ 4 L

Ⓒ 4.2 L   Ⓓ 8.4 L

5 A bag contains red, blue and green balls. The ratio of red balls to blue balls is 3 : 5 and there are twice as many green balls as blue balls. If there is a total of 90 balls in the bag, how many are green?

Ⓐ 23   Ⓑ 40

Ⓒ 45   Ⓓ 50

TOPIC TEST

SECTION II

Instructions • This section consists of 9 questions.
• Show all working.

Time allowed: 53 minutes

Total marks: 35

6 Convert:

a 24 m/s = _____ km/h

1 mark

b 3.6×10^5 W = _____ kW

1 mark

c 40 W = _____ J/second

1 mark

7 The distance-time graph for a moving object is shown on the graph below.

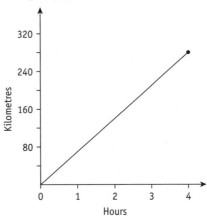

What is the speed of the object, to the nearest metres/second?

2 marks

_____

_____

8 The table shows an estimated number of kilojoules burned per kilogram of body mass **per 30 minutes** in different activities.

Activity	Energy used in 30 minutes
Walking: 6 km/h	9.22 kJ/kg
Cycling: 20 km/h	18.43 kJ/kg
Swimming: 50 m/min	20.73 kJ/kg
Jogging: 10 km/h	21.19 kJ/kg
Running: 16 km/h	32.25 kJ/kg

a Amber weighs 60 kg and jogs at 10 km/h for an hour. How much energy has she used, to the nearest kilojoule?

1 mark

_____

b Trent, who weighs 70 kg, drinks a 600-mL bottle of cola which contains 1080 kJ. For how long must Trent cycle at 20 km/h to burn off the energy contained in the bottle, to the nearest minute?

2 marks

_____

_____

c Mia, who weighs 54 kg, eats a chocolate bar which contains 241 kilocalories. For how long must Mia run at 16 km/h to burn off the energy contained in the chocolate bar, to the nearest minute? (1 kilocalorie = 4.184 kJ) **3 marks**

9 Carrie buys fuel at 162.9 cents/L. Her car uses an average of 7.4 L/100 km.

a What is the cost of fuel if Carrie drives 360 km? **2 marks**

b Carrie leaves home at 8:30 am and drives at an average speed of 82 km/h until she reaches her destination at 11:00 am. What is the cost of fuel used? **3 marks**

10 The diagram, drawn to scale, shows a paddock *ABCD*, with a small dam shown as *FPEQ*. The length of *DC* is 80 m.

a Find the area of the paddock, in square metres. **2 marks**

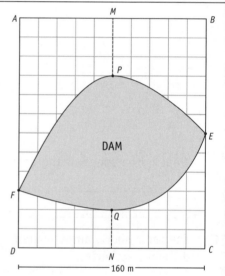

b Use applications of the trapezoidal rule to find the area of the dam. **3 marks**

c The average depth of the dam is 2.5 m. How many megalitres of water are in the dam? **1 mark**

11 An electricity company published the price of electricity available to consumers.

Period of day	Time	Price per kWh
Peak	Weekdays: 2 pm – 8 pm	53.911 cents
Shoulder	Weekdays: 7 am – 2 pm and 8 pm – 10 pm Weekends: 7 am – 10 pm	22.594 cents
Off-Peak	All other times	15.191 cents

a A portable heater uses 2400 W of electricity. What is the cost of running the heater for 45 minutes starting at 7 pm on a Tuesday? **2 marks**

b A dishwasher uses 1800 W of electricity and runs for 50 minutes. A family member turns the dishwasher on every night at 10 pm. What is the cost of electricity used in 4 weeks?   **2 marks**

_____

_____

12 A refrigerator is purchased for $1150 and has an energy rating sticker shown featuring the rate of the refrigerator's energy use.

If energy costs an average of $0.21/kWh, what is the total cost of the purchase and running of the refrigerator over 4 years?   **2 marks**

_____

_____

13 The area of a roof is 85 m² and all rain falling on the roof is caught by the gutters before draining to a water tank. If 48 mm of rain falls on the roof, how much water, in litres, is collected by the water tank?   **2 marks**

_____

_____

Source: Department of the Environment and Energy

14 The Basal Metabolic Rate (BMR) is the amount of energy expended while a person is at rest for 24 hours. The Harris-Benedict formula below can be used to calculate a BMR:

Gender	BMR Calculation
Women (kJ/day)	4.184 × [10 × weight (kg) + 6.25 × height (cm) – 5 × age (years) – 161]
Men (kJ/day)	4.184 × [10 × weight (kg) + 6.25 × height (cm) – 5 × age (years) + 5]

a Use the formula to calculate the BMR for a 48-year-old woman who has a mass of 65 kg and a height of 162 cm. Give your answer to the nearest kilojoule. _____

_____   **1 mark**

To determine a person's daily energy requirement (in kilojoules) the BMR is multiplied by an activity factor according to the description of their lifestyle (see the table below).

Lifestyle	Energy Requirement
Inactive	BMR × 1.2
Sedentary	BMR × 1.5
Moderately active	BMR × 1.6
Vigorously active	BMR × 2.3

b What is the daily energy requirement for a 28-year-old man with a mass of 78 kg and a height of 176 cm who has a moderately active lifestyle? _____

_____   **2 marks**

c The table shows information relating to twin brother and sisters, Jack and Jill. Which person has the greater daily energy need? _____

_____   **2 marks**

Name	Height (cm)	Mass (kg)	Age (years)	Lifestyle
Jack	168 cm	72 kg	29	Sedentary
Jill	165 cm	64 kg	29	Moderately active

CHAPTER 8
Statistical analysis: Bivariate data analysis

Excel MATHEMATICS STANDARD 2

Ch. 6, pp. 156–159

Constructing a scatterplot

QUESTION **1**   The table shows the number of weeks spent on a diet and the weight loss over that time for a group of six people.

Time (weeks)	4	5	7	10	12	15
Weight loss (kg)	1	3	2	3	4	3

a How many people:

   i were on a diet for more than 8 weeks?

   _____

   ii lost more than 2 kg?

   _____

b Use the data to draw a scatterplot on the graph.

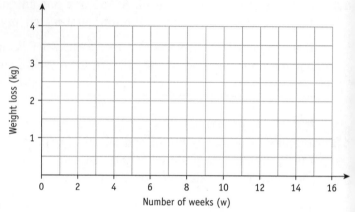

QUESTION **2**   The table below shows the maximum temperature across 10 days and the number of drinks purchased using a vending machine in a hospital.

Temperature (°C)	26	32	35	31	26	23	25	28	31	36
Number of drinks	24	34	48	40	28	18	24	29	36	44

a On how many days:

   i did the temperature exceed 30°?

   _____

   ii were more than 25 drinks sold?

   _____

b Draw a scatterplot of the data in the table.

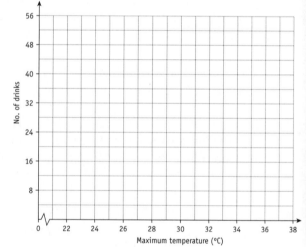

QUESTION **3**   The table below shows the height and handspan of eight female students.

Height (cm)	140	170	165	170	155	145	135	150
Handspan (cm)	16	18	21	22	18	17	15	19

Draw a scatterplot of the data in the table.

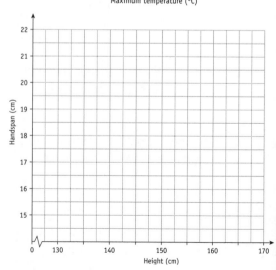

Statistical analysis: Bivariate data analysis

Excel MATHEMATICS STANDARD 2

Ch. 6, pp. 159–161

Correlation coefficients

QUESTION **1**

a What do correlation coefficients represent?

_____

_____

b What values can correlation coefficients have?

_____

c What is indicated by a positive correlation?

_____

d What is indicated by a negative correlation?

_____

e If the correlation is zero, what does this mean?

_____

QUESTION **2**   The following six scatter plots show relationships between two variables, x and y.

i 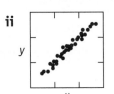 ii 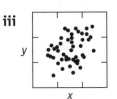 iii 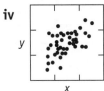 iv 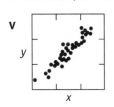 v 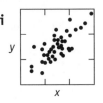 vi

Order these scatter plots in increasing strength of relationship; that is, with increasing correlation coefficients.

_____

QUESTION **3** The six diagrams show relationships between two variables, x and y.

i 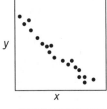   ii 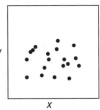   iii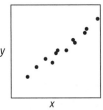

iv 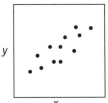   v 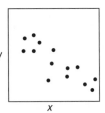   vi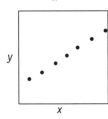

Match each diagram to the following correlation coefficients.

a $r = -0.9$ _____   **b** $r = -0.5$ _____   **c** $r = 0.0$ _____

d $r = 0.5$ _____   **e** $r = 0.9$ _____   **f** $r = 1.0$ _____

Statistical analysis: Bivariate data analysis

Calculating Pearson's correlation coefficients 1

QUESTION **1**   True or false?

a The value of any correlation coefficient, r, is $-1 \leq r \leq +1$. _____

b $r = -1$ and $r = +1$ if, and only if, the points lie exactly on a straight line. _____

c If the same amount is added to all of the x-values, the correlation coefficient is changed. _____

d If all of the x-values are multiplied by the same positive amount, the correlation coefficient is altered. _____

e If all of the x-values are multiplied by the same negative amount, the sign $(+/-)$ of the correlation coefficient changes. _____

QUESTION **2**   The following are scatter plots of some relationships.

i 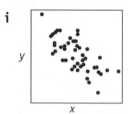   **ii** 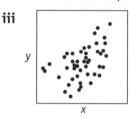   **iii** 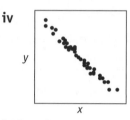   **iv** 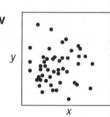   **v**

Identify the relationship showing:

a no correlation _____

b a weak positive correlation _____

c a weak negative correlation _____

d a strong positive correlation _____

e a strong negative correlation _____

QUESTION **3**   The following scatter plots show the relationship between biometric data on measuring the body.

i 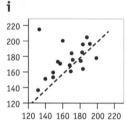   **ii** 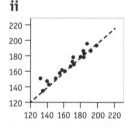   **iii** 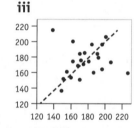   **iv** 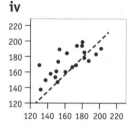   **v**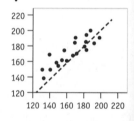

Match the plot with the following correlation coefficients.

a $r = 0.96$ _____   **b** $r = 0.87$ _____   **c** $r = 0.72$ _____   **d** $r = 0.45$ _____   **e** $r = 0.20$ _____

QUESTION **4**   The following shows a computer spreadsheet program where sets of values have been drawn on a scatter plot.

a Explain what is meant by the command =CORREL(A1:A19, B1:B19).

_____

_____

b In which cell is the correlation coefficient inserted? _____

c What is the correlation coefficient for this data, correct to two decimal places?

_____

(Note: In this course you are not expected to manually calculate the correlation coefficient. It is sufficient that you can obtain it by the use of appropriate technology.)

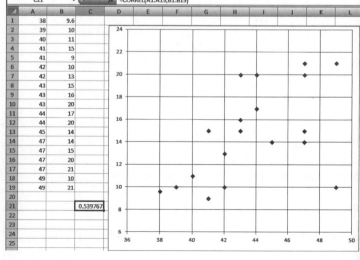

Statistical analysis: Bivariate data analysis

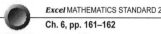
Calculating Pearson's correlation coefficients 2

QUESTION **1** If there is an obstruction in the pulmonary artery, the amount of carbon dioxide that can be carried is affected.

Pulmonary artery obstruction and carbon dioxide

Pulmonary artery obstruction (%)	CO$_2$ partial pressure
10	32
11	34
11	28
11	34
12	36
15	35
25	28
30	31
36	34
40	33
50	36
52	29
69	23
70	24
75	25
80	32
80	28
85	28
85	30
89	25

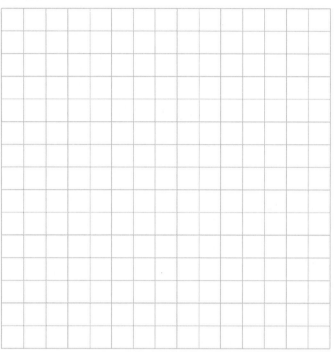

a Either manually on the grid provided above, or using appropriate technology, draw a scatter plot of this information.

b Use appropriate technology to calculate the correlation coefficient of the relationship, correct to two decimal places. _____

c What does the sign of this correlation coefficient indicate? _____

d Is this relationship strong, moderate or weak? _____

e Describe, in words, the relationship between pulmonary artery obstruction and CO$_2$ partial pressure.

_____

_____

f Draw by eye a straight line of fit on the scatter plot.

QUESTION **2** There is a relationship between the concentration of alcohol in someone's breath and that in their arteries.

Blood and breath alcohol concentration

Blood alcohol concentration (g/L)	0.0	0.1	0.2	0.3	0.4	0.5	0.6	0.7	0.8	0.9	1.0	1.1	1.2	1.3
Breath alcohol concentration (mg/L)	0.00	0.04	0.08	0.12	0.18	0.22	0.27	0.31	0.36	0.41	0.44	0.50	0.55	0.62

a Use appropriate technology to calculate the correlation coefficient. _____

b What does this value indicate? _____

Drawing a line of best fit by eye

QUESTION **1**   Use your ruler to draw a line of best fit by eye:

a
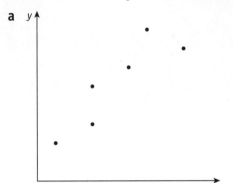

b
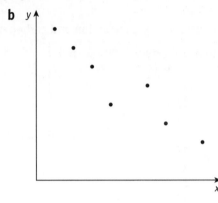

c
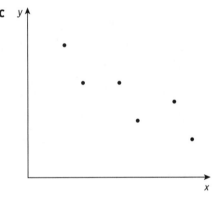

d
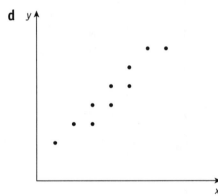

e
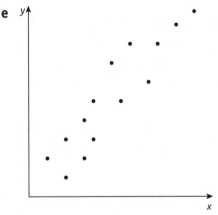

f
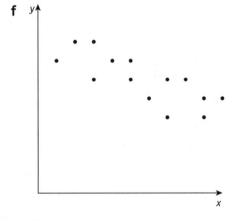

g
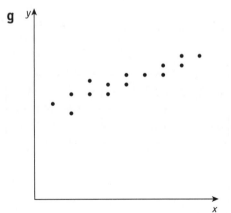

h
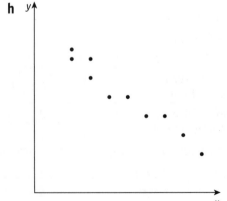

Statistical analysis: Bivariate data analysis

Equation of the line of best fit 1

QUESTION **1**   Find the equation of the line in the form $y = mx + c$ where:

a $m = 6$ and $c = 12$

b $m = 0.45$ and $c = -23$

c $m = \dfrac{4}{5}$ and $c = 8$

QUESTION **2**   Find the value of c in the line $y = 5x + c$ which passes through the point:

a (8, 63)

b (21, 54)

c (12.8, 3.6)

QUESTION **3**   Find the gradient of the line of best fit which passes through the points:

a (12, 18) and (22, 68)

b (8, 23) and (16, 25)

c (26, 63) and (39, 11)

QUESTION **4**   Find the equation of the line of best fit linking x and y, which passes through:

a (26, 37) and (51, 72)

b (12, 48) and (20, 16)

c (19, 101) and (51, 265)

QUESTION **5**   A line of best fit drawn on a scatterplot links basketballers' heights (h) to the average number of points (p) they scored in a match. The line passes through the points (187, 7) and (192, 15).

a Explain why the line has a gradient of 1.6.

b By substituting the point (187, 7) into the equation $p = 1.6h + c$, find the value of c.

QUESTION **6**   The number of skiers (s) each weekend at a ski resort depends on the depth of snow (d) in metres. A scatterplot records data over a series of days using d as the independent variable and s as the dependent variable. A line of best fit is drawn which passes through the points (1.6, 4300) and (2.4, 6400).

a Determine the equation of the line.

b In this context, what does the value of the constant c represent?

Statistical analysis: Bivariate data analysis

Equation of the line of best fit 2

QUESTION **1** Andrew investigated the relationship between the speed of his exercise bike and his pulse. After riding his bike for one minute at different speeds (km/h) he measured his pulse (beats/min). He recorded the data on a scatterplot and drew a line of best fit by eye.

a Andrew determined the equation of the line of best fit is $p = 3.8s + 65$.

What was his resting pulse, before he started any exercise?

_____

b Estimate his pulse when he is riding at 12 km/h.

_____

c Determine the speed he is riding if his pulse is 120 beats per minute.

_____

d How reliable do you think estimates outside this data would be? Justify your answer.

_____

_____

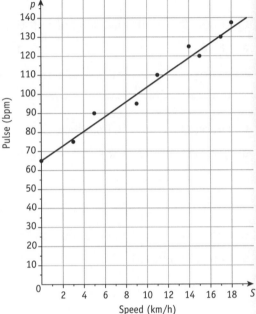

Bike speed and pulse rate

QUESTION **2** The heights (h) in centimetres and length of armspan (a) in centimetres of 12 students are recorded in the table below.

Student	A	B	C	D	E	F	G	H	I	J	K	L
height (h)	180	174	168	172	169	173	175	168	164	167	176	178
armspan (a)	176	175	171	173	168	172	171	172	165	169	172	175

a Use the data to draw a scatterplot using height as the independent variable and armspan as the dependent variable.

b Label the data for students J and L. Draw a line passing through J and L representing a line of best fit for the data for all 12 students.

c Use your line to estimate the:

i armspan of a student with a height of 176 cm

_____

_____

ii height of a student with an armspan of 170 cm

_____

_____

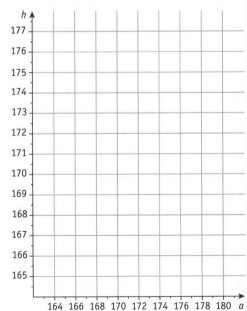

Statistical analysis: Bivariate data analysis

Using technology to find equation of regression line 1

QUESTION **1**   Use your calculator to find the equation of the least-squares regression line for the following sets of data:

a

Hours of study (*h*)	3	2	6	1	0	5
Test score (*s*)	78	76	91	48	63	84

b

Temperature in °C (*n*)	29	36	34	38	26	21
Water bottle sales (*S*)	24	27	35	32	17	8

c

Number of coffees (*n*)	3	5	1	2	0	3
Hours of sleep (*H*)	7.5	7.2	8.4	8.5	8.4	7.4

QUESTION **2**   The scatterplot shows the ankle circumference (*a*) and wrist circumference (*w*) of eight people.

a   Use your calculator to find the equation of the least-squares regression line for the data.

b   Use your equation to estimate the circumference of Ella's wrist if the circumference of her ankle is 21.5 cm.

c   Use your equation to estimate the circumference of Logan's ankle if the circumference of his wrist is 18.5 cm.

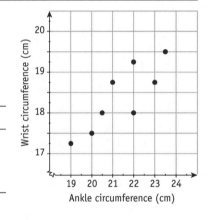

QUESTION **3**   The scatterplot shows the arm span (*s*) and height (*h*) of eight children aged between 10 and 13 years of age.

a   Use your calculator to find the equation of the least-squares regression line for the data.

b   Frida is 141 cm tall and is one of the children included in the group. Her twin brother Britton is 4 cm taller. Use your equation to estimate the length of Britton's arm span to the nearest centimetre.

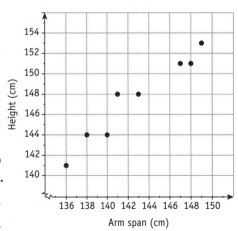

Statistical analysis: Bivariate data analysis

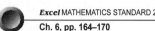

Using technology to find equation of regression line 2

QUESTION **1**   There is a strong relationship between the average height of parents and that of their children, when they are fully grown.

a Copy the following into a spreadsheet and use it to calculate the values shown and draw a scatter plot. (Heights are given to the nearest centimetre.)

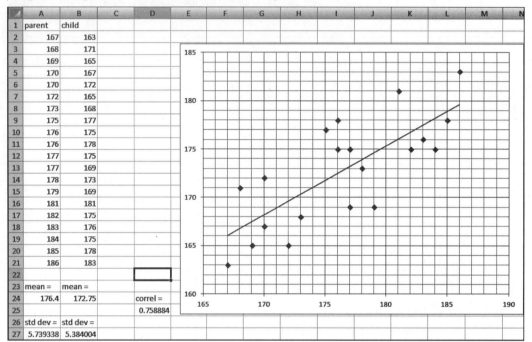

Click on the scatter plot and then click on Layout—Trendline—Linear Trendline. This inserts a line of best fit onto your scatter plot.

b The following describes how you can calculate the equation of the least-squares line of best fit. The equation of a straight line is given by $y = mx + b$, where m is the gradient and b is the y-intercept.

i   The gradient is found by: $gradient = correlation\ coefficient \times \dfrac{standard\ deviation\ of\ y\text{-}scores}{standard\ deviation\ of\ x\text{-}scores}$

Use this formula to calculate the gradient of your straight line, correct to two decimal places.

_____

ii   The y-intercept is found by: $y\text{-}intercept = $ mean of y-values $(\bar{y})$ – [gradient $\times$ mean of x-values $(\bar{x})$]

Use this formula to calculate the y-intercept of your straight line, correct to one decimal place.

_____

c   What is the equation of your straight line? _____

d   On a copy of your scatter plot, draw in the least-squares line of best fit.

e   How does your line compare to that generated by the computer? _____

f   Use your least-squares line of best fit to predict the average height of children whose parents are 174 cm.

_____

g   There is a reasonably high correlation between the average height of children and that of their parents. Is it true that parents' heights cause the heights of their children? Explain.

_____

Statistical analysis: Bivariate data analysis

TOPIC TEST

SECTION I

Instructions
- This section consists of 5 multiple-choice questions.
- Each question is worth 1 mark.
- Fill in only ONE CIRCLE for each question.

Time allowed: 7 minutes

Total marks: 5

1

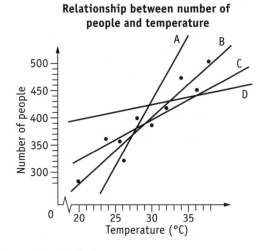

For the graph shown, the line of best fit is:

Ⓐ A   Ⓑ B   Ⓒ C   Ⓓ D

2 In writing the equation of this line in the form $y = mx + b$:

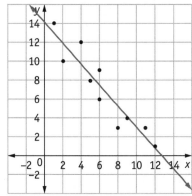

Ⓐ m is positive and $b = 14$ Ⓑ m is positive and $b = 13$

Ⓒ m is negative and $b = 14$ Ⓓ m is negative and $b = 13$

3 The graph shows the typing speed of a student. Based on the line of best fit, what would be the approximate typing speed, in words per minute, of a person who has practised for 4 weeks?

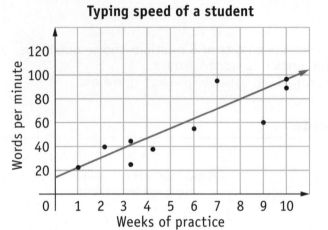

Ⓐ 40 Ⓑ 48 Ⓒ 62 Ⓓ 81

4 In the previous graph, the slope of the line of best fit represents:

Ⓐ the correlation between words per minute and practice

Ⓑ the initial typing speed of the student

Ⓒ the average typing speed of the student over the 10 weeks

Ⓓ the increase in words per minute for each additional week of practice

5 Using your calculator, what is the equation of the least-squares regression line for the data?

x	140	143	147	150
y	55	50	43	40

Ⓐ $y = 245.5 - 2.39x$

Ⓑ $y = 245.5 - 1.47x$

Ⓒ $y = 269.5 - 0.79x$

Ⓓ $y = 269.5 - 1.53x$

TOPIC TEST

SECTION II

Instructions
- This section consists of 5 questions.
- Show all working.

Time allowed: 53 minutes

Total marks: 35

6 The height and length of the arm span of eight students were measured. The results were recorded in the table.

Height (cm)	170	162	173	158	163	166	174	159
Arm span (cm)	169	156	176	160	164	161	170	163

a Calculate Pearson's correlation coefficient (r) for the data, correct to three decimal places. **2 marks**

_____

b Describe the strength of the association of the student's height and the length of their arm span. **1 mark**

_____

7 The graph shows the typing speed of a student.

a Calculate the slope of the line of best fit. **2 marks**

_____

b What is the y-intercept (vertical intercept) for this line? **1 mark**

_____

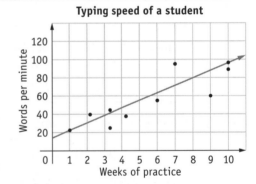

c What is indicated by the y-intercept for the line? **1 mark**

_____

_____

d Based on the slope of the line, by how many words per minute can the student expect to increase her or his speed for each additional week of practice? **1 mark**

_____

_____

e Using $WPM = mP + c$, where WPM = words per minute and P = weeks of practice, write an equation for the line. **1 mark**

_____

_____

f Will this curve keep on increasing with further practice? Explain. **2 marks**

_____

_____

_____

8 The graph shows data on the lengths of putts and the percentage of successful putts made by golfers during a number of tournaments.

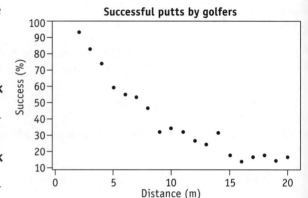

a Is the relationship between the two variables linear or not linear? **1 mark**

_____

b Which of the two variables is the independent variable? **1 mark**

_____

c Below what distance from the hole is the golfer almost certain to sink the ball? **1 mark**

_____

_____

d Above what distance from the hole do the chances of a successful putt remain the same? **1 mark**

_____

_____

e Around what distance from the hole is the chance of a successful putt about half? **1 mark**

_____

_____

9 Four scatter plots are shown.

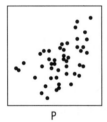
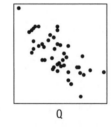
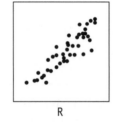
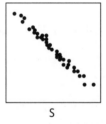

P   Q   R   S

The correlation coefficients are −0.99, −0.7, 0.5. and 0.9, though not necessarily in that order.

a Identify each scatter plot with its correlation coefficient. **4 marks**

_____

_____

b Which scatter plot shows:

i the greatest correlation? **1 mark**

_____

ii the least correlation? **1 mark**

_____

10 The following table shows the relationship between the blood glucose levels and age of several adults.

Age (x)	Glucose levels (y)
43	99
57	87
42	75
21	65
25	79
59	81

a Draw a scatter plot of these results on the grid provided. Place the age on the horizontal axis.   **3 marks**

b On your graph draw in a line of best fit.
                                        1 mark

c Calculate the mean of the x-scores ($\bar{x}$).   **2 marks**

_____

_____

d Calculate the mean of the y-scores ($\bar{y}$).   **2 marks**

_____

_____

e The correlation coefficient (r) for these scores is 0.53, the standard deviation of the x-scores is 15.75, and the standard deviation of the y-scores is 11.45.

 i Use the formula $gradient = r \times \dfrac{standard\ deviation\ of\ y\text{-}scores}{standard\ deviation\ of\ x\text{-}scores}$ to calculate the gradient of the line of best fit.   **2 marks**

_____

_____

 ii Use the formula $y\text{-intercept} = \bar{y} - (gradient \times \bar{x})$ to find the y-intercept of the line of best fit.   **2 marks**

_____

_____

f Write the equation of the line of best fit in the form $y = gradient \times x + y\text{-intercept}$.   **1 mark**

_____

_____

CHAPTER **9**

Statistical analysis: The normal distribution

Standard deviation and the *z*-score

QUESTION **1**   Beth sat for a test. The mean mark for the test was 6.4. The *z*-score for Beth's mark was 2. Briefly explain the significance of this result.

_____

_____

_____

_____

QUESTION **2**   On a particular test the mean mark was 67 and the standard deviation was 5. Carrie had a *z*-score of −1. What was Carrie's mark on the test?

_____

_____

_____

QUESTION **3**   The following table shows the *z*-scores relating to certain marks on a test.

Mark				76	80		
z-score	−3	−2	−1	0	1	2	3

a What is the mean?   **b** What is the standard deviation?

_____   _____

_____   _____

c Complete the table.

QUESTION **4**   A set of scores had a mean of 86.5 and a standard deviation of 3.7. Complete the table.

Mark							
z-score	−3	−2	−1	0	1	2	3

QUESTION **5**   On a particular test the standard deviation was 7. Tahlia's *z*-score was −2 and Ivanka's *z*-score was 1. If Ivanka scored 56, find:

a the mean   **b** Tahlia's score

_____   _____

_____   _____

QUESTION **6**   Ken sat for an examination. His results showed he scored 87% with a *z*-score of −1. Do you think Ken did well in the exam? Briefly comment.

_____

_____

_____

_____

Statistical analysis: The normal distribution

Excel MATHEMATICS STANDARD 2
Ch. 7, pp. 180–182

Calculating z-scores

QUESTION **1**   In a class test the mean mark was 72 and the standard deviation was 3. Using the formula $z = \dfrac{x - \mu}{\sigma}$, where z = z-score, x = score, μ = mean and σ = standard deviation, calculate the z-score for a mark of 87.

_____

_____

_____

QUESTION **2**   In an examination the mean was 70 and the standard deviation was 5. Calculate the z-scores for marks of:

a 60

_____

_____

_____

b 89

_____

_____

_____

c 93

_____

_____

_____

d 58

_____

_____

_____

QUESTION **3**   In a Maths test, the mean is 65 and the standard deviation is 5. What mark is equivalent to a z-score of 3?

_____

_____

_____

QUESTION **4**   The number of hours spent on home study per week by a group of 22 students is given below.

14	20	17	16	11	12	15	14	20	27	29
17	12	8	23	13	14	18	19	22	23	25

a Find correct to two decimal places:

i the mean

_____

_____

ii the standard deviation

_____

_____

b Michael spends 24 hours on home study each week. Express this as a z-score based on the above scores (correct to one decimal place).

_____

_____

Statistical analysis: The normal distribution

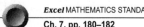
Using z-scores to compare results

QUESTION **1**   Amanda in her yearly examination scored 78 in Mathematics, 73 in English and 80 in Economics. The mean and standard deviation of the results in each subject are shown below.

Subject	Mean	Standard deviation
Mathematics	70	3
English	65	4
Economics	69	5

a Calculate Amanda's z-score for each subject.

_____

_____

b List Amanda's subjects from best to worst based on her z-scores.

_____

_____

QUESTION **2**   Ben achieved 76 marks in an English exam in which the mean was 64 and the standard deviation was 6. He also scored 71 marks in Mathematics in which the mean was 58 and the standard deviation was 10.

a Find his z-score in each subject.

_____

_____

_____

b In which subject was his result better? Justify your answer.

_____

_____

_____

QUESTION **3**   Adam scored 68 in an English exam in which the mean was 54 and the standard deviation was 4. He scored 76 in a Mathematics test in which the mean was 67 and the standard deviation was 5.

a Calculate his z-score in each subject.

_____

_____

b In which subject was his performance better?

_____

_____

_____

Statistical analysis: The normal distribution

Properties of the normal distribution

QUESTION 1 In a normal distribution, which three measures of central tendency are all equal?

_____

_____

QUESTION 2 The number of cars rolling off an assembly line was recorded over a month. The data was found to be normally distributed. The mean number of cars was 350.

a What was the mode?

_____

_____

b What was the median?

_____

_____

QUESTION 3 The scores out of 20 in a spelling test are recorded below:

13 14 14 15 15 16 16 17 17 17 17 18 18 18 18 19 19 19 20 20

a What is the mean? _____

b What are the modes? _____

c What is the median? _____

d Is the data normally distributed? Justify your answer.

_____

_____

_____

QUESTION 4 For each histogram, decide whether the data could be normally distributed.

a

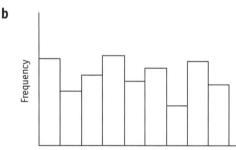

b

c

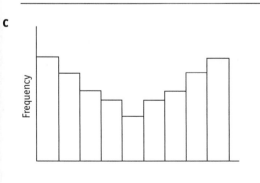

d

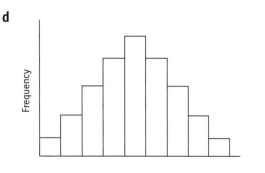

Statistical analysis: The normal distribution

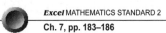

Normally distributed data 1

QUESTION **1**   In a normal distribution, what percentage of scores will have *z*-scores:

a between −1 and 1?

b between −2 and 2?

c between −3 and 3?

d between 0 and 1?

e between −2 and 0?

f between −2 and 1?

g greater than 1?

h less than −3?

QUESTION **2**   Data collected on the mass in grams of packets of biscuits produced at a factory is normally distributed. The mean is 260 g and the standard deviation is 5 g.

a Complete the table.

Mass in g			255	260			
z-score	−3	−2	−1	0	1	2	3

b What percentage of packets have a mass between 255 g and 265 g? _____

c What percentage of packets have a mass less than 260 g? _____

d What percentage of packets have a mass more than 250 g? _____

e The packets of biscuits are labelled 'Weight: 250 g'. Why do you think this is?

QUESTION **3**   A manufacturer guarantees her product for 100 hours. If the mean life is 112 hours and the standard deviation is 4, what percentage of the product can the manufacturer expect to have to replace under the guarantee? (Assume a normal distribution.)

Statistical analysis: The normal distribution

Normally distributed data 2

QUESTION **1** The heights of 300 students are normally distributed. The mean height is 173 cm and the standard deviation is 3 cm. Find the expected number of students whose heights are between 170 cm and 176 cm.

_____

_____

_____

_____

_____

QUESTION **2** A machine produces rods of mean diameter 7.000 cm and standard deviation 0.030 cm. Within what interval will the diameters almost certainly lie?

_____

_____

_____

_____

_____

QUESTION **3** Consider the rods described in the previous question. If three rods in a batch of 100 are found to have diameters of 7.098 cm, what can we conclude?

_____

_____

_____

_____

_____

_____

QUESTION **4** The contents of jars containing peanuts are to have a mean weight of 750 g with a standard deviation of 2.5 g. Seven jars were found to contain 758 g, 754 g, 759 g, 738 g, 765 g, 752g and 763 g. Which jars, if any, have contents that differ from the mean by more than four standard deviations?

_____

_____

_____

_____

_____

_____

Statistical analysis: The normal distribution

Determining probabilities using a statistical table

Use this cumulative normal distribution table to answer the questions below.

z	.0	.1	.2	.3	.4	.5	.6	.7	.8	.9
0.	0.5000	0.5398	0.5793	0.6179	0.6554	0.6915	0.7257	0.7580	0.7881	0.8159
1.	0.8413	0.8643	0.8849	0.9032	0.9192	0.9332	0.9452	0.9554	0.9641	0.9713
2.	0.9772	0.9821	0.9861	0.9893	0.9918	0.9938	0.9953	0.9965	0.9974	0.9981
3.	0.9987	0.9990	0.9993	0.9995	0.9997	0.9998	0.9998	0.9999	0.9999	1.0000

QUESTION **1**   Find the probability of a z-score:

a   less than 1

b   less than –1

c   between –2 and 2

QUESTION **2**   Find:

a $P(z \leq 2.1)$

b $P(1.4 \leq z \leq 1.7)$

c $P(-1.8 \leq z \leq 2.4)$

QUESTION **3**   A company surveyed the amount of time it took to assemble a product. The times were normally distributed with a mean of 16 minutes and a standard deviation of 2.4 minutes. A product is chosen at random. What is the probability that it took between 10 and 19.6 minutes to assemble the product?

QUESTION **4**   A certain brand of hand sanitiser is sold in 120-mL bottles. In a quality control check the mean was found to be 122 mL and the standard deviation 2.5 mL. What percentage of bottles contain less than the advertised capacity?

QUESTION **5**   A ball pit contains 2000 balls. The mean diameter of each ball in the pit is 8 cm and the standard deviation is 0.2 cm. Estimate the number of balls with a diameter less than 7.5 cm.

QUESTION **6**   A supermarket advertises beef mince in packets of 500 g. A quality checking process shows the mean mass is 485 g with a standard deviation of 10 g. What percentage of packets are less than the advertised mass?

QUESTION **7**   Oliver and Harry are both 18 years old. Oliver has a height of 173 cm and Harry is 6 cm taller than Oliver. Studies have shown the mean height of 18-year-old boys living in the country is 176 cm with a standard deviation of 2 cm. What percentage of 18-year-old boys have a height between Oliver and Harry?

QUESTION **8**   The speed limit outside a school is 40 km/h. A police officer measured the speed of passing vehicles over a period of time. She found the set of data to be normally distributed with a mean speed of 37 km/h and a standard deviation of 2.5 km/h. What is the probability that a vehicle passed the school at a speed greater than 40 km/h?

Statistical analysis: The normal distribution

TOPIC TEST

SECTION I

Instructions
- This section consists of 5 multiple-choice questions.
- Each question is worth 1 mark.
- Fill in only ONE CIRCLE for each question.

Time allowed: 7 minutes

Total marks: 5

1 In a small country town, the age of the population is normally distributed. The mean age is 36 years and the standard deviation is 12 years. The percentage of the population between the ages of 36 years and 60 years is closest to:

(A) 36

(B) 47.5

(C) 68

(D) 95

2 These statistics were obtained from Year 12 Maths and English tests. What mark in Maths would be equivalent to a mark of 78 in English?

Subject	Mean	Standard deviation
Maths	55	12
English	66	8

(A) 67

(B) 71

(C) 73

(D) 75

3 The mean of a set of scores is 38.5 and the standard deviation is 3.2. What is the z-score of a mark of 36.9?

(A) −2

(B) −0.5

(C) 0.5

(D) 2

4 The weights of 80 hen's eggs are normally distributed with a mean of 68 g and a standard deviation of 4 g. How many of these eggs are expected to weigh between 68 g and 76 g?

(A) 32

(B) 36

(C) 38

(D) 48

5 A class of students received their results from a Biology examination. The mean of the marks is 78 and a standard deviation of 4 cm. If Jerome's mark represents a z-score of 1.5, what was his examination result?

(A) 84

(B) 85

(C) 86

(D) 87

Instructions   • This section consists of 10 questions.
                    • Show all working.

Time allowed: 53 minutes   **Total marks: 35**

6   Tests were held in Maths and English and the marks for 10 students are recorded below.

Maths	67	70	82	75	68	88	78	71	88	86
English	68	86	76	84	74	72	90	84	62	53

a Find the mean and the standard deviation of the Maths marks.   **2 marks**

b Find the mean and the standard deviation of the English marks.   **2 marks**

c Kelly scored 76 in English. Find the z-score corresponding to this mark.   **1 mark**

d Kelly scored 78 in Maths. Which was the better result? Justify your answer.   **3 marks**

7   A factory packs pins into boxes that are labelled 'Contents 1000'. In fact the number of pins in boxes packed at that factory is normally distributed with mean 1015 and standard deviation 7.5. If a shipment contains 2000 boxes of pins, how many boxes would you expect to have less than the stated contents?

                                                                                      3 marks

8 The weights of boxes of WondaWeet breakfast cereal are normally distributed. The mean is 796 g and the standard deviation is 8 g.

  a What is the *z*-score of a box of WondaWeet with a weight of 800 g?   **1 mark**

  _____

  b What is the weight of a box that has a *z*-score of −2.3?   **1 mark**

  _____

  c WondaWeet boxes are labelled as having a weight of 780 g. In a shipment of 1000 boxes, how many boxes would be likely to weigh less than 780 g?   **2 marks**

  _____

  _____

9 The results of three class tests are normally distributed. The means and standard deviations are displayed in the table.

	Mean	Standard deviation
Test 1	70	5
Test 2	72	2
Test 3	68	?

  a Adeline scored 72 in Test 1 and 74 in Test 2. She thinks that she performed better in Test 2. Do you agree? Justify your answer using appropriate calculations.   **2 marks**

  _____

  _____

  b In Test 3 Adeline scored 78 which she calculated was a *z*-score of 2.5. What was the standard deviation of the results in Test 3?   **2 marks**

  _____

  _____

10 The normal distribution shown has a mean of 70 and a standard deviation of 5.

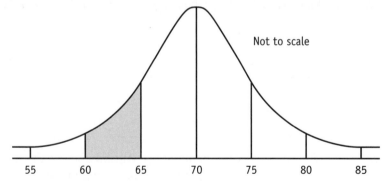

Not to scale

55   60   65   70   75   80   85

  a What is the *z*-score of 83?   **1 mark**

  _____

  _____

  b What percentage of the data lies in the shaded region?   **2 marks**

  _____

  _____

11 Glenda's class sits two Modern History tests. The results for students in her class on the first test are listed:

78, 69, 81, 77, 71, 75, 73, 72, 69, 65

    a The standard deviation of the first test is 5 (to the nearest whole). What is the mean of the results? **1 mark**

_____

    b Glenda scored 82 on the first test. On the second Modern History test, the mean for the class was 66 and the standard deviation was 10. Calculate the mark that Glenda needed to obtain in the second test to ensure that her performance relative to the class was maintained. **3 marks**

_____

_____

_____

12 The resting pulses, in beats/minute, of 400 people are found to be normally distributed with a mean of 68 and a standard deviation of 6. Find the number of people whose resting pulse is:

    a between 56 and 80? **1 mark**

_____

    b more than 80? **1 mark**

_____

13 A mobile speed camera vehicle uses a radar unit to measure speeds of vehicles on a road. The speeds recorded are normally distributed with a mean of 80 km/h and a standard deviation of 5 km/h. What is the probability that a car picked at random is travelling at more than 85 km/h? **2 marks**

_____

_____

_____

14 The mean life of a shipload of batteries is 1200 hours and the standard deviation is 80 hours. A battery is selected at random. What is the probability that the battery's life is:

    a at least 960 hours? **1 mark**

_____

    b between 1040 hours and 1280 hours? **1 mark**

_____

_____

15 In a class test Grace scored 64 which was two standard deviations below the mean of the class results. In the same test her friend Camilla scored 76 which was one standard deviation above the mean. By solving a pair of simultaneous equations, find the mean and standard deviation of the class results. **3 marks**

_____

_____

_____

_____

CHAPTER 10

Networks: Introduction to networks

Excel MATHEMATICS STANDARD 2
Ch. 8, pp. 199–201

Identifying network terminology

QUESTION **1**   For the networks shown, state:

a

b

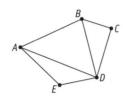

c

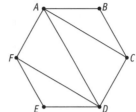

d

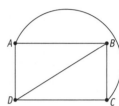

i the number of vertices

_____

ii the number of edges (arcs)

_____

iii the degree of vertex *C*

_____

iv a vertex adjacent to *B*

_____

QUESTION **2**   Draw a network diagram with these features:

a vertices *A*, *B* and *C*, where each vertex has degree 2

b vertices *P*, *Q*, *R* and *S*, where each vertex has degree 2

c vertices *W*, *X*, *Y* and *Z*, where each vertex has degree 3

QUESTION **3**   For the directed networks shown, state:

a

b

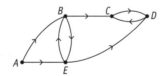

c

i the number of vertices

_____

_____

ii the number of edges (arcs)

_____

_____

iii the degree of vertex *C*

_____

_____

QUESTION **4**

a Name the isolated vertex. _____

b What is the weight of edge *AB*? _____

c What is the degree of *B*? _____

d What is the weight of path *BCD*? _____

e What is the weight of circuit *BCDB*? _____

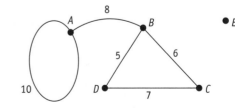

Networks: Introduction to networks

Networks and tables 1

QUESTION **1**   Use the tables to add weights to the edges of the network diagrams:

a

	A	B	C	D
A	–	6	10	7
B	6	–	5	–
C	10	5	–	8
D	7	–	8	–

b

	G	H	J	K	L
G	–	5	–	9	6
H	5	–	7	–	4
J	–	7	–	8	5
K	9	–	8	–	7
L	6	4	5	7	–

c

	P	Q	R	S	T	U	V
P	–	3	–	–	–	–	11
Q	3	–	4	–	–	–	6
R	–	4	–	7	8	–	9
S	–	–	7	–	5	–	–
T	–	–	8	5	–	8	–
U	–	–	–	–	8	–	3
V	11	6	9	–	–	3	–

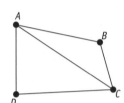

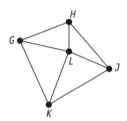

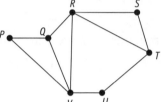

QUESTION **2**   Use the network diagrams to complete the tables:

a

	P	Q	R	S
P				
Q				
R				
S				

b

	F	G	H	J	K
F					
G					
H					
J					
K					

c

	A	B	C	D	E	F
A						
B						
C						
D						
E						
F						

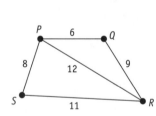

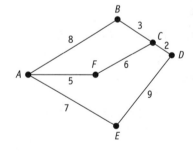

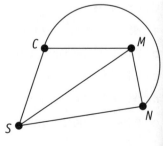

QUESTION **3**   The table shows the distances by air between the Hunter Valley airports: Cessnock (*C*), Maitland (*M*), Newcastle (*N*) and Singleton (*S*). Complete the network diagram to represent the data in the table.

Flight distances (km)				
	Cessnock	**Maitland**	**Newcastle**	**Singleton**
Cessnock	–	24	54	34
Maitland	24	–	32	39
Newcastle	54	32	–	68
Singleton	34	39	68	–

Networks and tables 2

QUESTION 1   Use the network diagrams to complete the tables:

a

	To:		
From:	**X**	**Y**	**Z**
X			
Y			
Z			

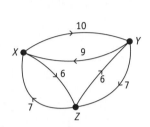

b

	To:			
From:	**A**	**B**	**C**	**D**
A				
B				
C				
D				

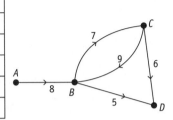

c

	To:					
From:	**P**	**Q**	**R**	**S**	**T**	**U**
P						
Q						
R						
S						
T						
U						

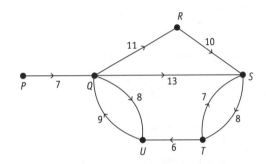

QUESTION 2   Use the tables to add weights to the edges of the network diagrams:

a

	To:			
From:	**P**	**Q**	**R**	**S**
P	–	4	–	–
Q	5	–	–	7
R	–	6	–	–
S	–	8	–	–

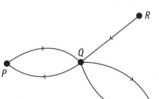

b

	To:				
From:	**A**	**B**	**C**	**D**	**E**
A	–	2	4	–	
B	2	–	–	–	–
C	–	–	–	–	3
D	–	5	4	–	–
E	–	–	–	3	–

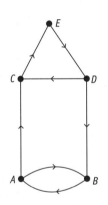

c

	To:				
From:	**V**	**W**	**X**	**Y**	**Z**
V	–	3	–	–	5
W	4	–	5	–	–
X	–	–	–	6	–
Y	–	–	7	–	8
Z	4	–	–	–	–

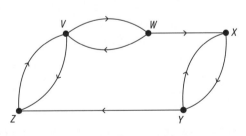

QUESTION 3   Use the table to complete the network diagram by using arrows and writing the weights on each edge.

	To:						
From:	**A**	**B**	**C**	**D**	**E**	**F**	**G**
A	–	12	–	–	6	5	–
B	–	–	15	–	–	–	–
C	–	–	–	6	–	–	–
D	–	–	7	–	–	–	8
E	7	–	–	8	–	–	–
F	–	–	–	–	5	–	4
G	–	–	6	–	–	3	–

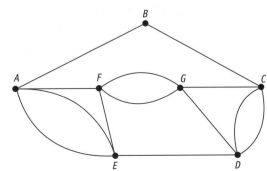

Networks: Introduction to networks

Maps and networks

QUESTION **1**   The sketches show islands in the middle of a river joined to the riverbanks by bridges. For example, in part **a** there are two bridges from *A* to *B*. Complete the network diagrams:

a

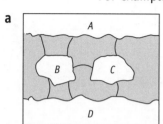

b

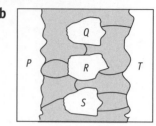

QUESTION **2**   Use the maps to complete the network diagrams:

a

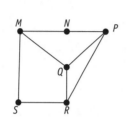

b

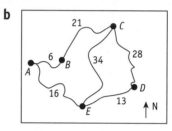

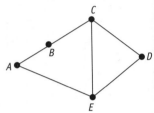

QUESTION **3**   Draw a network diagram to represent the roads between the towns *A*, *B*, *C*, *D* and *E*, if
- Town *A* is 32 km from town *B* and 43 km from town *E*
- Town *B* is 54 km from town *D* and 29 km from town *C*
- Town *D* is 41 km from town *C* and 34 km from town *E*

QUESTION **4**   A 'round–robin competition' is where each team plays the other teams in their 'pool' once. Draw network diagrams to show the games played for a pool of:

a   four teams: *A*, *B*, *C* and *D*

b   six teams: *P*, *Q*, *R*, *S*, *T* and *U*

QUESTION **5**   Three airlines are named according to their base city and can only fly from their base airport to and from two other airports. Airline *A* flies to and from *B* and *E*, *C* flies to and from *B* and *E*, and *D* flies to and from *C* and *E*. The cost of a ticket for each airline is the same for any of its routes. Airline *A* charges $80, *C* charges $70 and *D* charges $90. Draw a weighted network diagram to represent the flight routes and costs.

Networks: Introduction to networks

Paths

QUESTION **1**   The following network diagrams are to be walked so that every edge is to be travelled once, and only once.

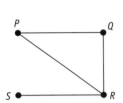

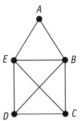

a Write the possible start/finish vertex. _____   **b** Write the start and finish vertices. _____

QUESTION **2**   In the diagrams name the different paths that are possible to travel from *A* to *E*.

a   **b**   **c**   **d**

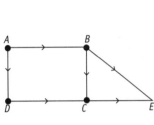   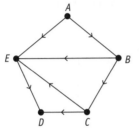   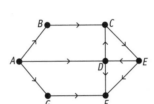   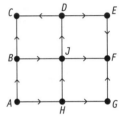

_____   _____   _____   _____

_____   _____   _____   _____

QUESTION **3**   Here are two network diagrams. Simon needs to travel from *A* to *B*. He is not allowed to backtrack—in this case, Simon always moves towards the right or towards the top of the diagram. How many paths are possible?

a

b

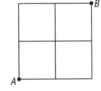

_____   _____

QUESTION **4**   How many different paths are possible between *A* and *C*, if backtracking is not allowed?

a   **b**

   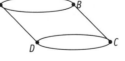

_____   _____

c

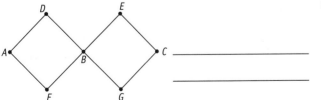

d

_____   _____

_____   _____

_____   _____

Networks: Introduction to networks

Shortest paths

QUESTION **1** If all dimensions on these networks are in metres find, by calculation, the shortest path and write the length of this path:

a from *J* to *N*

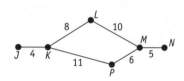

b from *A* to *E*

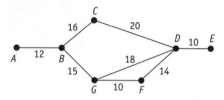

_____

_____

c from *Q* to *T*

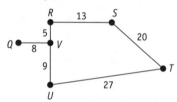

d from *A* to *D*

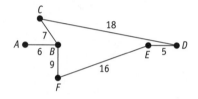

_____

_____

e from *M* to *R*

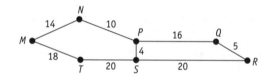

f from *T* to *X*

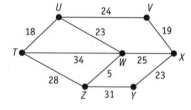

_____

_____

QUESTION **2** The times (in minutes) to travel between locations are shown on the networks below. Find the shortest time to travel between:

a *A* to *D*

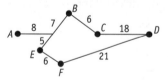

b *P* to *S*

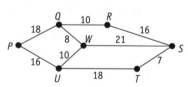

_____

_____

c *W* to *Y*

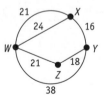

d *M* to *R*

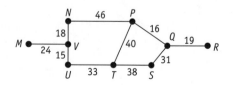

_____

_____

Networks: Introduction to networks

Spanning trees

QUESTION **1**   For each network below, by removing edges, draw two possible spanning trees.

a

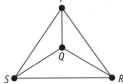

b

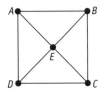

QUESTION **2**   Using the weighted network on the right, find the weight of each of these spanning trees:

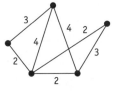

a

_____

_____

b

_____

_____

c

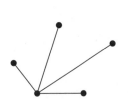

_____

_____

QUESTION **3**   Use the weighted network to the right, to find the weight of each of these spanning trees:

a

_____

_____

_____

b

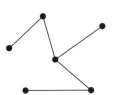

_____

_____

_____

c

_____

_____

_____

QUESTION **4**   Use the weighted network to the right, to find the weight of each of these spanning trees:

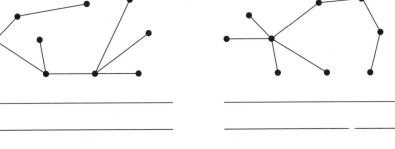

a

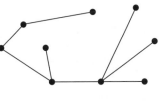

_____

_____

_____

b

_____

_____

_____

Networks: Introduction to networks

Minimum spanning tree

QUESTION **1**   Paisley used Kruskal's algorithm to calculate the minimum spanning tree for this network.

a She used a table to help her. Complete Paisley's table:

Edge	Weight
PT	1
QS	2
QT	
QR	

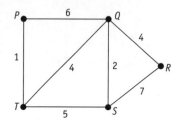

c Draw the minimum spanning tree.

b What is the weight of the minimum spanning tree?

_____

QUESTION **2**   Nathan used Prim's algorithm to find the minimum spanning tree for the following network.

a Nathan used a table to help him. Complete his table:

Action	Weight	Vertex visited
Start at G	–	G
Use GA		A
Use AF		F
Use AB		B
	4	
		D
Use DE		E

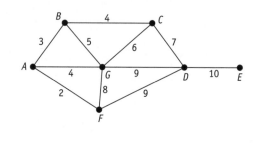

b What is the weight of the minimum spanning tree?   **c** Draw the minimum spanning tree.

_____
_____
_____
_____

QUESTION **3**   For the networks below find the weight of the minimum spanning tree:

a _____   **b** _____

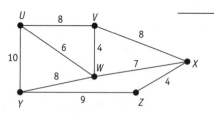

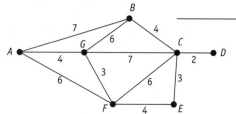

c _____   **d** _____

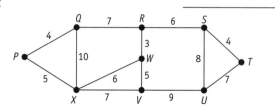

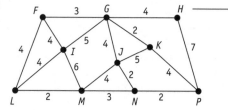

Networks: Introduction to networks

Excel MATHEMATICS STANDARD 2
Ch. 8, pp. 206–209

Solving problems involving minimum spanning trees

QUESTION **1**   Five towns are to be joined to the city of Alexander with fibre–optic cable. Use the network diagram to determine the minimum length of cable required.

_____

_____

_____

_____

_____

_____

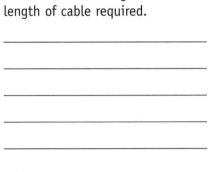
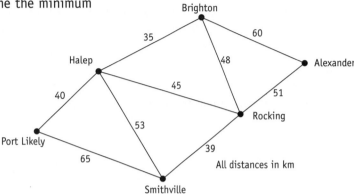

QUESTION **2**   A village has unsealed roads which become very muddy after rain. The mayor has decided to pave some roads. What will be the minimum length of roads she needs to pave to ensure that every person living and working in the village can walk to and from their home without walking through mud?

_____

_____

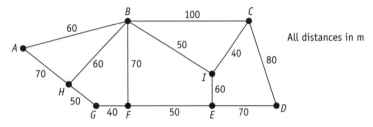

QUESTION **3**   A security system is to be installed in a department store.

a What is the length of the minimum spanning tree for the network?

_____

b The cost of the installation is $85/metre. What is the minimum cost of the installation?

_____

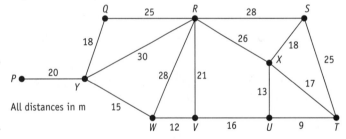

QUESTION **4**   A newly opened botanical gardens has pathways between seven significant points of interest (POIs). The committee in charge of the gardens wishes to install water bubblers at these POIs by laying water pipes along pathways. The cost of laying the pipes is $45/metre and each bubbler costs $580.

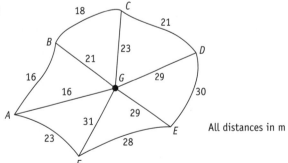

a What is the minimum cost of laying the pipes and providing the seven bubblers?

_____

b Suppose the committee decides to close the feature at B and block all paths leading to it. This means there will only be six bubblers at the other POIs. How much money is saved by the decision?

_____

Networks: Introduction to networks

TOPIC TEST

Instructions
- This section consists of 5 multiple-choice questions.
- Each question is worth 1 mark.
- Fill in only ONE CIRCLE for each question.

Time allowed: 7 minutes   **Total marks: 5**

1   In the network diagram, how many vertices have an odd degree?

Ⓐ   3

Ⓑ   4

Ⓒ   5

Ⓓ   9

2   The table shows the friendships between four girls: Abbie (*A*), Belinda (*B*), Charlie (*C*) and Didi (*D*).

A network diagram is to be drawn where each vertex represents a girl and an edge joining vertices represents a friendship. Which of these is the correct network diagram?

	A	B	C	D
A		✓		✓
B	✓		✓	✓
C		✓		✓
D	✓	✓	✓	

Ⓐ 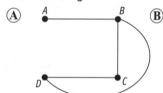   Ⓑ 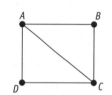   Ⓒ 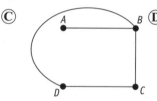   Ⓓ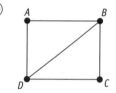

3   In the directed network on the right, starting at *P*, which of these vertices can be reached?

Ⓐ   *A*   Ⓑ   *B*

Ⓒ   *C*   Ⓓ   *D*

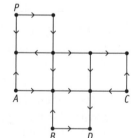

4   Which of these is the shortest path to travel from *A* to *E*?

Ⓐ   *AGHFDE*   Ⓑ   *ABFDE*

Ⓒ   *AGHJE*   Ⓓ   *AGHJDE*

5   The minimum spanning tree for the network below includes the edge with weight labelled *p*. The total weight of all edges for the minimum spanning tree is 20. What is the value of *p*?

Ⓐ   *p* = 1   Ⓑ   *p* = 2

Ⓒ   *p* = 3   Ⓓ   *p* = 4

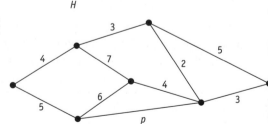

TOPIC TEST
SECTION II

Instructions • This section consists of 8 questions.
• Show all working.

Time allowed: 53 minutes **Total marks: 35**

6 For the network, state:

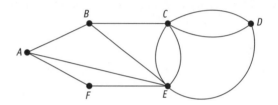

a the number of vertices _____ **1 mark**

b the degree of vertex *C* _____ **1 mark**

c the name of the vertices adjacent to *E* _____ **1 mark**

7 The table lists the travel time, in minutes, between six locations.

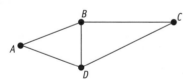

		To:				
		A	**B**	**C**	**D**	**E**	**F**
From:	**A**	–	8	–	–	–	5
	B	–	–	7	–	–	–
	C	–	–	–	5	6	–
	D	–	–	9	–	8	–
	E	6	9	8	–	–	–
	F	–	–	–	–	8	–

a Use the table to complete the network diagram by using arrows and writing the weights on each edge. **3 marks**

b What is the minimum travel time from:

i *B* to *E*? _____ **1 mark**

ii *D* to *A*? _____ **1 mark**

8 These networks represent streets. If a delivery van needs to drive every street once only, identify a possible route that needs to be taken by the driver. **1 mark each**

a

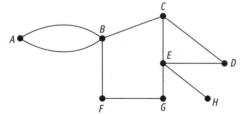

_____

_____

c

_____

_____

9 a Draw a network diagram to represent the roads between the eight towns *A, B, C, D, E, F, G* and *H* if:
* Town *B* is 12 km from town *A*, 15 km from town *C*, 8 km from town *D*
* Town *E* is 8 km from town *C*, 7 km from town *D* and 9 km from town *G*
* Town *H* is 14 km from town *G* and 10 km from town *C*   **2 marks**

b If all roads are two–way, what is the shortest distance from town *B* to town *G*?   **1 mark**

10 Identify by drawing a minimum spanning tree (MST) on the following networks and state the weight of the MST: **3 marks each**

a

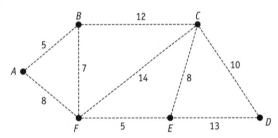

b

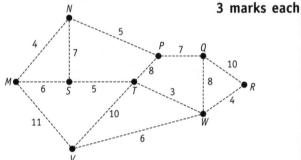

c

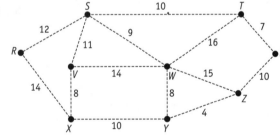

11 A university requires seven computer servers to communicate with each other through a connected network of cables across the campus. The servers are named *A, B, C, D, E, F* and *G* and are shown on the network diagram on the right. The edges on the graph represent proposed cables that would connect the computer servers. The numbers on the edges shows the cost, in dollars, of installing each cable.

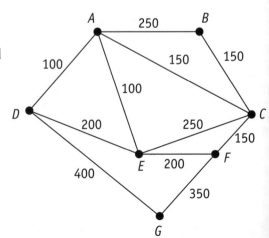

a What is the cheapest cost, in dollars, of installing cables between server *D* and server *C*?   **1 mark**

b The proposed network needs to be checked by walking along its entire length. To avoid walking along a section more than once, at which server should the inspection start and where should it finish?

1 mark

_____

c The cheapest installation ensuring that each server connects to another server is by using a minimum spanning tree. Draw the minimum spanning tree on the diagram and write down the length. **2 marks**

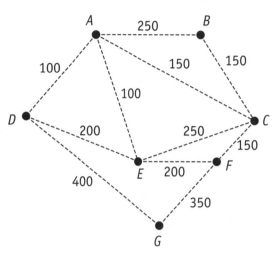

_____

d The university's IT manager has decided to reduce the number of servers to six. What is the change in installation costs if the manager removes server A from the minimum spanning tree? **1 mark**

_____

12 A new theme park is being designed with nine rides. On the network diagram on the right, the vertices represent the locations of the rides. The numbers on the edges represent the distances, in metres, between the rides.

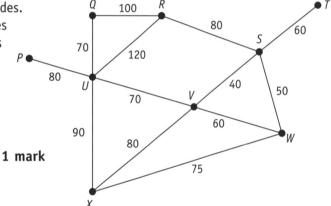

a Electrical cables are required to power the rides and these cables will be located using the network diagram. What is the minimum length of cabling required to join S to U? **1 mark**

_____

Cables will form a connected graph and the shortest length of cable will be used.

b What term is given to the network used where the length of cable is minimised? **1 mark**

_____

c Use the graph on the right to show the cabling used and find the length.

2 marks

_____

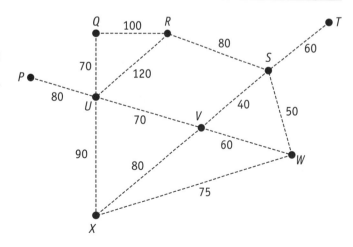

13 The network in the diagram below indicates the main road system between seven towns. A computer company wishes to install a computer network between these towns, using cables laid alongside the roads and designed so that all places are connected to the main computer located at town *A*.

Distance between towns (km)						
	A	**B**	**C**	**D**	**E**	**F**	**G**
A							
B	12						
C	–	10					
D	7	6	6				
E	–	–	5	9			
F	8	–	–	5	–		
G	–	–	–	8	4	7	

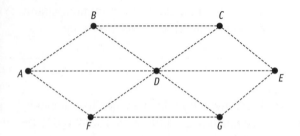

a Use the table to write weights on the edges of the network. **1 mark**

b Use a minimum spanning tree to find the length of cable required. **2 marks**

CHAPTER **11**

Networks: Critical path analysis

Excel MATHEMATICS STANDARD 2
Ch. 9, pp. 219–221

Activity charts and networks

QUESTION **1** Draw a network diagram to show the following:

a activity *P* has to finish before activity *Q* and activity *R* can start

b activity *P* and activity *Q* have to finish before activity *R* can start

c activity *P* has to finish before activity *Q* can start, and activity *Q* has to finish before activity *R* can start

QUESTION **2** Use the network diagram to complete the activity table.

Activities	Time	Prerequisites
A		
B		
C		
D		
E		
F		
G		

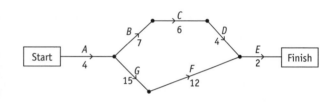

QUESTION **3** Here is an activity table for preparing scrambled eggs on toast. Complete the network.

Code	Activities	Time (s)	Prerequisites
A	Crack eggs into a bowl	20	None
B	Add milk and salt	5	A
C	Beat mixture	20	B
D	Heat in microwave	120	C
E	Toast 2 slices of bread	60	None
F	Spread butter on toast	10	E
G	Place scrambled eggs on toast	5	D, F

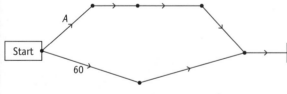

QUESTION **4** The activities needed to replace a broken window pane are given below, but are **not** listed in the correct order.

Code	Acivities	Time (min)	Prerequisites
T	Put in new pane	2	U
U	Putty into the empty frame	5	R
R	Remove broken pane	5	Q, S
P	Phone shop to order glass	5	None
V	Sweep up broken glass	3	W
Q	Collect pane from shop	30	P
S	Buy putty	20	None
W	Putty around the new pane	2	T

Networks: Critical path analysis

Identifying the critical paths

QUESTION **1**   For the following networks, identify the critical path and give its length:

a

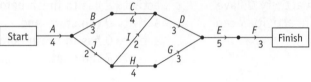

_____

_____

_____

_____

_____

_____

b

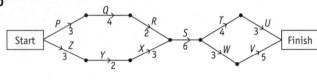

_____

_____

_____

_____

_____

_____

c

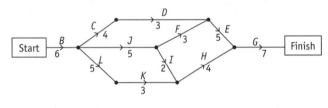

_____

_____

_____

_____

_____

_____

d

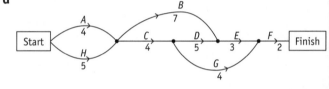

_____

_____

_____

_____

_____

_____

e

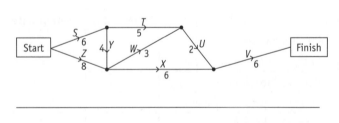

_____

_____

_____

_____

_____

f

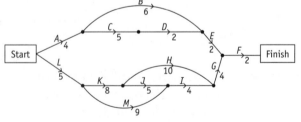

_____

_____

_____

_____

_____

Networks: Critical path analysis

Forward scanning and EST

QUESTION **1**   Use forward scanning to write the earliest starting time (EST) for each activity in these networks and identify the length of the critical path:

a

b

QUESTION **2**

a   On the network diagram, all measurements are in minutes.

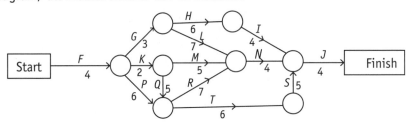

i   What is the length of the critical path?

_____

ii Use forward scanning to write the earliest starting time (EST) for each activity in the network.

iii If the project is to be completed by 10:26 am, what is the earliest starting time for activity:

A *Q*?   **B** *N*?   **C** *J*?

_____   _____   _____

_____   _____   _____

_____   _____   _____

b   On the network diagram, all measurements are in days.

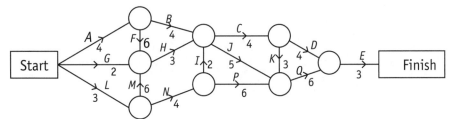

i   What is the length of the critical path?

_____

ii Use forward scanning to write the earliest starting time (EST) for each activity in the network.

iii If the project is to be completed by the end of the work day on 30 March, what is the earliest starting date for activity:

A *H*?   **B** *C*?   **C** *Q*?

_____   _____   _____

Networks: Critical path analysis

Backward scanning and LST

QUESTION **1**   Use backward scanning to write the latest starting time (LST) for each activity in these networks and identify the length of the critical path:

a

b

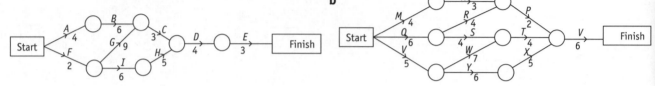

QUESTION **2**

a On the network diagram, all measurements are in days.

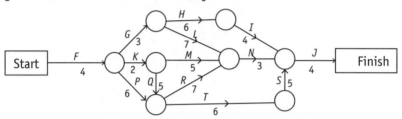

i What is the length of the critical path?

_____

ii Use backward scanning to write the latest starting time (LST) for each activity in the network.

iii If the project is to commence on 1 August, what is the latest starting date for activity:

  A *Q*?   **B** *S*?   **C** *J*?

_____   _____   _____

_____   _____   _____

_____   _____   _____

b On the network diagram, all measurements are in minutes.

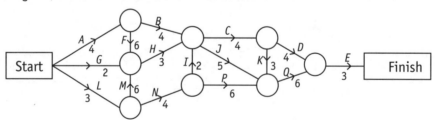

i What is the length of the critical path?

_____

ii Use backward scanning to write the latest starting time (LST) for each activity in the network.

iii If the project is to commence at 2 pm, what is the latest starting time for activity:

  A *H*?   **B** *K*?   **C** *Q*?

_____   _____   _____

Networks: Critical path analysis

Excel MATHEMATICS STANDARD 2

Ch. 9, pp. 225–227

Float time

QUESTION **1**

a Use forward and backward scanning to write the earliest and latest starting time for each activity in the network. All measurements are in minutes.

b What is the critical path?

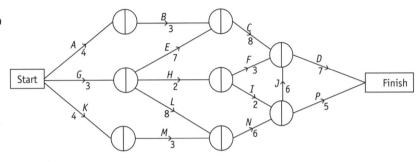

_____

c The project is to commence at 9:00.

  i What is the time the project is expected to be finished? _____

  ii What is the earliest starting time for activity:

    A *H*? _____   **B** *C*? _____

  iii What is the latest starting time for activity:

    A *C*? _____   **B** *N*? _____

d What is the float time for activity:

  i *B*? _____   **ii** *F*? _____

e Between which times can these activities commence?

  i *M* _____   **ii** *F* _____

QUESTION **2**

a Use forward and backward scanning to write the earliest and latest starting time for each activity in the network. All measurements are in hours.

b What is the critical path?

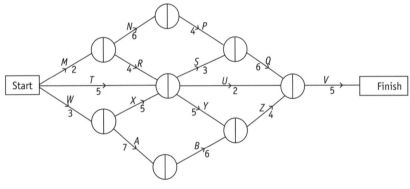

_____

c The project is to commence at 8 am Monday.

  i What is the time the project is expected to be finished? _____

  ii What is the earliest starting time for activity:

    A *P*? _____   **B** *B*? _____

  iii What is the latest starting time for activity:

    A *X*? _____   **B** *Q*? _____

d What is the float time for activity:

  i *R*? _____   **ii** *U*? _____

e Between which times can these activities commence?

  i *R* _____   **ii** *Q* _____

Networks: Critical path analysis

Excel MATHEMATICS STANDARD 2

Ch. 9, pp. 227–231

Maximum flow/minimum cut

QUESTION **1**   For each of the networks with source *S* and sink *T*, find the maximum flow across each cut:

a

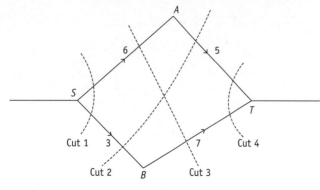

b

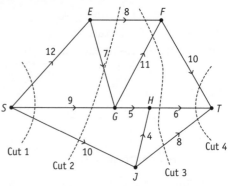

_____

c

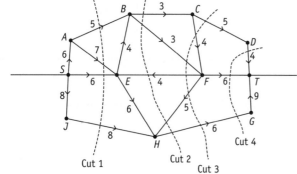

_____

_____

QUESTION **2**   In each of the networks below use the minimum cut to find the maximum flow from source (*S*) to sink (*T*):

a

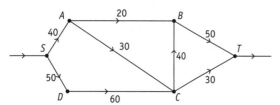

b

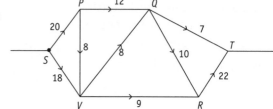

_____

_____

c

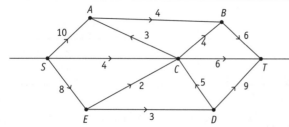

QUESTION **3**   The network shows the maximum rates of flow (in vehicles per hour) between towns *S*, *A*, *B*, *C*, *D* and *T* in the direction from *S* to *T*.

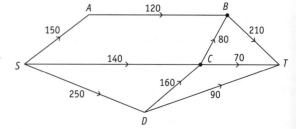

a Find the maximum traffic flow from *S* to *T*.

b When this maximum flow occurs, how many vehicles pass:

  i along *SA*? _____   **ii** through *C*? _____

Networks: Critical path analysis

TOPIC TEST

SECTION I

Instructions
- This section consists of 5 multiple-choice questions.
- Each question is worth 1 mark.
- Fill in only ONE CIRCLE for each question.

Time allowed: 7 minutes

Total marks: 5

1   What is the capacity of the cut in this network?

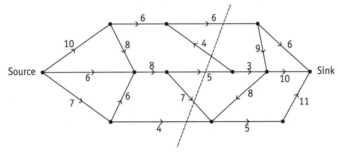

Ⓐ   7

Ⓑ   18

Ⓒ   22

Ⓓ   26

The table lists the earliest start time (EST) and latest start time (LST), in hours, for activities in a project and is used to answer Questions 2 and 3.

Activity	EST	LST
P	0	0
Q	3	3
R	5	7
S	9	9
T	12	12
U	15	15

2   Which of these are the activities that lie on the critical path?

Ⓐ   *PQRSTU*

Ⓑ   *PQSTU*

Ⓒ   *QRSTU*

Ⓓ   *QSTU*

3   What is the float time for activity *R*?

Ⓐ   2 hours

Ⓑ   3 hours

Ⓒ   5 hours

Ⓓ   7 hours

4 The table lists the activities for a project.

Activity	Immediate prerequisite(s)
A	None
B	A
C	A
D	A
E	B
F	C, D
G	E, F
H	G

Which of these directed networks represents the project?

Ⓐ   Ⓑ

Ⓒ   Ⓓ

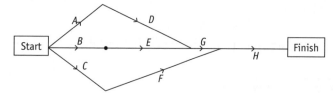

5 The directed network diagram for a project is given below.

What are all the activities that need to be completed before activity *R* can start?

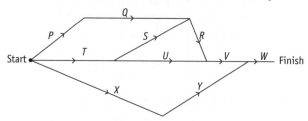

Ⓐ   *P* and *Q*   Ⓑ   *T* and *S*

Ⓒ   *P, Q, S* and *T*   Ⓓ   *P, Q, S, T* and *U*

TOPIC TEST

SECTION II

Instructions
- This section consists of 7 questions.
- Show all working.

Time allowed: 53 minutes

Total marks: 35

6 The diagram shows a simple directed network of roads, with measurements in vehicles/minute.

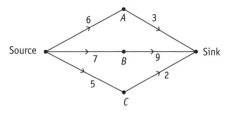

a What is the maximum flow of vehicles on the path from source to sink through:

i *A*? _____ **1 mark**

ii *B*? _____ **1 mark**

iii *C*? _____ **1 mark**

b Draw in the minimum cut and determine the maximum flow of vehicles from source to sink? **1 mark**

_____

_____

7 The network represents the flow from source to sink. Jenny needs to find the maximum flow and has already drawn two cuts through the network.

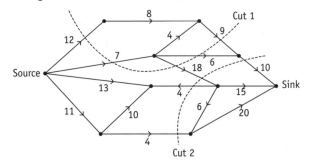

a Explain why Cut 1 is not a valid cut for determining the maximum flow. **1 mark**

_____

_____

b Explain why the capacity of Cut 2 is **not** 36. **1 mark**

_____

_____

c Jenny realises she has not drawn the minimum cut. Draw in the minimum cut, labelling it as Cut 3, and determine the maximum flow from source to sink. **2 marks**

_____

_____

8 Two cuts have been drawn across the network where S = source and T = sink. Cut 1 has a capacity of 31 and Cut 2 has a capacity of 23.

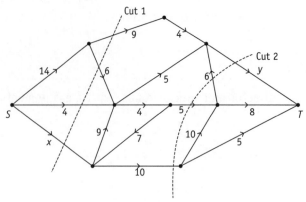

a What is the value of x? **1 mark**

b What is the value of y? **1 mark**

c With the use of another cut, determine the minimum flow from source to sink. **1 mark**

9 The network diagram shows a camping ground where S = entrance and T = exit. There are one-way roads in the camping ground shown as edges on the network and the amenities blocks are shown as vertices A to J. Each road has a capacity expressed in cars per minute.

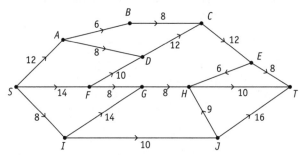

a What number of cars can pass through the entrance per minute? **1 mark**

b What is the maximum flow of cars per minute through the camping ground? **2 marks**

c Another road is to be built from C directly to T for cars to travel to the exit. The new road will have a capacity of 12 cars per minute. Draw the new road on the network diagram and determine how much the maximum flow for the camping ground has increased following the construction of the new road. **2 marks**

10 An activity table shows a construction project which has nine activities. All times are in weeks.

Activity	Immediate prerequisite(s)	Duration in weeks	Earliest start time (EST)
A	None	4	0
B	None	3	0
C	None	2	0
D	A	6	4
E	C	3	2
F	A	5	4
G	D, B, E	4	
H	C	6	2
I	F, G, H	3	

a Two entries are missing from the activity table. What is the EST for activity:

i G? _____ **1 mark**

ii I? _____ **1 mark**

b A directed network diagram is drawn to represent the project's activities. Complete the missing information. **2 marks**

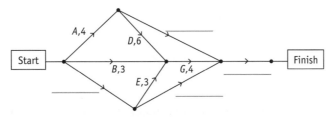

c List all the activities that need to be completed before activity G can start. **1 mark**

_____

_____

d What is the shortest time this project can be completed in? **1 mark**

_____

_____

e Write down the critical path for this network. **1 mark**

_____

_____

11 The directed network diagram represents a project with 10 activities where all measurements are in minutes.

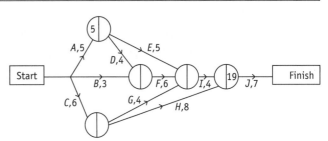

a Use forward and backward scanning to write the earliest starting time (EST) and latest starting time (LST) for each activity in the network. Use the left half of the circle for EST and the right half for LST. **2 marks**

_____

_____

b What is the critical path? **1 mark**

_____

c If the starting time is 10:30 am, what is the:

  i earliest time the project will complete? **1 mark**

_____

_____

  ii latest time to start activity _G_? **1 mark**

_____

_____

12 A project of building a children's playground involves 13 activities and a directed network diagram is used to represent the project, where all measurements are in weeks.

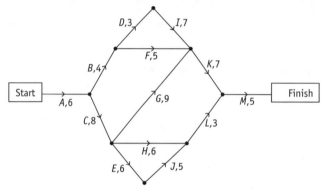

a Write down the critical path and the minimum number of weeks it will take for the project to be completed. **3 marks**

_____

_____

_____

b What is the float time for activity _I_? **1 mark**

_____

_____

_____

c _P_ is a dummy activity that needs to be completed after _B_ but before _C_. Represent activity _P_ on the network diagram above. **1 mark**

d Additional funding has meant that activity _G_ can be reduced by up to 5 weeks at a cost of $1200 per day. What is the maximum cost for reducing the completion time of the project? **2 marks**

_____

_____

_____

_____

CHAPTER 12

Sample HSC Examination 1

Total time: 2 hours and 30 minutes   **Total marks: 100**

SECTION I   **Marks: 15**

Instructions   • Attempt Questions 1 to 15.
 • Allow about 25 minutes for this section.
 • Each question is worth 1 mark.
 • Fill in only ONE CIRCLE for each question.

1 Which of these relationships shows a strong positive association?

Ⓐ    Ⓑ 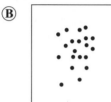   Ⓒ    Ⓓ

2 Energy is used at the rate of 20 joules per second. The power developed is:

Ⓐ   100 W   Ⓑ   25 W   Ⓒ   20 W   Ⓓ   5 W

3 As shown in the figure, a square is drawn in a circle of radius 6 cm.
The area of the shaded region is given by:

Ⓐ $\pi \times 12^2 - 12^2$ Ⓑ $\pi \times 6^2 - 12^2$

Ⓒ $\pi \times 6^2 - 6^2$ Ⓓ $\pi \times 6^2 - 12 \times 6$

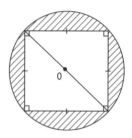

4 A car that was purchased for $39 900 is worth $20 400 after 5 years.
The annual amount of depreciation, using the straight-line method, is:

Ⓐ $3900   Ⓑ $4080   Ⓒ $7980   Ⓓ $12 060

5 2.5 g of a medicine is used to make a 200–mL solution. The concentration of this medicine, in mg/mL, is:

Ⓐ   0.125   Ⓑ   1.25   Ⓒ   12.5   Ⓓ   125

6 Use the sine rule to find the length of the side x correct to one significant figure.

Ⓐ   7 cm   Ⓑ   5 cm

Ⓒ   4 cm   Ⓓ   8 cm

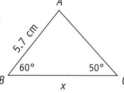

7 Lauren's z–score on a particular test was 1.5. If the class average and standard deviation were 64 and 8 respectively, Lauren's mark was:

Ⓐ   52   Ⓑ   65.5   Ⓒ   76   Ⓓ   86

8 Saccio earns commission selling musical instruments and equipment. He is paid a retainer of $100 per week as well as 5% commission on sales up to $10 000 and 7% commission on additional sales over $10 000. What does he earn in a week where he sells $12 500 worth of goods?

Ⓐ $675   Ⓑ $775   Ⓒ $875   Ⓓ $975

9 The cost of hiring a venue involves a fixed cost of $300 then varies directly with the number of people in attendance. If it costs $450 for 30 people, how much would it cost to hire the venue for 40 people?

Ⓐ $480   Ⓑ $490   Ⓒ $500   Ⓓ $550

10 A new laptop was purchased for $1800 on 15 June using a credit card. Simple interest is charged at a rate of 23.42% p.a. for purchases using the credit card. No other purchases were made and there is no interest–free period. Interest is charged on both the date of purchase and date of payment. What was the total amount owing on 7 July the same year?

Ⓐ $1826.56   Ⓑ $1827.72   Ⓒ $2656.41   Ⓓ $2771.90

11 Steve wants to buy a caravan at a cost of $60 000. He has savings of $40 000 but borrows the remainder. He is charged 8% p.a. flat–rate interest over 5 years. Which of these is closest to the monthly repayment on his loan?

Ⓐ $270   Ⓑ $370   Ⓒ $470   Ⓓ $570

12 A project involves four activities. One of the activities is named Activity X. The latest start time for Activity X is 10 days and the float time is 3 days. Which of these is the earliest start time for Activity X?

Ⓐ 7 days   Ⓑ 10 days   Ⓒ 13 days   Ⓓ 30 days

13 What is the equation of the line drawn on the number plane?

Ⓐ $C = 20n + 200$ Ⓑ $C = 25n + 200$

Ⓒ $C = 40n + 200$ Ⓓ $C = 200n + 40$

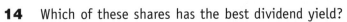

14 Which of these shares has the best dividend yield?

Ⓐ share price = $2.60, dividend per share = $0.16

Ⓑ share price = $5.20, dividend per share = $0.29

Ⓒ share price = $22.70, dividend per share = $1.55

Ⓓ share price = $48.10, dividend per share = $2.85

15 The minimum spanning tree for the network below includes the edge with weight labelled p.

The total weight of all edges for the minimum spanning tree is 20.

What is the value of p?

Ⓐ $p = 1$ Ⓑ $p = 2$

Ⓒ $p = 3$ Ⓓ $p = 4$

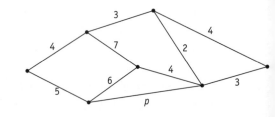

Sample HSC Examination 1

SECTION II

Marks: 85

Instructions
- Attempt Questions 16 to 34.
- Allow about 2 hours and 5 minutes for this section.
- Answer the questions in the spaces provided. These spaces provide guidance for the expected length of response.
- Your responses should include relevant mathematical reasoning and/or calculations.

QUESTION **16** (5 marks)

The diagram shows a river of width x metres.

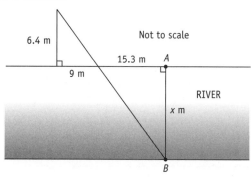

a Use similar triangles to find the width of the river.

2 marks

_____

_____

_____

b The average depth of the river at AB is 2.1 m. What volume of water, in kilolitres, flows past AB every minute if the water is flowing at 1.6 m/s?

3 marks

_____

_____

_____

_____

QUESTION **17** (5 marks)

The diagram shows three towns A, B and C. Town B is 250 km due west of C and town A is due north of town B. The bearing of town A from town C is 300°.

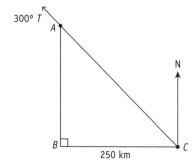

Sample HSC Examination 1

a Explain why angle *ACB* is 30°.   **1 mark**

---

b How far south of town *A* is town *B*? Give your answer to the nearest kilometre.   **2 marks**

---

c At 9:00 am a plane is flying directly overhead town *A* towards town *C*. If the plane flies at 400 km/h, at what time will it be directly overhead town *C*?   **2 marks**

Question 18 (4 marks)

Solve the following equations:

a $7x - 20 = 3x + 16$ **2 marks**

---

b $\sqrt{x + 3} = 8$ **2 marks**

Question 19 (5 marks)

A radial survey of a field is given.

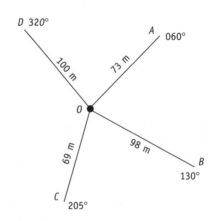

a Find the size of $\angle AOB$.   **1 mark**

---

b Calculate the area of $\triangle AOB$ to the nearest square metre.   **2 marks**

_____

_____

_____

_____

c Find the distance from A to B to the nearest metre.   **2 marks**

_____

_____

_____

_____

QUESTION **20** (6 marks)

a Solomon invests $25 000 in an account earning 6% p.a. interest, compounded quarterly.
How much is his investment worth, to the nearest whole dollar, at the end of 5 years?   **2 marks**

_____

_____

_____

_____

b Sally invests $3000 at the end of every 6 months in an account that earns 8% p.a. interest,
compounded 6-monthly. Using the table below, calculate the amount her investment is worth,
to the nearest dollar, at the end of 5 years.   **2 marks**

Future value of $1				
Interest rate per period				
Period	3%	4%	5%	6%	10%
1	1.0000	1.0000	1.0000	1.0000	1.0000
2	2.0300	2.0400	2.0500	2.0600	2.1000
3	3.0909	3.1216	3.1525	3.1836	3.3100
4	4.1836	4.2465	4.3101	4.3746	4.6410
5	5.3091	5.4163	5.5256	5.6371	6.1051
10	11.4639	12.0061	12.5779	13.1808	15.9374
20	26.8704	29.7781	33.0660	36.7856	57.2750

_____

_____

_____

_____

_____

_____

c How much more would Solomon need to have invested to have the same amount as Sally at the end of the 5 years? Give your answer to the nearest dollar. **2 marks**

_____

_____

_____

_____

QUESTION **21** (8 marks)

The table gives an average water use per person per day.

Use	Litres/day
Bath/shower	72
Sink	18
Toilet	35
Washing clothes	45
Washing dishes	29
Cooking	8
Miscellaneous	6
Total	

a Complete the table to insert the value for total. **1 mark**

b Some people will look at this table and argue that they don't use this much water. How can you respond? **1 mark**

_____

c How much water is used in the sink over a year? **1 mark**

_____

d How much water (in kilolitres) does the average person use in a year? **1 mark**

_____

e One of these areas uses 21.1% of the daily water use. Which is it? **1 mark**

_____

f What percentage of water is spent on washing dishes? **1 mark**

_____

g A water-efficient toilet can save about 20% on a person's water use of that device.

   i What is the daily saving in this area? **1 mark**

_____

   ii What is the annual saving in this area? **1 mark**

_____

Sample HSC Examination 1

QUESTION **22** (2 marks)

The distance, d metres, that an object falls is proportional to the square of the time, t seconds. An object dropped from a plane falls 45 m in 3 seconds. How far will it fall in 8 seconds?　　**2 marks**

_____

_____

_____

_____

QUESTION **23** (5 marks)

Brendan is currently paying an average of $150 per month for his household electricity. He is looking into purchasing a solar panel system which will reduce his reliance on the electricity grid. The initial cost for the system is $6000 as well as a $240 per year maintenance cost. He expects to reduce the cost of his existing monthly electricity bill by 40%.

a　Let $C_1 = 150n$ be Brendan's existing cost of electricity for n months. Explain why $C_2 = 6000 + 110n$ is the projected cost of Brendan's electricity if he installs the new solar panel system.　　**2 marks**

_____

_____

_____

b　Determine the time it will take for Brendan to recoup the cost of the solar panel system and start saving money.　　**3 marks**

_____

_____

_____

_____

QUESTION **24** (4 marks)

A company manufactures cylindrical pipes all of length 70 cm. The approximate capacity, in litres, of the pipes for different diameters is shown by the graph.

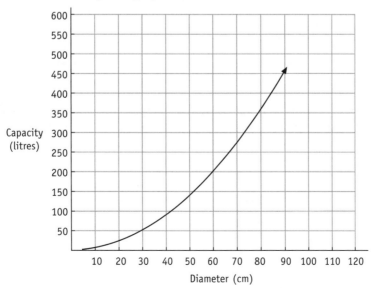

Sample HSC Examination 1

a What would be the diameter of a pipe with capacity 100 L? **1 mark**

b Carmel predicted that a pipe with diameter 120 cm would have a capacity of 600 L.
Do you agree with this prediction? Briefly comment. **2 marks**

c If the capacity can be approximated using the formula $C = 0.055d^2$, find the capacity
when $d = 120$. **1 mark**

QUESTION **25** (4 marks)

Tom purchased a tractor for $80 000.

a Use the declining-balance formula to find the salvage value of the tractor after 10 years if it depreciates
in value by 12% p.a. Leave your answer to the nearest dollar. **2 marks**

b Tom also calculated the salvage value of the tractor after 10 years using a straight–line method of
depreciation of $6000 p.a. What is the difference in the amount of depreciation using both
methods? **2 marks**

QUESTION **26** (3 marks)

A plane leaves Melbourne (UTC+10) at 8:30 am on Wednesday and arrives in Tokyo (UTC+8) at 5:00 pm
that evening. If the flight distance is 8160 km what is the average speed of the aeroplane, to the nearest
kilometre per hour? **3 marks**

Sample HSC Examination 1

QUESTION **27** (4 marks)

To determine whether muscle mass reduces as men age, a nutritionist surveyed three men in each of four age groups: 50s, 60s, 70s and 80s. The results are recorded in the table.

Muscle mass of men in different age groups												
Age in years (x)	56	52	68	73	64	79	82	86	51	63	73	86
Muscle mass in kg (y)	25	26	24	24	26	21	20	18	28	26	25	20

a Comment on the association of age and muscle mass, using a calculation to support your conclusion. **1 mark**

b What is the equation of the least-squares regression line for the data? **2 marks**

c Use your equation to estimate the muscle mass of a 70-year-old man. **1 mark**

QUESTION **28** (6 marks)

The table below details the present-value interest factors to compare annuities of $1.

Table of present-value interest factors						
	Interest rate per period					
Period	0.50%	1.00%	2.00%	4.00%	6.00%	8.00%
16	15.3399	14.7179	13.5777	11.6523	10.1059	8.8514
20	18.9874	18.0456	16.3514	13.5903	11.4699	9.8181
24	22.5629	21.2434	18.9139	15.2470	12.5504	10.5288
36	32.8710	30.1075	25.4888	18.9083	14.6210	11.7172
48	42.5803	37.9740	30.6731	21.1951	15.6500	12.1891
64	54.6543	47.1029	35.9214	22.9685	16.2665	12.4093
120	90.0735	69.7005	45.3554	24.7741	16.6514	12.4988
240	139.5808	90.8194	49.5686	24.9980	16.6667	12.5000

a What amount of money needs to be invested today, earning interest of 4% p.a, compounded 6–monthly, to provide for an annuity of $40 000 every 6 months for the next 24 years? **2 marks**

b Preston has two choices for a loan of $150 000. Loan A can be taken over a period of 20 years at 6% p.a., compounded monthly, or Loan B is for a period of 16 years at 8% p.a., compounded quarterly. Loan A has monthly instalments and Loan B has quarterly instalments. What is the:

Sample HSC Examination 1

i amount of each instalment? **2 marks**

_____

_____

_____

ii difference in the interest paid on each of the loans? **2 marks**

_____

_____

_____

QUESTION **29** (3 marks)

The suggested maximum heart rate (MHR) is 220 beats per minutes minus your age.

a What is the age of a person if their suggested MHR is 165 beats per minute? **1 mark**

_____

_____

b An alternative method to determine a person's maximum heart rate (MHR), in beats per minute, is to use the formula MHR = 208 − 0.7a, where a is the person's age in years. Use this formula to determine the age of a person if their suggested MHR is 165 beats per minute, to the nearest year. **2 marks**

_____

_____

QUESTION **30** (2 marks)

The body mass index can be calculated from $BMI = \dfrac{\text{weight} \left(kg \right)}{\text{height} \left(m \right) \times \text{height} \left(m \right)}$

A man has a BMI of 29 and a height of 1 m 80 cm. Calculate his weight. **2 marks**

_____

_____

QUESTION **31** (4 marks)

A project requires activities A to J to be completed, as shown in the table.

Activity	Immediate prerequisite(s)	Duration in days
A	None	4
B	None	3
C	A	5
D	A	
E	B, D	8
F	B, D	
G	F	
H	C, E, G	6
I	F	2
J	H, I	4

The minimum completion time for the project is 28 days by using the critical path *ADEHJ*. The earliest start time for *G* and *I* is day 13. The float time for activity *G* is 1 day. Draw a directed network diagram and complete the table by finding the duration of activities *D*, *F* and *I*.   **4 marks**

_____

_____

_____

_____

_____

_____

QUESTION **32** (8 marks)

The Cross family have a backyard swimming pool which is 10 m long and 5 m wide. The depth of the pool varies as shown on the diagram.

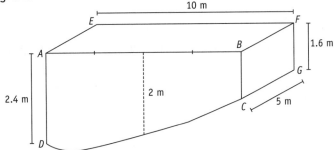

a Use the trapezoidal method to show that the area of *ABCD* is approximately 20 m².   **2 marks**

_____

_____

b The Cross family pays $2.30/kL for their domestic water. The pool is presently at 80% of total capacity and the level of water needs to be 'topped up' to a level of 90% of its total capacity. Calculate the cost of the water needed.   **2 marks**

_____

_____

c The hose used to fill the pool discharges water at the rate of 100 L /minute. How long will it take to top up the level of the poolwater from 80% capacity to 90% capacity?   **2 marks**

_____

_____

d The table shows the level of energy used for different rated pool pumps.

Pool pump and energy use						
Horsepower	0.75	1	1.5	2	2.5	3
kW	1.26	1.72	2.14	2.25	2.62	3.17

To maintain water quality the family run their 1.5-horsepower pool pump for two sessions each day: from 7 am to 10 am and from 4:30 pm to 7:00 pm.

If the average cost of the Cross family's electricity is 27.6 c/kWh, what is the cost of electricity used in a year to run the pool pump, to the nearest dollar? **2 marks**

_____

_____

_____

QUESTION **33** (4 marks)

The length of human pregnancies is approximately normally distributed with a mean of 266 days and a standard deviation of 16 days.

a What is the z–score of a pregnancy that lasts 258 days? **1 mark**

_____

_____

b What percentage of pregnancies have a length between 250 days and 298 days? **1 mark**

_____

_____

c In a random sample of 200 pregnancies, how many women have a pregnancy that lasts less than 282 days? **2 marks**

_____

_____

QUESTION **34** (3 marks)

The network shows the maximum rates of flow (in vehicles per minute) from city S to city T passing through seven towns.

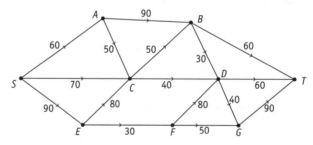

a Find the maximum traffic flow from S to T. **1 mark**

_____

b A new road is to be built directly from town E to town G which will have a capacity of 60 vehicles per minute. What will be the new maximum flow? **1 mark**

_____

c Once this new road is built, what impact will closing the road from A to B for roadworks have on the maximum possible flow of vehicles from S to T per minute? **1 mark**

_____

Sample HSC Examination 2

Total time: 2 hours and 30 minutes **Total marks: 100**

SECTION I **Marks: 15**

Instructions
- Attempt Questions 1 to 15.
- Allow about 25 minutes for this section.
- Each question is worth 1 mark.
- Fill in only ONE CIRCLE for each question.

1 The graph shows the typing speed for a student.

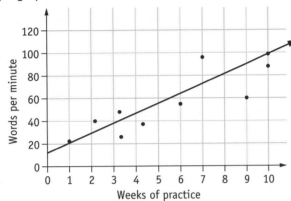

Based on the line of best fit, what would be the approximate typing speed, in words per minute, of a person who has practised for 8 weeks?

Ⓐ 40 Ⓑ 48 Ⓒ 62 Ⓓ 81

2 A concrete pipe has an inner diameter of 20 cm and is 3 cm thick. What volume of concrete is used to make a pipe section 15 m long?

Ⓐ 0.3 m^3 Ⓑ 0.43 m^3 Ⓒ 3251.55 m^3 Ⓓ 6078.98 m^3

3 In the triangle drawn, the value of y is given by:

Ⓐ $y = 9\cos 63°$ Ⓑ $y = 9\sin 63°$

Ⓒ $y = \dfrac{9}{\cos 63°}$ Ⓓ $y = \dfrac{9}{\sin 63°}$

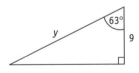

4 Matthew took out a loan of $9000 at the flat interest rate of 8% p.a. over a term of 36 months. How much will he have to repay?

Ⓐ $6840 Ⓑ $11 337 Ⓒ $11 160 Ⓓ $2160

5 The equation of this graph could be:

Ⓐ $y = x^2 + 3$ Ⓑ $y = x^3 + 3$

Ⓒ $y = \dfrac{3}{x}$ Ⓓ $y = 3^x$

6 A map is drawn using a scale of 1 : 250 000. The towns of Marabin and Cosalletti are 75 km apart. What is the distance between the two towns on the map?

Ⓐ 1.875 cm Ⓑ 3 cm Ⓒ 18.75 cm Ⓓ 30 cm

Sample HSC Examination 2

7   Xavier graphed the lines $y = 2x - 4$ and $y = 5 - x$ on a number plane. What is the point of intersection of the two lines?

(A)   (1, –2)   (B)   (1, 4)   (C)   (3, 1)   (D)   (3, 2)

8   A network diagram is drawn by connecting edges to vertices.
How many vertices have an odd degree?

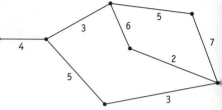

(A)   3   (B)   4

(C)   5   (D)   7

9   Which of these is closest to the future value of an investment of $12 000 at 8% p.a., compounded quarterly, for 3 years?

(A) $14 880   (B) $15 117   (C) $15 219   (D) $19 301

10   Justin owns 200 shares in Company X. Each share is priced at $12.50 and Justin receives a total dividend of $80. What is the dividend yield per share?

(A)   3.2%   (B)   5.6%   (C)   7.8%   (D)   15.6%

11   If $N = k(2.5)^3$, what is the value of k when $N = 312.5$?

(A)   2   (B)   12   (C)   16   (D)   20

12   When in use, an appliance uses 840 W. How much power is consumed in one week if the appliance is used every morning from 7:20 to 8:40?

(A)   7.056 kWh   (B)   7.84 kWh   (C)   7.96 kWh   (D)   8.635 kWh

13   A credit card has a simple interest rate of 0.042% per day with no interest–free period. What is the interest charged on a purchase of $1856 for 13 days, to the nearest cent?

(A) $10.13   (B) $10.17   (C) $10.19   (D) $10.21

14   The table is used to add weights to the network diagram. What is the value of t?

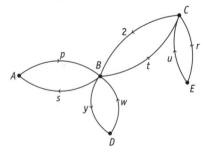

| | | To: | | | |
		A	B	C	D	E
From:	**A**	–	3	–	–	–
	B	2	–	4	3	–
	C	–	5	–	–	2
	D	–	2	–	–	–
	E	–	–	4	–	–

(A)   2   (B)   3   (C)   4   (D)   5

15   Which of these is closest to the volume of the triangular prism?

(A)   64.8 cm³   (B)   194.3 cm³

(C)   388.5 cm³   (D)   777.0 cm³

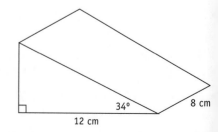

Sample HSC Examination 2

Instructions
- Attempt Questions 16 to 36.
- Allow about 2 hours and 5 minutes for this section.
- Answer the questions in the spaces provided. These spaces provide guidance for the expected length of response.
- Your responses should include relevant mathematical reasoning and/or calculations.

QUESTION **16** (3 marks)

The weight of the contents of cans of a particular brand of dog food is normally distributed with mean 757 g and standard deviation 3.5 g. There are 24 cans per carton. In a shipment of 20 cartons of this dog food, how many cans would you expect to have less than the labelled weight of 750 g?   **3 marks**

_____

_____

_____

_____

_____

_____

_____

_____

QUESTION **17** (7 marks)

The points P, Q and R on the diagram represent three towns. Q is due west of P. The bearing of R from P is 240° and the bearing of R from Q is 205°. The distance from Q to R is 58 km.

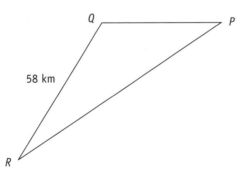

a What is the size of $\angle PQR$?   **2 marks**

_____

_____

b What is the size of $\angle QPR$?   **2 marks**

_____

_____

_____

Sample HSC Examination 2

c Find the distance from *P* to *R*, to the nearest kilometre.

2 marks

d What is the bearing of *P* from *R*?

1 mark

QUESTION **18** (2 marks)

a A car travels at 90 km/h for $2\frac{1}{4}$ hours and at 110 km/h for $1\frac{3}{4}$ hours.

Find the total distance travelled.

1 mark

b If this distance is travelled on 50 L of petrol how far would the car travel on 35 L of petrol?

1 mark

QUESTION **19** (7 marks)

The graph shows the line of best fit in an experiment where the burning time of a candle was measured.

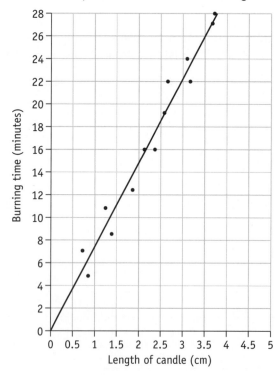

a Name the dependent variable.

1 mark

b What is the *y*–intercept of this line? **1 mark**

c What is the significance of the *y*–intercept? **1 mark**

d What is the gradient of the line, correct to one decimal place? **2 marks**

e Write the equation of the line in the form $y = mx + c$ in terms of the given variables. **2 marks**

QUESTION **20** (2 marks)

If the average peak rate for electricity is $0.48 per kilowatt–hour, calculate the cost of running a 200–watt TV for 7 hours and a 180–watt computer for 8 hours during peak time. **2 marks**

QUESTION **21** (4 marks)

A class of Year 12 students recorded their bodyweight and displayed the data in the back-to-back stem-and-leaf plot shown:

a Determine the upper and lower quartiles for the boys' data. **2 marks**

Boys		Girls
	4	9
6 2	5	3 4 6 7 8 9
8 7 4 2 1 0	6	0 0 2 3 8
5 5 4 0	7	2 5
1	8	
7	9	

b Show if there is an outlier in the boys' data. **2 marks**

QUESTION **22** (2 marks)

Ben invests $5000 into a savings fund. Interest is paid at the rate of 6.5% p.a. compounded monthly on this amount. How much will the investment be worth at the end of 25 years? (Give your answer to the nearest dollar.) **2 marks**

QUESTION **23** (2 marks)

In a certain state the stamp duty for a new private car is as shown. **2 marks**

Car value	Stamp duty
$600 or less	$20
$601 to $35 000	3% ($3 for every $100 or part thereof)
$35 001 to $40 000	$1050 + 11% for the proportion over $35 000
$40 001 and over	4% ($4 for every $100 or part thereof)

Sample HSC Examination 2

How much **more** in stamp duty is paid for a vehicle costing $40 000 than one costing $20 000?

_____

_____

QUESTION **24** (7 marks)

Tim wants to fence a small rectangular yard for his dog. He intends to use the back wall of his shed as one side and an existing fence as another side so that he only needs to fence two sides as shown in the diagram. He has enough materials to fence 8 m. The length of one side is x m.

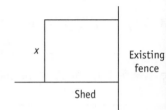

a Show that the area A m^2 of the yard is given by $A = 8x - x^2$. **2 marks**

_____

_____

_____

The graph of $A = 8x - x^2$ is a parabola as shown below.

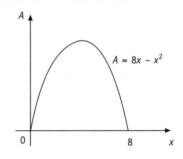

b What value of x will make the area a maximum? **1 mark**

_____

_____

c What is the largest possible area of the yard? **1 mark**

_____

_____

d What shape is the yard when the area is a maximum? **1 mark**

_____

_____

e Tim decides his dog needs a bigger yard. He has worked out the maximum area for different lengths of fence. These results are shown in the table.

Length of fence (l)	10	12	14	16	18	20	22	24
Maximum area (M)	25	36	49	64	81	100	121	144

Write an equation that describes the relationship between M and l. **2 marks**

_____

_____

Sample HSC Examination 2

QUESTION 25 (4 marks)

The network diagram shows a project where the weights are in days and the starting date is 1 July.

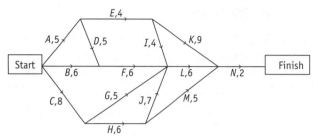

a By forward and backward scanning, find the critical path. **2 marks**

_____

b What is the earliest date the project can be completed? **1 mark**

_____

c Determine the float time for activity F. **1 mark**

_____

QUESTION 26 (3 marks)

Calculate the difference in the surface area of a tennis ball (radius 3.5 cm) and a soccer ball (radius 10 cm). Give your answer correct to two significant figures. **3 marks**

_____

_____

QUESTION 27 (4 marks)

Students in two classes recorded how many sit-ups they could complete in one minute. The results are shown on the box-and-whisker plots below.

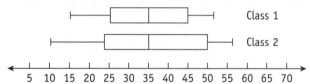

a Describe the general shape of the data for class 1. **1 mark**

_____

b What percentage of students in class 2 completed between 35 and 50 sit-ups? **1 mark**

_____

c Given that there is an equal number of students in both classes, compare and contrast the results. **2 marks**

_____

QUESTION 28 (2 marks)

The angle of depression made by a ladder against a wall is 70°. If a 3-m ladder positioned at the same spot reaches 1.5 m lower down the wall, calculate its angle of elevation to the nearest degree. **2 marks**

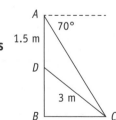

_____

_____

_____

Sample HSC Examination 2

QUESTION **29** (6 marks)

Michelle and Holly decide to set aside regular sums of money to save for future expenses. Use the table below to answer the following questions.

Future value of $1					
Interest rate per period					
Period	3%	4%	5%	6%	10%
1	1.0000	1.0000	1.0000	1.0000	1.0000
2	2.0300	2.0400	2.0500	2.0600	2.1000
3	3.0909	3.1216	3.1525	3.1836	3.3100
4	4.1836	4.2465	4.3101	4.3746	4.6410
5	5.3091	5.4163	5.5256	5.6371	6.1051
10	11.4639	12.0061	12.5779	13.1808	15.9374
20	26.8704	29.7781	33.0660	36.7856	57.2750

a Michelle chooses to set aside $600 every 6 months. If she earns 10% interest per annum, how much will she have in 5 years? **2 marks**

_____

_____

_____

b If Holly saves $1200 per year, how much will her investment amount to in 5 years, if interest is charged at the same rate? **1 mark**

_____

_____

_____

c Both girls have a savings goal of $10 000. How much more would they each have to put into their savings account to reach their goal in 5 years? Answer to the nearest dollar. **3 marks**

_____

_____

_____

QUESTION **30** (3 marks)

What is the perimeter of *ABCD*, to the nearest centimetre? **3 marks**

_____

_____

_____

_____

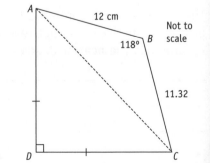

Sample HSC Examination 2

The table shows the daily cost of gas used by a household.

Cost of gas for domestic users per day	
Breakdown	**Cost (in cents/Mj)**
First 41 MJ	3.90
Next 49 MJ	2.20
Next 189 MJ	2.17
Next 2466 MJ	2.16
Daily supply charge	58.25

a Show that the weekly cost for a family who use 65 MJ/day is $18.97. **2 marks**

_____

_____

b A household of four people use an average of 160 MJ/day. What is the cost of gas used by each person in one year? **3 marks**

_____

_____

_____

QUESTION **32** (7 marks)

The population of people living on an island is increasing exponentially. The population of the island is modelled using the formula $P = 30\,000(1.035)^t$, where P is the population and t is the number of years after 2018.

a What was the initial population (in 2018)? **1 mark**

_____

b Complete the table of values below using $P = 30\,000(1.035)^t$. **1 mark**

t	0	5	10	15	20	25
P		35 631	42 318		59 694	

c Draw the population graph for the table of values. **2 marks**

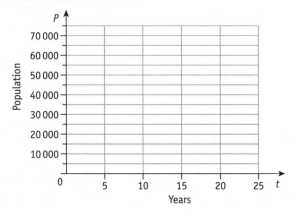

d Use the graph to estimate the population in 2030, to the nearest 10 000.　　　　**1 mark**

_____

_____

e Estimate the time taken for the population to reach 55 000.　　　　**1 mark**

_____

_____

f Use your calculator to estimate the population in 2050.　　　　**1 mark**

_____

_____

QUESTION **33** (2 marks)

The diagram represents a scale drawing of the roof of a large factory where AB = 80 m.

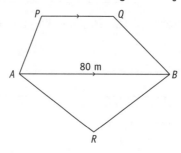

All the rain that falls on the roof is collected in a water tank. If 20 mm of rain falls on the roof, how much water will be collected, in kilolitres?　　　　**2 marks**

_____

_____

_____

QUESTION **34** (5 marks)

A school has 10 classrooms that require access to water. The classrooms are represented by vertices A to J on the network diagram below. Water is presently piped to vertex X. The dotted edges represent possible water pipe routes between adjacent classrooms. The weights on edges represent the length of pipe required, in metres.

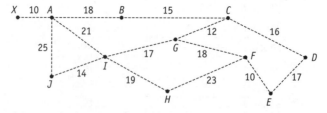

All classrooms are to be connected using the smallest length of pipe possible. The cost of the water pipe plus laying is $123.40/m.

The principal used a minimum spanning tree to determine the lowest cost of water pipe required. However, the price was too expensive. She decided to reduce costs by not connecting classroom B

to the water supply. What will be the savings for the school under the new plan of not connecting classroom *B*?   **5 marks**

_____

_____

_____

QUESTION **35** (5 marks)

The diagram shows a truncated cone where a small cone has been removed from the top of a larger cone. The original large cone had a height of 4 m and a diameter of 2 m. The height of the truncated cone is now 75% of its original height.

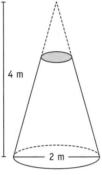

a Explain why the area of the shaded cross section is $\dfrac{\pi}{16}$ m².   **2 marks**

_____

_____

_____

b What is the volume of the truncated cone, correct to three significant figures?   **3 marks**

_____

_____

_____

QUESTION **36** (3 marks)

Jimmy is planning to buy a bike and is considering the salvage value of the bike after 4 years to help him make a choice.

a One bike costs $3400 and the bike reduces in value by 20 cents per kilometre ridden on the bike. If Jimmy averages 6 km per day every day, what is the value after 3 years?   **1 mark**

_____

_____

b Another bike is priced at $4600 but is depreciated at 23% p.a. Jimmy thinks that this bike will be worth more than the first bike after 3 years. Do you agree? Support your answers with calculations.   **2 marks**

_____

_____

_____

Sample HSC Examination 3

Total time: 2 hours and 30 minutes   **Total marks: 100**

SECTION I   **Marks: 15**

Instructions
- Attempt Questions 1 to 15.
- Allow about 25 minutes for this section.
- Each question is worth 1 mark.
- Fill in only ONE CIRCLE for each question.

1   What is the bearing of P from Q?

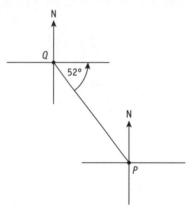

    Ⓐ S52°E   Ⓑ N52°W   Ⓒ S38°E   Ⓓ N38°W

2   What is the gradient of the line $y = 3 - 2x$?

    Ⓐ 3   Ⓑ −2   Ⓒ $\dfrac{3}{2}$ Ⓓ $-\dfrac{2}{3}$

3   A set of eight scores has a lower quartile and 14 and an upper quartile of 20. Which of these is an outlier for the data set?

    Ⓐ 5   Ⓑ 6   Ⓒ 29   Ⓓ 30

4   Two hundred students sat an examination and the results were normally distributed. Kate gained a z–score of +1. Which of these is closest to the number of students who scored higher than Kate?

    Ⓐ 32   Ⓑ 47   Ⓒ 64   Ⓓ 68

5   The point (5, 200) lies on the parabola with equation $y = kx^2$. What is the value of k?

    Ⓐ $k = \sqrt{40}$ Ⓑ $k = 8$ Ⓒ $k = 16$ Ⓓ $k = 40$

6   What is the value of the correlation coefficient, correct to two decimal places?

Student results in Maths and Science tests						
Maths	48	65	87	69	83	62
Science	57	61	72	70	78	63

    Ⓐ 0.67   Ⓑ 0.69   Ⓒ 0.90   Ⓓ 0.93

7 The scale on an aerial photo is given as 1:250 000. Two mountain peaks are 5 cm apart on the photo. What is the actual distance between the two peaks in kilometres?

(A) 1.25 km   (B) 5 km   (C) 12.5 km   (D) 50 km

8 Jolinda takes out a loan for $320 000 over a period of 30 years at an interest rate of 5.5% p.a. She plans to make monthly repayments of $1760. She uses a spreadsheet to monitor her interest paid and the balance owing after each repayment.

Loan table				
	Amount:	$320 000.00		
	Annual interest rate:	5.50%		
	Monthly repayment:	$1760.00		
n	Principal (P)	Interest (I)	$P + I$	$P + I - R$
1	$320 000.00	$1466.67	$321 466.67	$319 706.67
2	$319 706.67	$1465.32	$321 171.99	$319 411.99
3	$319 411.99		$320 875.96	$319 115.96
4	$319 115.96		$320 578.58	$318 818.58
5	$318 818.58	A		

What is the value of **A**?

(A) $1461.25   (B) $1461.82   (C) $1461.98   (D) $1462.18

9 A car is purchased for $32 890. It will depreciate at the rate of 18% p.a. Using the declining-balance method, which of these is closest to the salvage value of the car after 5 years?

(A) $12 194   (B) $14 263   (C) $18 627   (D) $20 696

10 Telea's car has an average fuel consumption rate of 7.9 L/100 km. What is the fuel cost of a trip of 380 km, to the nearest cent, if the cost of the fuel is 149.9 c/L?

(A) $31.16   (B) $31.20   (C) $44.95   (D) $45.00

11

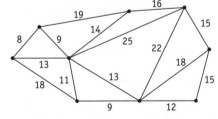

Daniel used the network diagram above to draw this spanning tree.

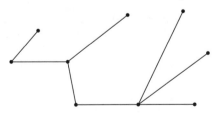

Which of these is the total weight of Daniel's spanning tree?

(A) 8   (B) 84   (C) 97   (D) 107

12 The probability of winning a game is $\frac{5}{8}$. Which expression represents the probability of losing two consecutive games?

(A) $\frac{5}{8} \times \frac{5}{8}$
(B) $\frac{5}{8} \times \frac{4}{7}$
(C) $\frac{3}{8} \times \frac{3}{8}$
(D) $\frac{3}{8} \times \frac{2}{7}$

13 The results of an analysis of reasons given by workers who arrive late to the office over a 6–month period are displayed below. A Pareto chart is to be drawn for the data.

Reasons for lateness to work			
Reasons	**Frequency**	**Cumulative frequency**	**Cumulative percentage**
Traffic	40		
Slept in	28		p
Low on petrol	8		
Family issues	4		

What is the value of p?

(A) 28
(B) 68
(C) 80
(D) 85

14 The network diagram represents a system of sewerage pipelines connecting the 'Source' to the 'Sink'. Sewerage travels in the direction of the arrows, and the maximum flow is represented as weights on edges, measured in kL/minute.

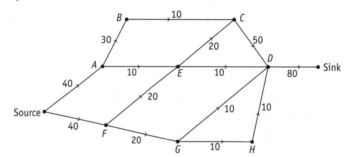

At present the flow capacity of the network is not maximised. Which of these pipelines should be built to ensure maximum flow capacity is met?

(A) *BC* with capacity 20 kL/minute
(B) *GH* with capacity 10 kL/minute
(C) *BC* with capacity 10 kL/minute
(D) *FD* with capacity 20 kL/minute

15 The value of *T* varies directly with the square of *n*. It is known that $T = 160$ when $n = 20$. What is the value of *T* when $n = 30$?

(A) 240
(B) 300
(C) 360
(D) 420

Sample HSC Examination 3

SECTION II

Marks: 85

Instructions
- Attempt Questions 16 to 34.
- Allow about 2 hours and 5 minutes for this section.
- Answer the questions in the spaces provided. These spaces provide guidance for the expected length of response.
- Your responses should include relevant mathematical reasoning and/or calculations.

QUESTION **16** (5 marks)

Rose runs a chocolate cupcake stall. If n = number of cupcakes sold, the cost (C) and revenue (R) equations each day are as follows:

$C = 24 + 1.6n$

$R = 3.2n$

a How many cupcakes does Rose need to sell to break even? **1 mark**

_____

_____

b What will be her loss if she only sells 12 cupcakes? **2 marks**

_____

_____

c To increase sales, Rose decides to improve the quality of ingredients as well as sell her cupcakes in individual boxes. Her fixed costs rise by $12 and the cost per cupcake increases by 40 cents. If Rose sells each cupcake now for $5, how much profit will she make when selling 24 cupcakes? **2 marks**

_____

_____

QUESTION **17** (2 marks)

Three years ago Jenny bought 400 shares at $2.60 per share. They are now worth $3.80 per share. In the past year Jenny received a total dividend of $91.20. What is the current dividend yield on these shares? **2 marks**

_____

_____

_____

QUESTION **18** (3 marks)

On 12 March Cassie bought a sofa costing $1940 using a credit card. Simple interest was charged at a rate of 20.65% p.a. for purchases. There is no interest-free period. The period for which interest was charged included the date of purchase and date of payment. Cassie made no other purchases on her card. What amount was paid when the account was paid in full on 16 April? **3 marks**

_____

_____

_____

Sample HSC Examination 3

QUESTION **19** (8 marks)

The diagram shows three towns A, B and C. Town A is due west of Town B. The bearing of Town A from Town C is 306° and the bearing of Town C from Town B is 216°. The distance between A and B is 480 km.

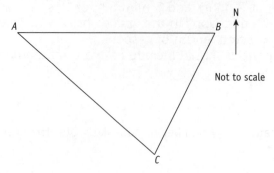

a Mark the given information on the diagram and explain why ∠ACB = 90°.   **2 marks**

b A plane flies at an average speed of 340 km/h between the three towns. How long does the flight between B and C take? Give your answer to the nearest minute.   **3 marks**

c Another plane takes off from A and flies on a bearing of 024°, before turning around and flying, for 590 km, to B. On what bearing should the pilot fly the plane to land at B?   **3 marks**

QUESTION **20** (3 marks)

The table below shows the monthly repayments per $1000 on a bank loan for various annual interest rates.

Term	5.5%	6.0%	6.5%	7%	7.5%	8.0%
20 years	$6.8684	$7.1643	$7.4581	$7.7506	$8.0560	$8.3669
30 years	$5.6754	$5.9955	$6.3233	$6.6503	$6.9921	$7.3404

Dorothy is borrowing $327 000 for 20 years at 6.5% p.a.

a Find her monthly repayment, to the nearest cent.   **1 mark**

b Use this monthly repayment to find the amount of interest Dorothy pays.   **2 marks**

Sample HSC Examination 3

The radius of the circle, centre O, is 8 cm. The size of angle OQP is 100°.

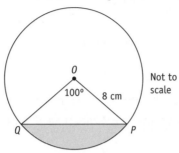

a Explain why the area of triangle OQP is 31.51 cm², correct to two decimal places. **2 marks**

_____

_____

_____

b Find the area of the shaded segment, correct to three significant figures. **2 marks**

_____

_____

_____

QUESTION **22** (2 marks)

The formula for the drip rate, in drops/minute, for a particular medication is given as:

$$\text{Drip rate} = \frac{\text{total volume to be given (in mL)}}{\text{time (in minutes)}} \times \text{drop factor}$$

A patient requires 1200 mL of medication over a 6-hour period. If the drop factor is 15 calculate the drip rate in drops/minute. **2 marks**

_____

_____

QUESTION **23** (3 marks)

To investigate the relationship between age and height a group of nine students were surveyed.

Age v height of males	
Age in years (x)	Height in cm (y)
7	123
9	133
11	151
13	160
8	123
12	158
10	141
5	108
6	118

Sample HSC Examination 3

a Find the equation of the least-squares regression line for the data. **1 mark**

_____

_____

b Use the equation to estimate the height of a 4-year-old boy. **1 mark**

_____

_____

c Asha is 152 cm tall. Use the equation to estimate the time it will take him to grow another 8 cm. Give your answer to the nearest month. **1 mark**

_____

_____

QUESTION **24** (2 marks)

A station manager used the capture-recapture technique to estimate the number of feral buffalo she had on her property. She captured, tagged and released 16 of the buffalo. Later, she caught 30 buffalo at random and found that four had been tagged. What is the estimate for the total number of buffalo on her property? **2 marks**

_____

_____

_____

_____

_____

_____

QUESTION **25** (3 marks)

A certain brand of car battery has a mean life of 3.4 years, and a standard deviation of 0.4 years. A survey of 4000 customers was conducted by a consumer organisation. Using the cumulative normal distribution table, estimate the number of customers who had a car battery that lasted between 3 and 4 years. **3 marks**

z	.0	.1	.2	.3	.4	.5	.6	.7	.8	.9
0.	0.5000	0.5398	0.5793	0.6179	0.6554	0.6915	0.7257	0.7580	0.7881	0.8159
1.	0.8413	0.8643	0.8849	0.9032	0.9192	0.9332	0.9452	0.9554	0.9641	0.9713
2.	0.9772	0.9821	0.9861	0.9893	0.9918	0.9938	0.9953	0.9965	0.9974	0.9981
3.	0.9987	0.9990	0.9993	0.9995	0.9997	0.9998	0.9998	0.9999	0.9999	1.0000

_____

_____

_____

_____

_____

_____

QUESTION **26** (5 marks)

The diagram shows a scale drawing of a rectangular paddock and a dam. The dam has an average depth of 2.8 m.

Find the approximate amount of water in the dam, to the nearest megalitre.   **5 marks**

_____

_____

_____

_____

_____

_____

_____

_____

_____

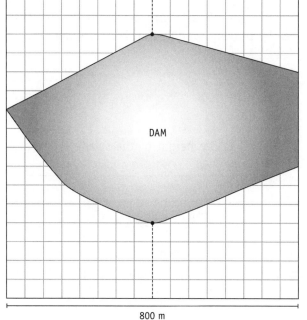

DAM

800 m

QUESTION **27** (5 marks)

An electricity company published the price of electricity available to consumers.

Period of day	Time	Price per kWh
Peak	Weekdays: 2 pm – 8 pm	53.911 cents
Shoulder	Weekdays: 7 am – 2 pm and 8 pm – 10 pm Weekends: 7 am – 10 pm	22.594 cents
Off–peak	All other times	15.191 cents

a Keith irons his clothes every Sunday night. He starts ironing at 10:15 pm and finishes at midnight. If his iron uses 1200 W of electricity, what is the cost over a fortnight, to the nearest cent?   **2 marks**

_____

_____

b Bridgett washes two loads of washing every Saturday morning from 7:30. For a cold-water cycle she uses 0.3 kWh of electricity per load, but when Bridgett selects a warm-water cycle she uses 4.5 kWh per load. How much money does Bridgett save by using cold water rather than warm water over 5 years?   **3 marks**

_____

_____

Sample HSC Examination 3

QUESTION **28** (6 marks)

Violet and her classmates measured the heights of trees in their own high school playground and at the nearby primary school. The data sets were displayed on two box–plots.

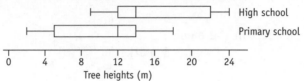

a What was the height of the smallest tree at the primary school?   **1 mark**

_____

_____

_____

_____

b Both schools had 24 trees over 12 m tall. How many trees were in each playground?   **2 marks**

_____

_____

_____

_____

_____

c Compare and contrast the two data sets by referring to the skewness of the distributions and the measures of location and spread.   **3 marks**

_____

_____

_____

_____

_____

QUESTION **29** (4 marks)

A farmer registered 75 mm of rain in his rain gauge after a thunderstorm. The farmer's hayshed has a rectangular roof measuring 16 m by 12 m. All the water that fell on to the roof drained to an empty cylindrical tank with a diameter of 4.6 m. What was the depth of water in the tank after the storm, to the nearest centimetre?   **4 marks**

_____

_____

_____

_____

_____

_____

_____

Sample HSC Examination 3

QUESTION **30** (3 marks)

A table of future values for an annuity of $1 is shown.

Table of future value interest factors								
	Interest rate per period							
Period	**0.50%**	**1.00%**	**1.50%**	**2.00%**	**3.00%**	**4.00%**	**5.00%**	**6.00%**
1	1.0000	1.0000	1.0000	1.0000	1.0000	1.0000	1.0000	1.0000
2	2.0050	2.0100	2.0150	2.0200	2.0300	2.0400	2.0500	2.0600
3	3.0150	3.0301	3.0452	3.0604	3.0909	3.1216	3.1525	3.1836
4	4.0301	4.0604	4.0909	4.1216	4.1836	4.2465	4.3101	4.3746
5	5.0503	5.1010	5.1523	5.2040	5.3091	5.4163	5.5256	5.6371
6	6.0755	6.1520	6.2296	6.3081	6.4684	6.6330	6.8019	6.9753
7	7.1059	7.2135	7.3230	7.4343	7.6625	7.8983	8.1420	8.3938
8	8.1414	8.2857	8.4328	8.5830	8.8923	9.2142	9.5491	9.8975

Justin is paid an annual salary of $103 200 and he contributes 9.5% of his salary into a superannuation account at the end of each year. At the contribution stage his fund manager charges $2800 each year for fees. If the remainder of the money earns interest of 5% p.a. what will be the balance in his fund after 6 years?

3 marks

QUESTION **31** (2 marks)

The cost per passenger of hiring a bus is inversely proportional to the number of passengers on the bus. If there are 24 passengers, the cost per passenger is $16. What is the cost per passenger when there are 32 passengers?

2 marks

QUESTION **32** (4 marks)

Oscar is buying a car with a purchase price of $23 500. As Oscar does not have a trade-in he pays a deposit of 15%. The balance is borrowed from a finance company with 36 monthly repayments of $655.60 each.

a What is the total amount that Oscar will end up paying for the car?

2 marks

b What is the annual simple interest rate being charged by the finance company? Give your answer to one decimal place.

2 marks

Sample HSC Examination 3

QUESTION **33** (6 marks)

The speed of a car (s, in km/h) and the time taken (t, in hours) is shown in the table.

t	4	6	8	10	12
s	90	60	45	36	30

a Use the number plane to graph the curve representing the relationship between t and s. **2 marks**

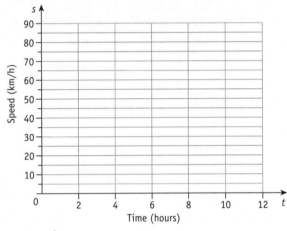

b A hyperbolic model in the form $s = \dfrac{k}{t}$ describes the situation. What is the value of k? **1 mark**

_____

_____

_____

c Use the model to find the speed of the car if the time taken is 5 hours. **1 mark**

_____

_____

_____

d If the car travels an average speed of 15 m/s, find the time taken, in hours and minutes. **2 marks**

_____

_____

_____

QUESTION **34** (6 marks)

The table shows an estimated number of kilojoules burned per kilogram of body mass per 30 minutes in different activities.

Activity	Energy used in 30 minutes
Walking at 6 km/h	9.22 kJ/kg
Cycling at 20 km/h	18.43 kJ/kg
Swimming at 50 m/min	20.73 kJ/kg
Jogging at 10 km/h	21.19 kJ/kg
Running at 16 km/h	32.25 kJ/kg

Sample HSC Examination 3

a Dayle weighs 68 kg and cycles at an average speed of 20 km/h for 45 minutes. How much energy has she used, to the nearest kilojoule? **2 marks**

_____

_____

_____

_____

b George, who weighs 83 kg, eats a hamburger from a fast-food restaurant which contains 870 kilocalories. For what distance must George walk at 6 km/h to burn off the energy contained in the hamburger, to the nearest kilometre? (1 kilocalorie = 4.184 kJ) **4 marks**

_____

_____

_____

_____

_____

_____

QUESTION **35** (4 marks)

The network diagram represents a project consisting of 16 activities shown as *A* to *P*. All measurements are in hours and the project commences on Monday midday and all activities can run at any time of the day or night.

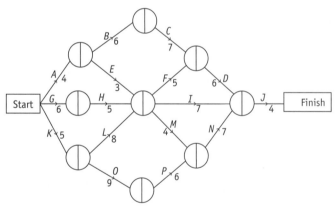

a Use forward and backward scanning to write the earliest starting time (EST) and latest starting time (LST) for each activity in the network.

For example, (10|6) represents an activity's EST of 10 and an LST of 6. **2 marks**

b What is the earliest the project can be completed? **1 mark**

_____

c What is the float time for activity *H*? **1 mark**

_____

QUESTION **36** (5 marks)

A solid is made up of a cone and a hemisphere.

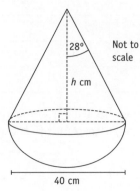

28°

Not to scale

h cm

40 cm

a Show that the height of the cone, correct to one decimal place, is 37.6 cm.   **2 marks**

_____

_____

b Hence, find the volume of the solid, correct to three significant figures.   **3 marks**

_____

_____

_____

Answers

Chapter 1—Financial mathematics: Investments

Page 1 **1 a** 0.5% **b** 1.5% **c** 3% **d** 2% **2 a** 0.75% **b** 0.625% **3 a** 2% **b** 1.25% **4 a** 60 months **b** 12 quarters
c 16 six-months **d** 6 four-months **5 a** 16 quarters **b** 2.25% **6 a** 10% **b** 10.8% **c** 13% **d** 16.79%

Page 2 **1 a** $720 **b** $3360 **c** $14 400 **d** $354 **e** $384.38 **f** $14 760 **g** $21 125 **h** $13 530 **2 a** $600 **b** $3600
3 a 4.63 years **b** 4.43 years **4 a** 5.56% **b** 16.67%

Page 3 **1 a** $4500 **b** $2777.78 **2 a**

n	0	1	2	3	4	5	6	7	8	9	10
4% p.a.	I	0	20	40	60	80	100	120	140	160	180	200
7% p.a.	I	0	35	70	105	140	175	210	245	280	315	350
9% p.a.	I	0	45	90	135	180	225	270	315	360	405	450

b

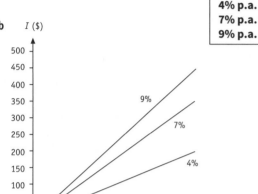

Page 4 **1 a** $10 960.69 **b** $2960.69 **2 a** $2469.49 **b** $5594.33 **c** $30 653.59 **d** $7748.87 **e** $205 651.82 **f** $1388.53
Page 5 **1 a** $4764.06 **b** $15 280.15 **2 a** $5832 **b** $13 381.03 **c** $19 965 **d** $15 109.02 **3 a** $5723.08 **b** $30 825.95
Page 6 **1 a** $8236.71 **b** $3350.24 **c** $29 065.89 **d** $59 665.44 **2 a** $35 143.71 **b** $67 884.05
Page 7 **1 a** $2500 **b** $6400 **c** $12 000 **2 a** $3325.29 **b** $2871.87 **3 a** $13 021.77 **b** $12 996.78
Page 8 **1 a** $2814.20 **b** $6701.20 **c** $20 426.40 **d** $10 247.25 **2 a** $7306.74 **b** $13 319.13
Page 9 **1 a** $1700 **b** 9 years **c** $1200 **d** The future value will increase at a faster rate. The future value doubles approximately
every 4 years, so after 14 years it will be close to $12 000. **2 a** 18% p.a. becomes 9% per six months. Using the formula $A = P(1 + r)^n$
then $A = 1000(1 + 0.09)^n = 1000(1.09)^n$ where n is the number of six-month periods.
b

n	2	4	6	8	10	12	14	16	18	20
A($)	1188	1412	1677	1993	2367	2813	3342	3970	4717	5604

c

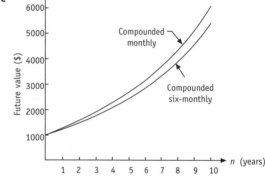

d The difference will increase, the future value is greater for the investment
which has the interest compounded monthly.

Page 10 **1 a** $15.15 **b i** $12 701.11 **ii** $32 312.55 **c i** $5402.22
ii $32 176.19 **2 a** $34 676.14 **b i** $31 370.62 **ii** $30 478.23 **iii** $34 115.38
iv $300 000

Page 11 **1** $399 408 **2** $40 119 **3** $581.56 **4** 13.23% **5** $211 598
6 $7102.73 **7 a** $768.75 **b** $2.54

Page 12 **1 a** $30 660 **b** $469.90 **c** $92.10 **2** 61 cents **3 a** $360
b $60 900 **c** $2100 **4** $2.18

Page 13 **1 a** 5% **b** 5.5% **2** 5.29% **3 a** $2.50 **b** 5% **4** $4.75 **5** If the recent trend continues the shares should reach a
value of $2.60. However, shares can quickly change in value so predictions are very unreliable.

Pages 14—17 **1** A (3200 × 0.0425 × 1.25) **2** D (16 000(1.003)^{24}) **3** A ($\frac{\$0.28}{\$4.20}$ × 100% = 6.7% which is highest)
4 C (230(1.026)^5 – 230) **5** C (Difference between 10 000(1.004)^{60} and 10 000(1.0045)^{60}) **6 a i** $5000 × 1.407 = $7035

Answers

ii $3400 × 1.062 = $3610.80 **b i** $12 000 × 2.144 – $12 000 = $13 728 **ii** $9600 × 1.051 – $9600 = $489.60

7 a $16 000(1.04)^7 = $21 054.91 **b** $24 000(1.005)^{60} = $32 372.40 **c** $8000(1.02)^{16} = $10 982.29 **d** $11 400(1.0075)^{36} = $14 918.56

8 a $\dfrac{\$6000}{1.05^{12}} = \$3341.02$ **b** $\dfrac{\$15\,000}{1.01^{80}} = \$6766.77$ **c** $\dfrac{\$9500}{1.005^{120}} = \$5221.51$ **d** $\dfrac{\$32\,000}{1.004^{300}} = \$9661.31$

9 a $5000(1.04)^{18} = $10 129 **b** $5000(1.04)^{65} = $63 994 **10 a** $\dfrac{\$120\,000}{1.005^{180}} = \$48\,898$ **b** $\dfrac{\$500\,000}{1.005^{360}} = \$83\,021$

11 a $6.80 × 5000 + 0.6 × $6.80 × 5000 ÷ 100 + 0.025 × $6.80 × 5000 × 0.025 = $35 054 **b** 0.045 × $7.20 × 5000 = $1620
c The total amount received was $33 750 from the sale of the shares plus $1620 dividends; $35 370, a profit of $316

CHAPTER 2—Financial mathematics: Depreciation and loans

PAGE 18 **1 a** 0.22 **b** 0.165 **c** 0.1875 **2 a** 15% **b** 23.5% **c** 9.8% **3 a i** $S = 28\,500(1 - 0.2)^2 = \$18\,240$
ii $S = 28\,500(1 - 0.2)^5 = \$9339$ **b** $12\,600 = V_0(1 - 0.12)^6$. $V_0 = 12\,600 ÷ 0.88^6 = \$27\,132$ **c** $19\,500 = 37\,800(1 - r)^4$.

So $(1 - r)^4 = \dfrac{19\,500}{37\,800} = 0.5159$. Taking the fourth root of both sides, $1 - r = 0.8475$. This gives $r = 1 - 0.8475 = 0.1525$, or $15\frac{1}{4}$%.

d $14\,400 = 45\,000(1 - 0.15)^n$. So $0.85^n = \dfrac{14\,400}{45\,000} = 0.32$. Now you need to try various values of n to get as close as possible to

answering $0.85^n = 0.32$. This gives $n = 7$ years.

4

Year	Net book value ($)	Depreciation ($)	Final value ($)
1	30 000	0.12 × 30 000 = 3600	30 000 – 3600 = 26 400
2	26 400	0.12 × 26 400 = 3168	26 400 – 3168 = 23 232
3	23 232	0.12 × 23 232 = 2788	23 232 – 2788 = 20 444
4	20 444	0.12 × 20 444 = 2453	20 444 – 2453 = 17 991
5	17 991	0.12 × 17 991 = 2159	17 991 – 2159 = 15 832
6	15 832	0.12 × 15 832 = 1900	15 832 – 1900 = 13 932
7	13 932	0.12 × 13 932 = 1672	13 932 – 1672 = 12 260
8	12 260	0.12 × 12 260 = 1471	12 260 – 1471 = 10 789

a The amount becomes less in subsequent years. This is because the same percentage of depreciation applies to a lesser book value.
b With the straight-line method the amount of depreciation remains the same from year to year.
PAGE 19 **1 a** $20 000 **b** $20 000 – $12 000 = $8000 **c** With $S = 12\,000$, $V_0 = 20\,000$, $n = 1$, then $12\,000 = 20\,000(1 - r)^1$.
This gives $1 - r = \dfrac{12\,000}{20\,000} = 0.6$, whence $r = 1 - 0.6 = 0.4$. So $r = 40\%$. **d** $S = 20\,000(1 - 0.4)^6 = \$933.12$ **e** Extending the graph to

the 6th year should give a value just under $1000. **2 a** $18 000 **b** $14 000 **c** 4 years (where the curves intersect on the graph)

d Not necessarily. Ryan's car might be worth more than Bella's according to the depreciation schedule, but this doesn't take into account potential accidents, car maintenance level or the type of car, which all affect its value.
PAGE 20 **1 a** $8000 **b** $466.67 **2 a** $600 **b** $2400 **c** $1080 **d** $3480 **e** $96.67 **3 a** $14 780 **b** $246.33
PAGE 21 **1 a** $9675 **b** $22 575 **c** $376.25 **2 a** $78 750 **b** $4775 **3 a** $12 600 **b** 6.5% p.a.
PAGE 22 **1 a** $298 570.77 **b i** $299 052.33 **ii** $1619.87 **iii** $300 672.20 **iv** $298 812.20 **c i** $1860 × 6 = $11 160
ii $300 000 – $298 570.77 = $1429.23 **2 a** $18 553.33 **b i** $17 102.81 **ii** $26.11 **iii** $5372.78 **c** $148.42 **d** Mia has paid the
loan out. **e** $891.83

PAGE 23 **1 a i** 260 × $7.4581 = $1939.11 **ii** 312 × $8.3669 = $2610.47 **iii** 435 × $5.6754 = $2468.80
b i 385 × $7.1643 × 240 – $385 000 = $276 981 **ii** 482.5 × $6.9921 × 360 – $482 500 = $732 028 **c i** $2175.12 ÷ 270 = $8.056.
From the table, this is 7.5% **ii** $1929.64 ÷ 340 = $5.6754. From the table, this is 5.5% **d i** 327 × $6.9921 = $2286.42
ii $2286.42 × 360 = $823 111.20 **iii** $823 111.20 – $327 000 = $496 111.20 **e** 245 × ($8.3669 – $7.4581) = $222.66
2 a 460 × $6.3233 = $2908.72 **b** $2908.72 × 360 – $460 000 = $587 139 **c** New repayment = $2908.72 + $307.65 = $3216.37.
$3216.37 ÷ 460 = $6.9921. From the table, this is 7.5%
PAGE 24 **1 a** $280 000 **b** 21 years **c i** $2398 × 12 × 30 = $863 280 **ii** $863 280 – $400 000 = $463 280
2 a 6 years **b i** $1199 × 26 × 24 = $750 000 **ii** $750 000 – $400 000 = $350 000 **3 a** $280 000 – $80 000 = $200 000
b i $2398 × 12 × 18 + $200 000 = $717 968 **ii** $463 280 – ($717 968 – $400 000) = $145 312

PAGE 25 **1 a** $10 000 **b i** $10 000 – $4627.18 = $5372.82 **ii** 11.50% ÷ 365 = 0.03151% **c** $\dfrac{139}{4627.18} × 100\% = 3.0\%$

2 a 18% ÷ 365 = 0.049 315% **b** 27 days **c** $960 (1 + 0.000 493 15)^{27} = $972.86 **d** $12.86

Answers

3 a $13.2\% \div 365 = 0.03616\%$ **b i** $\$216.80 \times 1.0003616^{14} - \$216.80 = \$1.10$ **ii** $\$104.90 \times 1.0003616^5 - \$104.90 = \$0.19$
c $\$186.70 \times 1.0003616^{22} + \$217.90 + \$187.20 \times 1.0003616^8 + \$105.09 = \$698.92$ **d** $0.96 \times \$698.92 = \$670.96$

PAGE 26   **1 a** $\$416.40$ **b** $\$8.00$ **2 a** $\$143.93$ **b** $\$120.00$

PAGES 27–30   **1** B ($\$26\,990 \times 0.84^4$)   **2** D   **3** C ($\$1250 + \$1250 \times 0.0004438 \times 16$)   **4** D ($\$910 \times 12 \times 4 - 0.8 \times \$41\,250$)
5 B ($[\$18\,000 + \$18\,000 \times 0.08 \times 10] \div 120$)   **6 a i** $\$2300$ **ii** 0.058877%
b $\$125 \times 0.00054767 \times 15 + \$340 \times 0.00054767 \times 12 = \$3.26$ **c** $\$7694.62$ **d** $0.01 \times \$2305.38 + \$5.38 = \$28.43$
7 a i $\$32\,956.25$ **ii** $\$56.58$ **b** $\$351$ **c** The loan is completely paid out in the 17th repayment **d** $\$1621.28$
8 a $310 \times \$7.068 = \$2191.08$ **b** $\$2476.44 \div 360 = \$6.879$. From the table, this is 5.5% p.a. **c** $2278.78 \div \$5.558 \times 1000 = \$410\,000$
d $340 \times \$6.321 \times 12 \times 30 = \$773\,690.40$ **e** $400 \times \$8.056 \times 12 \times 20 - \$400\,000 = \$373\,376$
f $460 \times \$5.678 \times 12 \times 30 - \$460\,000 = \$480\,276.80$ and $460 \times \$6.879 \times 12 \times 20 - \$460\,000 = \$299\,441.60$ gives a saving of
$\$180\,835.20$ **g** Original: $280 \times \$5.368 = \$1503.04$, New: $200 \times \$7.164 = \$1432.80$. Decrease of $\$70.24$
9 a $\$42\,500 \times 0.82^3 = \$23\,433.14$ **b** $\$42\,500 \times 0.82^5 \times 0.88^5 = \$8315.18$

CHAPTER 3—Financial mathematics: Annuities

PAGE 31   **1 a i** $\$630$ **ii** $\$661.50$ **iii** $\$694.58$ **iv** $\$729.30$ **b i** $\$2715.38$ **ii** $\$315.38$ **2 a** $\$600$ **b** It has been immediately
withdrawn. **c** 5 months **d** $\$103.81$ **e** The first amount invested earns interest for 5 months so, using the compound interest formula, its
value is given by $100(1.0075)^5$. The second amount earns interest for 4 months so its value is $100(1.0075)^4$ and so on. The last amount
earns no interest so its value is 100. The total value of the investment is the sum of these amounts. **f** $\$611.36$
PAGE 32   **1 a** $\$35\,766.50$ **b** $\$3556.92$ **c** $\$1301.00$ **d** $\$27\,642.60$ **2 a** No **b** Short by $\$310$ **c** $\$1300.39$ per month for 6 months
PAGE 33   **1 a** $\$23\,145.60$ **b** $\$4346.63$ **c** $\$5462.80$ **2** $\$22\,392.38$ **3 a** $\$15\,027.43$ **b** $\$15\,137.13$
PAGE 34
1 a b $\$1293.04$ **2 a b** $\$17\,325.50$

Future value of $1				
Interest rate per period				
Period	3%	4%	5%	6%	10%
1	1.0000	1.0000	1.0000	1.0000	1.0000
2	2.0300	2.0400	2.0500	2.0600	2.1000
3	3.0909	3.1216	3.1525	3.1836	3.3100
4	4.1836	4.2465	4.3101	4.3746	4.6410
5	5.3091	5.4163	5.5256	5.6371	6.1051
10	11.4639	12.0061	12.5779	13.1808	15.9374
20	26.8704	29.7781	33.0660	36.7856	57.2750

Present value of $1				
Interest rate per period				
Period	3%	4%	5%	6%	10%
1	0.9709	0.9615	0.9524	0.9434	0.9091
2	1.9135	1.8861	1.8594	1.8334	1.7355
3	2.8286	2.7751	2.7233	2.6730	2.4869
4	3.7171	3.6299	3.5460	3.4651	3.1699
5	4.5797	4.4518	4.3295	4.2124	3.7908
10	8.5302	8.1109	7.7217	7.3601	6.1446
20	14.8775	13.5903	12.4622	11.4699	8.5136

PAGE 35   **1 a** $\$32\,097.06$ **b** $\$641\,941.20$ **c** $\$241\,941.20$ **2 a** Repayment $= \$17\,923.33$ Total $= \$448\,083.25$
b Repayment $= \$28\,829.72$ Total $= \$432\,445.80$ **c** If she can afford it, Bank B's loan will save her $\$15\,637.45$ in interest and she will
repay it 10 years sooner than Bank A's loan.
PAGE 36   **1** $\$253.93$ **2 a** $\$4483.90$ **b** $\$67\,258.50$ **3** $\$6489.35$ **4 a** $\$1751.17$ **b** $\$232\,956.30$
PAGE 37   **1 a** $\$5255.36$ **b** $\$9819.79$ **2 a** $\$2833.43$ **b** $\$170\,630.80$ **c** No. The total to be repaid over 6 years excluding fees and
charges is $\$174\,133.44$, so Jason would be $\$3502.64$ worse off.
PAGES 38–42   **1** C ($\$2000 \times 3.1216$)   **2** A ($\$10\,000 \div 6.4684$)   **3** B ($\$25\,000 \times 6.2098$)   **4** C ($\$2000 \times 42.5803$)   **5** D
6 a i $\$5000 \times 8 = \$40\,000$ **ii** $\$5000 \times 8.4328 = \$42\,164$ **iii** $\$2164$ **b i** $\$198\,990 \div 6.6330 = \$30\,000$
ii $\$44\,212.35 \div 6.8019 = \$6500$ **c** $\$4800 \div 8.1414 = \$590$ **d** Contribution $= 0.095 \times \$106\,500 - \$2400 = \$7717.50$
Balance $= \$7717.50 \times 9.5491 = \$73\,695.18$ **7 a i** $\$5000 \times 155.2069 = \$776\,034.50$ **ii** $\$32\,000 \times 34.7609 = \$1\,112\,348.80$
iii $\$25\,000 \times 56.2543 = \$1\,406\,357.50$ **b i** A: $\$80\,000 \div 139.5808 = \$573.14$, B: $\$80\,000 \div 164.4385 = \$486.50$
ii $\$486.50 \times 300 - \$573.14 \times 240 = \$8396.40$ more for loan B **c** $380\,000 \div 97.2183 - 380\,000 \div 124.2819 = \$851.16$
8 a i $\$18\,000 \times 9.8975 - \$18\,000 \times 8 = \$34\,155$ **ii** $\$9000 \times 20.1569 - \$9000 \times 16 = \$37\,412.10$
iii $\$4500 \times 40.6883 - \$4500 \times 32 = \$39\,097.35$ **iv** $\$1500 \times 122.8285 - \$1500 \times 96 = \$40\,242.75$
b Evan: $\$1500 \times 17.9324 - \$1500 \times 16 = \$2898.60$. Solomon: $\$500 \times 54.0978 - \$500 \times 48 = \$3048.90$. Solomon earns $\$150.30$ more
interest than Evan **c** Interest $= \$5000 \times 9.8975 - \$5000 \times 8 = \$9487.50$. Compounded amount $= \$49\,487.50$.
Hence, $\$49\,487.50 = P(1.06)^8$. $P = \$31\,049.07$

Answers

CHAPTER 4—Algebra: Simultaneous linear equations

PAGE 43   **1 a**

x	−1	0	1	2
y	−2	0	2	4

b

x	−1	0	1	2
y	0	1	2	3

c

x	−1	0	1	2
y	−3	−1	1	3

d

x	−1	0	1	2
y	6	5	4	3

e

x	−1	0	1	2
y	4	2	0	−2

f

x	−2	−1	0	1
y	−3	0	3	6

2

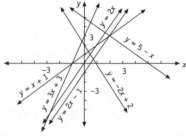

PAGE 44   **1 a** 5 **b** The fixed amount of the pocket money per week, $5 **c** 2 **d** Liam's mother pays him $2 per hour when he helps her. **2 a** 90 **b** Barton is 90 km from Aden. **c** −15 **d** Dorian rides at a constant 15 km/h. **e** $d = -15t + 90$

PAGE 45   **1 a i** $y = 20x$

x	0	10	20	30	40
y	0	200	400	600	800

ii $y = 600 - 10x$

x	0	10	20	30	40
y	600	500	400	300	200

b

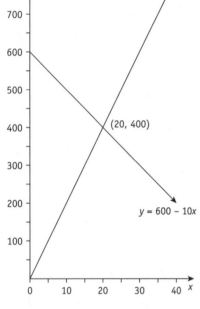

c (20, 400)

2 $y = 60 + 20x$

x	0	1	2	3	4	5	6	7
y	60	80	100	120	140	160	180	200

$y = 300 - 40x$

x	0	1	2	3	4	5	6	7
y	300	260	220	180	140	100	60	20

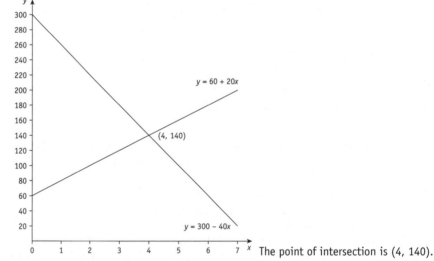

The point of intersection is (4, 140).

PAGE 46   **1 a** $C = 50 + 6m$ where $C =$ cost in dollars and $m =$ metres of turf. **b**
c Cost of 100 m $= 50 + 6 \times 100 = \$650$ **d** The model only calculates cost of the turf and delivery, not other costs such as labour.
2 a $C = 200 + 5n$ **b**

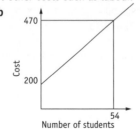

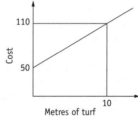

Answers

c Cost = 200 + 50 × 5 = $450 **d** Only 54 people can travel on the bus. Numbers greater than 54 require the hire of another bus, which may involve a higher booking fee.

PAGE 47 **1 a** $C = 60n$ **b** $C = 7x$ **2 a** $C = 4 + 2n$ **b** $28   **3** $P = 70 + 50n$ **4 a** $d = 70t$ **b** 420 km   **5 a** $80n$ is the distance travelled in n hours and this distance is being subtracted from 280 km. **b** 80 km   **6 a** $C = 120 + 8n$ **b** $S = 16n$ **7 a** $C = 1000 + 30n$ **b** $S = 200n$ **c** $P = 170n - 1000$ **8 a** $d = 60t$ **b** $d = 240 - 80t$

PAGE 48 **1 a** See graph **b** 40 **c** the cost of making each cake **d** $52.50 **e** See graph **f** See graph

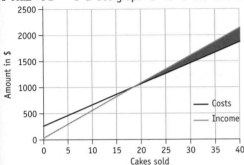

2 a 10 **b** Zone 2 **c** Zone 1 **d i** the cost of producing each T-shirt **ii** the fixed costs of production
e i the income from each shirt sold **ii** There is no income if no T-shirts are sold. **f** $I = 10x$ **g** $C = 5x + 50$

PAGE 49 **1 a** There is a one-off cost of $2400 and a cost of $40 for each person who attends.

b Each person who attends pays $120 per ticket. **c**
d 30 tickets **e** $3200
f No, the maximum profit is $5600.
2 a $13 **b** 1.5 cents/h
c

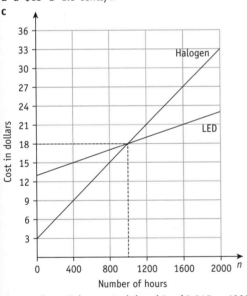

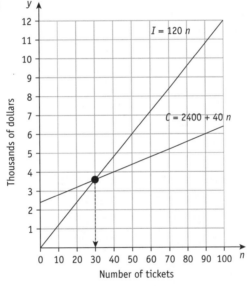

d 1000 h **e** Halogen: 2 globes $6 + $0.015 × 4000 = $66. LED: $13 + $0.005 × 4000 = $33. Cheaper by $33.

PAGES 50–53 **1** B **2** C **3** A **4** C **5** D **6 a i**

x	−1	0	1	2
y	−4	−1	2	5

ii

x	−1	0	1	2
y	4	5	6	7

b 3   **7 a** ii **b** iv **c** i **d** iii

Answers

8 a

Number of jugs	0	4	8	12	16	20
Cost ($)	8	20	32	44	56	68

b and **g**

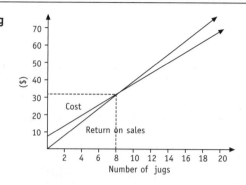

c 8, $8 is the fixed cost of making a jug of lemonade **d** 3, $3 is the additional cost per jug of lemonade **e** $50 **f** 16 jugs
h The lines intersect at (8, 32); the break-even point is where 8 jugs of lemonade are produced and sold.   **9 a** 4 cakes **b i** loss of $20
ii profit of $30 **c i** $I = 20n$ **ii** $C = 40 + 10n$ **10 a i** $C = 100 + 15n$ **ii** $S = 40n$
b $ **c** 4 dresses **d** $50

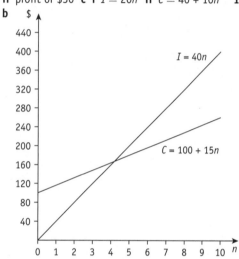

Chapter 5—Algebra: Non-linear relationships

1 a

x	0	0.5	1	2	3	4	5	6
y	1	1.41	2	4	8	16	32	64

b

x	0	0.5	1	1.5	2	2.5	3	3.5	4
y	1	1.73	3	5.20	9	15.59	27	46.77	81

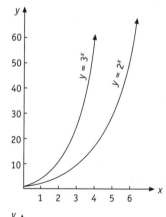

2 a

x	0	1	2	3	4	5	6	7	8
y	5	6	7.2	8.64	10.37	12.44	14.93	17.92	21.50

b

x	0	1	2	3	4	5	6	7
y	2	3.4	5.78	9.83	16.70	28.40	48.28	82.07

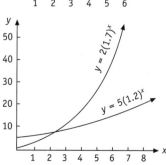

Answers

1 a $3430 **b** 9 years **c** $170 **2 a** $3400 **b** 1.9 years

PAGE 56 **1 a**

x	0	0.5	1	1.5	2	2.5	3	3.5	4
y	0	0.25	1	2.25	4	6.25	9	12.25	16

b

x	0	0.5	1	1.5	2	2.5	3	3.5	4
y	-3	-1.75	0	2.25	5	8.25	12	16.25	21

c

x	0	0.5	1	1.5	2	2.5	3	3.5	4
y	-5	-4.5	-3	-0.5	3	7.5	13	19.5	27

d

x	0	0.5	1	1.5	2	2.5	3	3.5	4
y	-4	-6.75	-8	-7.75	-6	-2.75	2	8.25	16

2

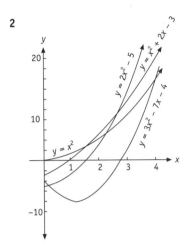

PAGE 57 **1 a**

x	0	0.5	1	1.5	2	2.5	3	3.5	4
y	-1	-1.75	-2	-1.75	-1	0.25	2	4.25	7

x	0	0.5	1	1.5	2	2.5	3	3.5	4
y	1	-1.75	-2	-1.75	-1	0.25	2	4.25	7

b Both graphs are identical, therefore the equations are the same.
$(x - 1)^2 - 2 = x^2 - 2x + 1 - 2 = x^2 - 2x - 1$ **2 a** 36 m **b** 20 m **c** 5 s

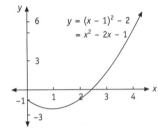

PAGE 58 **1 a**

l	0	4	8	12	16	20	24	28	32
A	0	128	224	288	320	320	288	224	128

b

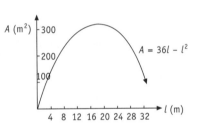

c 18 m **d** 324 m² **e** No, the area would be a negative number.

PAGE 59 **1 a**

x	0.25	0.5	1	2	4	8	16	32
y	32	16	8	4	2	1	0.5	0.25

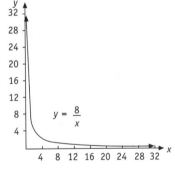

b

x	1	2	3	4	6	8	12	16	20	24
y	24	12	8	6	4	3	2	1.5	1.2	1

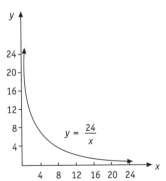

Answers

c

x	1	2	3	4	5	6	8	10	12
y	6	3	2	1.5	1.2	1	0.75	0.6	0.5

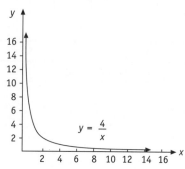

d

x	0.25	0.5	1	2	4	8	16
y	16	8	4	2	1	0.5	0.25

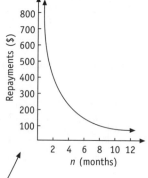

PAGE 60   **1 a** $75   **b** 5 months   **c** $6\frac{2}{3}$ months, Greg could pay $90 per month for 6 months and $60 in the seventh month.
d Yes, by using 48 months. $\frac{600}{48} = \$12.50$ per month over 4 years.

e i

n	1	2	3	4	5	6	7	8	10	12
R	840	420	280	210	168	140	120	105	84	70

ii

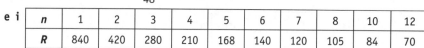

iii $27 per month

PAGE 61   **1 a** 72 **b** 9   **2 a** $y = \frac{96}{x}$ **b** 12 **c** $\frac{4}{3}$ **3** 6   **4** 4 hours   **5** 30 tables

PAGES 62–65   **1** D   **2** D   **3** A   **4** C   **5** C   **6 a** $k = \frac{7}{2}$ **b** 112 **c** $3584 = \frac{7}{2} 2^t$

means $2^t = 1024$. Hence, $t = 10$: after 10 years   **7** 1.8 m   **8 a**
b 280 m **c** 4.5 s   **9 a** exponential growth **b** 6 million
c 1995   **d** 10 million

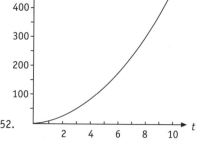

10 b

n	4	8	16	24	32	48	64
C	48	24	12	8	6	4	3

c

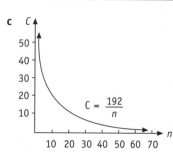

11 Let $f = \frac{k}{L}$.

As $4.2 = \frac{k}{0.6}$, then $k = 2.52$.

As $f = \frac{2.52}{L}$, subs $L = 0.5$ gives $f = 5.04$ times/s

12 a

t	0	1	2	3	4
h	0	3	4	3	0

Answers

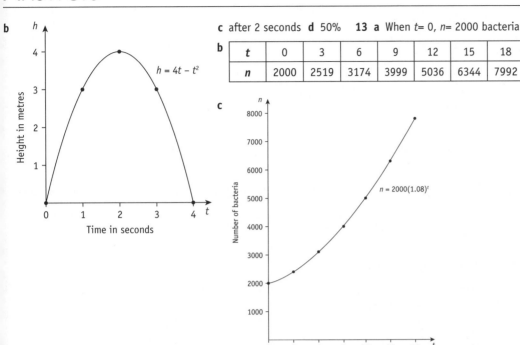

b

Height in metres / Time in seconds

$h = 4t - t^2$

c after 2 seconds **d** 50% **13 a** When $t = 0$, $n = 2000$ bacteria

b

t	0	3	6	9	12	15	18
n	2000	2519	3174	3999	5036	6344	7992

c

Number of bacteria / Number of years

$n = 2000(1.08)^t$

CHAPTER 6—Measurement: Non-right-angled trigonometry

PAGE 66 **1 a** 0.906 **b** 1.499 **c** 0.024 **2 a** 44° 26′ **b** 51° 19′ **c** 69° 33′ **3 a** 38.5 cm **b** 16.3 cm **c** 30.2 cm **d** 13.0 cm
e 15.9 cm **f** 11.3 cm **4 a** 36° 52′ **b** 67° 23′ **c** 61° 56′

PAGE 67 **1 a** 5.85 m **b** 16.72 m **2 a** 64 m **b** 52° 24′ **c** 45.86 m **3 a** 4 cm **b i** 15 cm **ii** 17 cm

PAGE 68 **1 a**   **b** 51° **2 a**   **b** 13 cm **c** 22° 37′

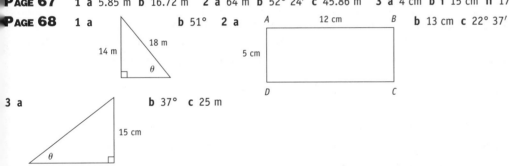

18 m / 14 m / θ

A 12 cm B 5 cm D C

3 a   **b** 37° **c** 25 m

15 cm / θ / 20 cm

PAGE 69 **1 a** 0.87 **b** −0.87 **c** −1.19 **d** −0.79 **e** 0.25 **f** 0.57 **2 a** 0.8660 −0.5000 −1.7321 **b** 0.7071 −0.7071 −1.0000
c 0.9903 −0.1392 −7.1154 **d** 0.2756 −0.9613 −0.2867 **e** 0.0872 −0.9962 −0.0875 **f** 0.7660 −0.6428 −1.1918
3 a pos **b** neg **c** neg **d** pos **e** pos **f** pos **g** pos **h** neg **i** pos **j** neg **k** neg **l** pos **m** pos **n** neg **o** neg **p** pos
4 a positive **b** negative **c** negative **5 a** 5.30 **b** 0.50 **c** −0.11 **d** 180.40

PAGE 70 **1 a** 9.03 cm **b** 10.91 cm **c** 31.43 m **d** 3.85 m **2 a i** 48° **ii** 3.31 m **b i** 127° **ii** 10.66 m

PAGE 71 **1 a** 50° **b** 34° **c** 22° **d** 35° **2 a** 71° **b** 53° **3** 77° 56′

PAGE 72 **1 a** 13.69 m **b** 22.85 cm **c** 5.19 km **d** 7.37 m **2 a** 10 cm **b** 13.02 cm

PAGE 73 **1 a** 25° **b** 132° **c** 28° **d** 50° **2 a** 80° **b** 52° **c** 48°

PAGE 74 **1 a** 13 cm² **b** 4 cm² **c** 15 cm² **d** 33 cm² **2 a** 139.6 cm² **b** 111.3 cm² **3** 15 cm

PAGE 75 **1 a** 39° **b** 9.4 cm **2** $a = 8.0$ m $b = 5$ m

PAGE 76 **1 b** 139.42 m **c** 131.01 m **2 a** 30° **b** 42° **c** 33.5 km

PAGE 77 **1 a** 126° **b** 230° **c** 051° **d** 312° **e** 204° **f** 148° **2 a** 166.59 km **b** 224.17 km **3** N 48° 49′ E
4 a 83.36 km **b** 86.32 km

Answers

1 a 90° **b** 180° **c** 45° **d** 45° **e** 45° **f** 135°

2 a 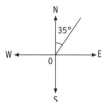 **b** 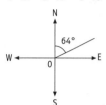 **c**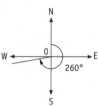

3 a 210°, S 30° W **b** 156°, S 24° E **c** 290°, N 70° W **4** 301° T or N 59° W **5** 1928 m **6** 7.07 km

PAGE 79 **1 a** $\angle BPC = 105°$, $\angle APC = 115°$ **b** 115.5 m **2 a** 105° **b** 2463.1 m²

PAGES 80–83 **1** B **2** A **3** D **4** B ($\frac{1}{2} \times x \times 26 \times \sin 58° = 220$. $11.025x = 220$. $x = 19.955...$) **5** D **6 a** 9 m **b** 13 m

7 a 59° **b** 46° **8** 329° **9 a** 13.7 m **b** 37° **10 b** 173.7 m **c** 171.0 m **11 a** 65.5 cm² **b** 131 cm² **12 a** 140° **b** 416.5 m²

c 85° **13** 74 m **14** $\frac{1}{2} \times x \times x \times \sin 30° = 9$. $\frac{x^2}{4} = 9$. $x^2 = 36$. $x = 6$ ($x > 0$)

CHAPTER 7—Measurement: Rates and ratio

PAGE 84 **1 a** $2.25 ÷ 4.4 = 0.5341 **b** $3.45 ÷ 1.75 = 1.9714 **c** $5.40 ÷ 6.4 = 0.8438 **d** $1.60 ÷ 4.2 = 0.3810

2 a $3.40 ÷ 6 = 0.5667 **b** $2.80 ÷ 5.1 = 0.5490 **c** $6.80 ÷ 3.9 = 1.7436 **d** $2.18 ÷ 12.5 = 0.1744

3

Store	Size	Price	Price/100 g
A	560 g	$7.90	$1.41
B	453 g	$6.45	$1.42
C	380 g	$5.80	$1.53
D	280 g	$4.90	$1.75
E	220 g	$3.75	$1.70

4 8-rolls: $0.73/roll, 12-rolls: $0.70/roll, 6-rolls: $0.68/roll, 24-rolls: $0.61/roll. **5** cashews: $3.00/100 g, hazelnuts: $3.10/100 g, pecans: $4.70/100 g, brazil nuts: $5.49/100 g **6** 4 for $2.85 as a dozen costs $8.55

PAGE 85 **1 a** $60 \times 1000 ÷ 60 ÷ 60 = 16.7$ m/s **b** $45 \times 1000 ÷ 60 ÷ 60 = 12.5$ m/s **c** $110 \times 1000 ÷ 60 ÷ 60 = 30.6$ m/s

2 a $12 \times 60 \times 60 ÷ 1000 = 43.2$ km/h **b** $34 \times 60 \times 60 ÷ 1000 = 122.4$ km/h **c** $18 \times 60 \times 60 ÷ 1000 = 64.8$ km/h

3 a tortoise: $60 ÷ 60 = 1$ m, hare: $36 \times 1000 ÷ 60 = 600$ m **b** The hare wins as the tortoise takes 30 seconds to complete the race, while the hare only takes 10 seconds. **4 a** $1\frac{5}{6} \times 90 = 165$ km **b** $165 ÷ 75 = 2.2$ h = 2 h 12 min. Hence, 6:37 pm

5 a Total speed is 190 km/h, Distance = $190 \times 0.5 = 95$ km **b** Time = $\frac{114}{190} = 0.6$ h = 36 min. Hence, 3:06 pm

6 a 60 m in 4 s = 15 m/s = 54 km/h **b** B: 20 m in 4 s = 5 m/s = 18 km/h. Difference is 36 km/h or 72 km in 2 hours

7 a $40 \times 1000 ÷ 60 ÷ 60 \times 0.95 = 11$ m **b** $90 \times 1000 ÷ 60 ÷ 60 \times 0.95 = 24$ m **c** $110 \times 1000 ÷ 60 ÷ 60 \times 0.95 = 29$ m

PAGE 86 **1 a** 64 bpm **b** 76 bpm **2 a** Average **b** 54–59 bpm **c** 62–65 bpm **3 a** 195 bpm **b** 175 bpm **c** 145 bpm

4 a $208 - 0.7(30) = 187$ bpm **b** $208 - 0.7(60) = 166$ bpm **c** $208 - 0.7(86) = 148$ bpm

5

Heart rates after activity based on age		
Target heart rate zone (bpm)		
Moderate activity	Intense activity	Maximum heart rate
Age 50-70% max.	70-85% max.	(bpm)
20	100–140	140–170	200
30	95–133	133–162	190
40	90–126	126–153	180
50	85–119	119–145	170
60	80–112	112–136	160
70	75–105	105–127.5	150

Answers

PAGE 87   **1 a** 40 **b** 120 **c** 10   **2 a** 1.8 kWh **b** 10.8 kWh **c** 2.88 kWh   **3 a i** $0.539 11 × 3 × 1.5 = $2.43

ii $0.225 94 × 3 × 1.5 = $1.02 **iii** $0.151 91 × 3 × 1.5 = $0.68 **b i** $0.151 91 × 1.8 × $\frac{2}{3}$ = $0.18 **ii** $0.225 94 × 1.8 × $\frac{2}{3}$ = $0.27

iii $0.539 11 × 1.8 × $\frac{2}{3}$ = $0.65 **c** It costs $0.94 more on weekdays than the weekend.

d i ($0.539 11 × 30 + $0.225 94 × 75 + $0.151 911 × 63) ÷ 168 = 25.41 c/kwh **ii** (20 − 12) × 154 ÷ 1000 × $0.2541 = $0.31.
It costs $0.31 more to run the halogen globe than the LED globe.
4 (4.5 − 0.3) × 2 × 52 × $0.225 94 = $98.69   **5** 0.95 × 0.1 × 24 × $0.216 × 7 = $3.45

PAGE 88   **1 a** 45 ÷ 6.5 = 6.9 L/100 km **b** 38 ÷ 5.86 = 6.5 L/100 km   **2 a** 7.6 × 3.8 = 28.88 L **b** 7.6 × 5.15 = 39.14 L
3 a 45 ÷ 8.3 × 100 = 542 km **b** 60 ÷ 1.729 ÷ 8.3 × 100 = 418 km   **4 a** 8.1 × 1.8 × $1.669 = $24.33
b 8.1 × 4.35 × $1.669 = $58.81   **5** (7.3 − 5.9) × 6.05 × $1.799 = $15.24   **6 a** 45 ÷ 1.549 ÷ 6.8 × 100 = 427 km
b i 7.9 × 2.9 × $1.439 = $32.97 **ii** 7.9 × 2.9 × $1.619 = $37.09 **c** ($1.549 − $1.439) × 6.9 × 4.8 = $3.64
d Lincoln: 60 ÷ 1.439 ÷ 8.3 × 100 = 502 km, Sarah: 60 ÷ 1.619 ÷ 7.7 × 100 = 481 km. Lincoln drove 21 km further.

PAGE 89   **1 a** 3:4 **b** 1:4 **c** 300:1 **d** 7:3 **e** 3:2 **f** 1:20   **2 a** 4:11 **b** 11:15   **3 a** 12 cm **b** 120 cm   **4** 90   **5 a** $45
b $84   **6 a** $n = 4$ **b** $n = 1.5$ **c** $n = 2.6$ **7 a** 190 mL **b** 4.94 L **c** 6.65 L

PAGE 90   **1 a** $7.50, $12.50 **b** 0.4 kg, 0.6 kg, 0.2 kg **c** 144 min, 240 min, 96 min   **2** 200 mL, 800 mL, 1000 mL
3 $8000, $7000, $5000   **4** 12 kg cement, 36 kg sand, 72 kg gravel   **5** $48 000   **6** 35 cm   **7 a** 20:15:18 **b** 3600   **8** 1.4 ha

PAGE 91   **1** Let x = total population of rabbits. From first catching = 60 out of x. From second catching = 4 out of 50 ∴ $\frac{60}{x} = \frac{4}{50}$.
$4x = 3000$ (by cross-multiplying), $x = 750$. There are 750 rabbits in the park.   **2** Let x = total population of frogs.
From first catching = 50 out of x. From second catching = 30 out of 140 ∴ $\frac{50}{x} = \frac{30}{140}$. $30x = 7000$ (by cross-multiplying), $x = 233$ (nearest
whole). There are about 233 frogs in the ecosystem.   **3** 1 hectare = 10 000 m². Area of section = 2 × 2 = 4 m². Let x = number of plants
in the paddock. $\frac{10000}{x} = \frac{4}{9}$. $4x = 90 000$ (by cross-multiplying), $x = 22 500$. There are about 22 500 sunflower plants in the paddock.
4 Let x = number of camels on the property. $\frac{32}{x} = \frac{6}{54}$. $6x = 1728$ (by cross-multiplying), $x = 288$. There are about 288 wild camels on the
property.   **5** Let x = number of seals. $\frac{80}{x} = \frac{12}{160}$. $12x = 12 800$ (by cross-multiplying), $x = 1067$ (nearest whole). As 108% = 1067,
then 100% = 1067 ÷ 108 × 100 = 988 (nearest whole). Population was about 988 in 2015.   **6** 45% = 0.45. Let x = number of crocodiles.
$\frac{36}{x}$ = 0.45. $0.45x = 36$ (by cross-multiplying), $x = 80$. There were about 80 crocodiles.

PAGE 92   **1 a** 1:1000 **b** 1:100 **c** 1:10 000 **d** 1:10 000 **e** 1:250 **f** 1:20 **g** 1:20 000 **h** 1:5 **i** 1:6000
2 a 1 m **b** 3 m **c** 5 m **d** 0.8 m **e** 0.6 m **f** 1200 m   **3 a** 8 m **b** 50 m **c** 6 km **d** 95 m **e** 8.3 km **f** 63.25 km
4 a 5 cm **b** 4 cm **c** 12.6 cm **d** 8 mm **e** 30 cm **f** 28.35 cm   **5 a** 1 km **b** 8.4 km **c** 26 cm

PAGE 93   **1 a** 30 m **b** 13 m **c** 390 m² **d** 3.5 m **e** 104 m²   **2 a** 1:45 **b** 1.26 m
3 a **b** 135 m

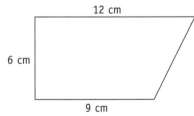

PAGE 94   **1** length = 20 m, width = 10 m (Remember the question asks for the dimensions of the swimming pool, not the brick
surrounds.)   **2** Approx. 6 m   **3** $P = 937 + 350 + 282 + 514 + 379 + 842 + 978 = 4282$ m   **4 a** 2700 m **b** 1200 m (This number is
approximate.) **c** $A = 50 × 50 = 2500$ m² **d** $A = 167 × 2500 = 417 500$ m² or 41. 75 ha **e** $A = 29 × 2500 = 72 500$ m² (This number is
approximate.) **f** $\frac{72 500}{417 500} × \frac{100}{1} = 17.4\%$

PAGE 95   **1 a** 8 m **b** sliding door **c** walk-in robe **d** 3.865 m by 2.93 m **e** 7 cm **f** 10 cm **g** south **h** 4835 **i** $89 900 **j** west

PAGE 96   **1 a** 260 km **b** 260 km **c** Around 85 km **d** C (The actual area is 48 670 km².)   **2 a** 34 m
b $A = 20 × 34 = 680$ m² (Your area could be slightly different.) **c** Around 150 m   **3 a** 15 km²
b Now 1 km² = 1 km × 1 km = 1000 m × 1000 m = 1 000 000 m². So this catchment area covers 15 000 000 m². Volume of water can be
found using $V = Ah = 15 000 000 × 0.075 = 1 125 000$ m³. Given 1 m³ = 1000 L, then 1 125 000 m³ = 1 125 000 000 L = 1125 ML.

Answers

1 a

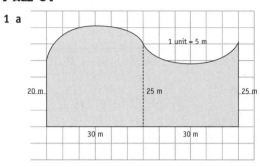

$\dfrac{30}{2}(20 + 2(25) + 25) = 1425$ m²

b

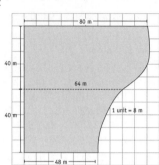

$\dfrac{40}{2}(80 + 2(64) + 48) = 5120$ m²

2 a 20 **b i** 80 m **ii** 40 m **iii** 20 m **iv** 80 m **v** 80 m **vi** 40 m **vii** 40 m

c

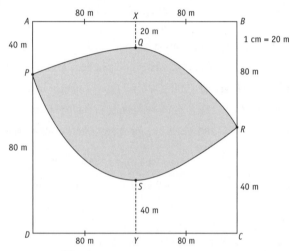

$160 \times 120 - (\dfrac{80}{2}[40 + 2(20) + 80 + 80 + 2(40) + 40]) = 4800$ m² **d** $4800 \times 2.4 = 11\,520$ kL which is close to 12 ML **3 a** $AP = 3$ units, $PE = 4$ units and so, by Pythagoras, $AE = 5$ units. As 5 units = 25 m, then $AP = 15$ m and $PE = 20$ m.

b

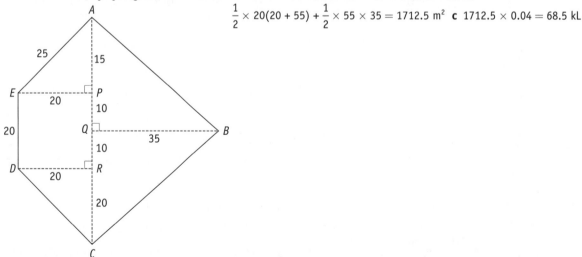

$\dfrac{1}{2} \times 20(20 + 55) + \dfrac{1}{2} \times 55 \times 35 = 1712.5$ m² **c** $1712.5 \times 0.04 = 68.5$ kL

PAGES 98–101 **1** C ($280 \div 80 \times 5$) **2** A ($68 \times 1000 \div 60 \div 60 \times 0.92$) **3** B ($3 \times 1.5 \times 3$)

4 D (1 unit = 25 m. $\dfrac{1}{2} \times 150 \times (100 + 250) \div 10\,000 \times 3.2$) **5** D (Ratio is 3:5:10. $90 \div 18 \times 10$) **6 a** $24 \times 60 \times 60 \div 1000 = 86.4$

b $3.6 \times 10^5 \div 10^3 = 3.6 \times 10^2$ **c** $40W = 40$ J/s **7** 280 km in 4 h = 70 km/h $70 \times 1000 \div 60 \div 60 = 19$ m/s

8 a $21.19 \times 60 \times 2 = 2543$ kJ **b** Let t = time. $18.43 \times 70 \times t = 1080$. $1290.1t = 1080$. $t = 0.8372$ (of half-hour) = 25 minutes

c Let t = time. $32.25 \times 54 \times t = 241 \times 4.184$. $1741.5t = 1008.344$. $t = 0.579$ (of half-hour) = 17 minutes

Answers

9 a $7.4 \times 3.6 \times \$1.629 = \$43.40$ **b** Distance $= 82 \times 2.5 = 205$ km. $7.4 \times 2.05 \times \$1.629 = \$24.71$
10 a 10 units $= 160$, 1 unit $= 16$ m. As $12 \times 16 = 192$, Area $= 192 \times 160 = 30\,720$ m^2

b $30\,720 - \dfrac{80}{2}[144 + 2(48) + 96 + 48 + 2(32) + 96)] = 8960$ m^2 **c** $8960 \times 2.5 = 22\,400$ kL $= 22.4$ ML

11 a $\$0.539\,11 \times 2.4 \times 0.75 = \$0.97$ **b** $\$0.151\,91 \times 1.8 \times \dfrac{5}{6} \times 7 \times 4 = \$6.38$

12 $\$1150 + \$0.21 \times 384 \times 4 = \$1472.56$ **13** $85 \times 0.048 = 4.08$ kL $= 4080$ L

14 a BMR $= 4.184 \times [10 \times 65 + 6.25 \times 162 - 5 \times 48 - 161] = 5278$ kJ
b BMR $= 4.184 \times [10 \times 78 + 6.25 \times 176 - 5 \times 28 + 5] = 7301.08$. Daily energy requirement $= 7301.08 \times 1.6 = 11\,682$ kJ
c Jack: $4.184 \times [10 \times 72 + 6.25 \times 168 - 5 \times 29 + 5] \times 1.5 = 10\,230$.
Jill $= 4.184 \times [10 \times 64 + 6.25 \times 165 - 5 \times 29 - 161] \times 1.6 = 9140$ ∴ Jack by 1090 kJ.

CHAPTER 8—Statistical analysis: Bivariate data analysis

PAGE 102 **1 a i** 3 **ii** 4 **b**

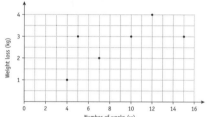

2 a i 5 **ii** 7 **b**

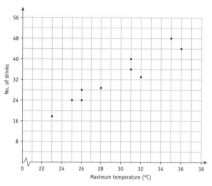

3

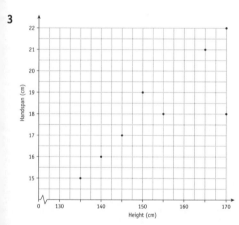

PAGE 103 **1 a** A measure of the degree of linear relationship between two quantities or variables; a summary of the strength of the linear association between the variables **b** Between, and including, −1 and +1 **c** A direct or positive relationship; as one variable increases, so does the other. **d** A negative relationship; as one variable increases, the other variable decreases.
e No relationship exists. **2** (iii), (iv), (vi), (i), (v), (ii) **3 a** (i) **b** (v) **c** (ii) **d** (iv) **e** (iii) **f** (vi)

PAGE 104 **1 a** True **b** True **c** False **d** False **e** True **2 a** (v) **b** (iii) **c** (i) **d** (ii) **e** (iv) **3 a** (ii) **b** (v)
c (iv) **d** (i) **e** (iii) **4 a** The '=' sign refers to a formula or calculation to follow. CORREL means a correlation coefficient is to be calculated. The values A1:A19 are where the values in the first array are to be found (from cell A1 to cell A19). The values B1:B19 are where the values in the second array are to be found. **b** Cell C21 (click in the cell that you want the correlation coefficient inserted, before you write the command.) **c** 0.54

PAGE 105 **1 a**

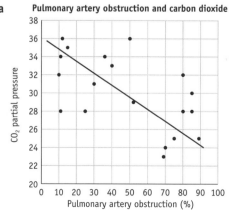

b −0.61 **c** There is a negative relationship. As the percentage obstruction increases, there is less CO_2 (lower partial pressure) getting through. **d** moderate **e** The greater the obstruction, the less CO_2 (and anything else for that matter) getting through. **f** See diagram to the left. Your line could vary a little from this.
2 a 0.9989 **b** Almost a perfect positive correlation

Answers

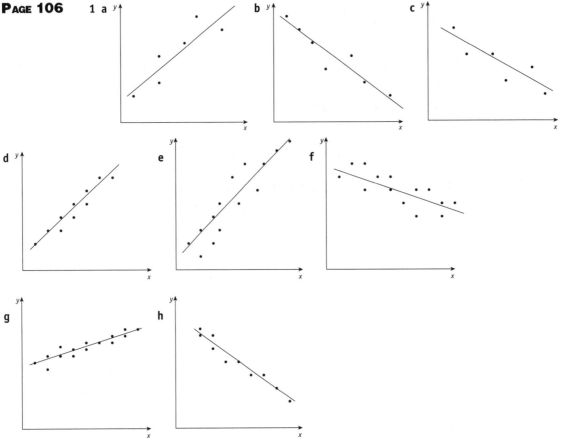

1 a $y = 6x + 12$ **b** $y = 0.45x - 23$ **c** $y = \frac{4}{5}x + 8$ **2 a** $63 = 5(8) + c$. This means $c = 63 - 40 = 23$. **b** $54 = 5(21) + c$.

This means $c = 54 - 105 = -51$. **c** $3.6 = 5(12.8) + c$. This means $c = 3.6 - 64 = -60.4$.   **3 a** gradient $= \dfrac{68 - 18}{22 - 12} = 5$

b gradient $= \dfrac{25 - 23}{16 - 8} = 0.25$ **c** gradient $= \dfrac{11 - 63}{39 - 26} = -4$ **4 a** gradient $= \dfrac{72 - 37}{51 - 26} = 1.4$. The equation is in the form $y = 1.4x + c$.

Substituting (26, 37) gives $37 = 1.4 \times 26 + c$. This means $c = 0.6$, so the equation is $y = 1.4x + 0.6$. **b** gradient $= \dfrac{16 - 48}{20 - 12} = -4$. The

equation is in the form $y = -4x + c$. Substituting (12, 48) gives $48 = -4 \times 12 + c$. This means $c = 96$, so the equation is $y = -4x + 96$.

c gradient $= \dfrac{265 - 101}{51 - 19} = 5.125$. The equation is in the form $y = 5.125x + c$. Substituting (19, 101) gives $101 = 5.125 \times 19 + c$. This means

$c = 3.625$, so the equation is $y = 5.125x + 3.625$.   **5 a** gradient $= \dfrac{15 - 7}{192 - 187} = 1.6$. The gradient is 1.6. **b** $7 = 1.6(187) + c$ means

$c = -292.2$ **6 a** gradient $= \dfrac{6400 - 4300}{2.4 - 1.6} = 2625$. The gradient is 2625. The equation is $s = 2625d + c$. Substituting (1.6, 4300) gives

$4300 = 2625(1.6) + c$. This means $c = 100$. **b** As $c = 100$, then 100 skiers will come to the resort even though there is no snow.

Answers

1 a 65 bpm **b** 111 bpm **c** 14 km/h **d** The model is only relevant for speeds up to 18 km/h. We cannot estimate Andrew's heart rate for any speed higher as we are not certain of his ability to ride faster, nor the health of his heart.

2 a b

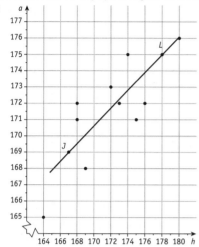

c i 174 cm **ii** 169 cm

1 a $s = 5.71h + 57.14$ **b** $S = 1.41n - 19.51$ **c** $H = 8.58 - 0.29n$

2 a

a	19	20	20.5	21	22	22	23	23.5
w	17.25	17.5	18	18.75	18	19.25	18.75	19.5

$w = 0.45a + 8.75$

b $w = 0.45(21.5) + 8.75 = 18.425$. Ella's wrist has a circumference of 18.425 cm. **c** $18.5 = 0.45a + 8.75$. This means $a = 21.67$ (2 dec. pl.). Logan's ankle has a circumference of 21.67 cm.

3 a

s	136	138	140	141	143	147	148	149
h	141	144	144	148	148	151	151	153

$h = 0.84s + 27.89$ **b** Britton is 145 cm tall. $145 = 0.84s + 27.89$. This means $s = 139.42$ (2 dec. pl.). Logan's arm span is about 139 cm.

1 a (performed electronically) **b i** gradient $(m) = 0.759 \times \dfrac{5.384}{5.739} = 0.71$

ii y-intercept $(b) = 172.75 - 0.71 \times 176.4 = 47.51$ **c** $y = 0.71x + 47.17$

d Use your line to determine some (x, y) values.
For example, when $x = 165$, $y = 164.32$; when $x = 190$, $y = 182.07$.

e The line calculated fitted exactly over the line generated by the computer.

f 171 cm **g** No, there is no causal relationship between the parents' average height and that of their children. Both factors are governed by genes. Taller parents will pass on those genes to their children allowing them to be tall as well. And while genes are one factor to consider, the environment plays a part, too. Undernourished children will not necessarily achieve their potential.

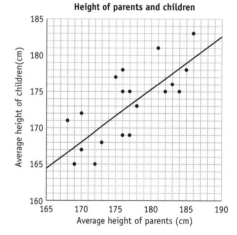

Height of parents and children

1 B **2** C **3** B **4** D **5** D **6 a** $r = 0.814$ **b** strong positive correlation **7 a** $m = \dfrac{(98 - 17)}{10} \approx 8$ **b** $b = 17$ **c** That the student could type around 17 words per minute before he or she started practice. **d** By around 8 words per minute each week. **e** $WPM = 8P + 17$ **f** No, a limit will be reached depending on hand-eye co-ordination and how quickly the student can move their fingers to the next letter.

8 a Not linear **b** Distance **c** From around 2 m **d** After about 15 m **e** 6 or 7 m

9 a P $= 0.5$; Q $= -0.7$; R $= 0.9$; S $= -0.99$ **b i** S **ii** P

Answers

10 a and **b**

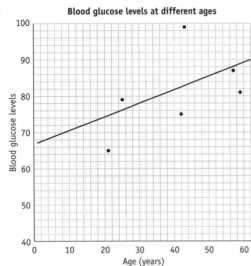

Blood glucose levels at different ages

(graph: y-axis "Blood glucose levels" from 40 to 100; x-axis "Age (years)" from 0 to 60)

c $\bar{x} = \dfrac{247}{6} = 41.17$

d $\bar{y} = \dfrac{486}{6} = 81$

e i gradient $(m) = 0.53 \times \dfrac{11.45}{15.75} = 0.39$
   ii y-intercept $= 81 - 0.39 \times 41.17 = 65$
f $y = 0.39x + 65$, or blood glucose level $= 0.39 \times$ age $+ 65$

CHAPTER 9—Statistical analysis: The normal distribution

PAGE 116 **1** Beth's score was two standard deviations above the mean mark. **2** 62 **3 a** 76 **b** 4

c

Mark	64	68	72	76	80	84	88
z-score	–3	–2	–1	0	1	2	3

4

Mark	75.4	79.1	82.8	86.5	90.2	93.9	97.6
z-score	–3	–2	–1	0	1	2	3

5 a 49 **b** 35 **6** Not compared with the others; his score is one standard deviation below the mean.

PAGE 117 **1** 5 **2 a** –2 **b** 3.8 **c** 4.6 **d** –2.4 **3** 80 **4 a i** 17.68 **ii** 5.36 **b** 1.2

PAGE 118 **1 a** Mathematics, $z = 2.67$; English, $z = 2$; Economics, $z = 2.2$ **b** Mathematics, Economics, English
2 a English, $z = 2$; Mathematics, $z = 1.3$ **b** Ben performed better in English as his z-score was higher. **3 a** English, $z = 3.5$;
Mathematics, $z = 1.8$ **b** Better in English

PAGE 119 **1** Mode, mean, median **2 a** 350 **b** 350 **3 a** 17 **b** 17, 18 **c** 17 **d** No, it is not symmetrical.
4 a and **d** have the correct shape.

PAGE 120 **1 a** 68% **b** 95% **c** 99.7% **d** 34% **e** 47.5% **f** 81.5% **g** 16% **h** 0.15%
2 a

Mass in g	245	250	255	260	265	270	275
z-score	–3	–2	–1	0	1	2	3

b 68% **c** 50% **d** 97.5% **e** Only 2.5% are likely to be
below this weight. **3** 0.15%

PAGE 121 **1** 204 **2** Between 6.910 cm and 7.090 cm **3** This is higher than expected, the machine should be reset.
4 738 g, 763 g and 765 g

PAGE 122 **1 a** 0.8413 **b** $1 - 0.8413 = 0.1587$ **c** $0.9772 - (1 - 0.9772) = 0.9544$ **2 a** 0.9821 **b** $0.9554 - 0.9192 = 0.0362$
c $0.9918 - (1 - 0.9641) = 0.9559$ **3** z-score for $10 = -2.5$, z-score for $19.6 = 1.5$. $P(-2.5 \leq z \leq 1.5) = 0.9332 - (1 - 0.9938) = 0.927$
4 z-score for $120 = -0.8$. $P(z \leq -0.8) = 1 - 0.7881 = 0.2119$, which is 21.19%. **5** z-score for $7.5 = -2.5$ $P(z \leq -2.5) = 1 - 0.9938$
$= 0.0062$. As $0.0062 \times 2000 = 12.4$, there are 12 balls **6** z-score for $500 = 1.5$ $P(z \leq 1.5) = 0.9332$. This means 93.32% of packets are
under 500 g. **7** z-score for $173 = -1.5$, z-score for $179 = 1.5$ $P(-1.5 \leq z \leq 1.5) = 0.9332 - (1 - 09332) = 0.8664$. This means 86.64% of
the boys. **8** z-score for $40 = 1.2$ $P(z \leq 1.2) = 1 - 0.8849 = 0.1151$.

PAGES 123–126 **1** B **2** C **3** B **4** C **5** A **6 a** Mathematics, $\mu = 77.3$, $\sigma = 7.86$; **b** English, $\mu = 74.9$, $\sigma = 11.05$
c $z = 0.10$ **d** For Mathematics $z = 0.09$ so English is slightly better. **7** 50 boxes **8 a** $\dfrac{800 - 796}{8} = 0.5$ **b** $-2.3 = \dfrac{x - 796}{8}$ $x = 777.6$ g
c $\dfrac{780 - 796}{8} = -2$. Hence, 2.5% Hence, 25 boxes. **9 a** Yes. 72 in Test 1 is a z-score of 0.4 while a 74 in Test 2 is a z-score of 1.
b $\dfrac{78 - 68}{\sigma} = 2.5$. Hence, $\sigma = 4$ **10 a** $\dfrac{83 - 70}{5} = 2.6$ **b** $-2 \leq z \leq -1$: $47.5\% - 34\% = 13.5\%$ **11 a** 73 **b** In Test 1 her z-score was 1.8.
She needs a mark of $66 + 18 = 84$ in Test 2. **12 a** $-2 \leq z \leq 2$ is 95% of scores. Hence, $0.95 \times 400 = 380$ **b** $z \geq 2$ is 2.5% of scores.
Hence, $0.025 \times 400 = 10$ **13** $z \geq 1$ is a probability of 16%. **14 a** $z \geq -3$ is a probability of 99.85% **b** $z = -2 \leq z \leq 1$ is a
probability of 81.5% **15** Two equations are $-2 = \dfrac{64 - \mu}{\sigma}$ and $1 = \dfrac{76 - \mu}{\sigma}$. Mean $= 72$, standard deviation $= 4$.

Answers

Chapter 10—Networks: Introduction to networks

1 a i 4 **ii** 6 **iii** 3 **iv** A, C, D **b i** 5 **ii** 7 **iii** 2 **iv** A, C, D **c i** 6 **ii** 9 **iii** 3 **iv** A, C **d i** 4 **ii** 6 **iii** 3 **iv** A, C, D

2 a

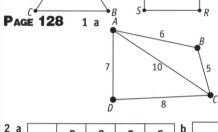

3 a i 4 **ii** 6 **iii** 3 **b i** 5 **ii** 8 **iii** 3 **c i** 3 **ii** 6 **iii** 4

4 a E **b** 8 **c** 3 **d** 13 **e** 18

1 a

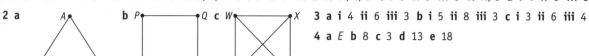

2 a

	P	Q	R	S
P	–	6	12	8
Q	6	–	9	–
R	12	9	–	11
S	8	–	11	–

b

	F	G	H	J	K
F	–	7	10	11	6
G	7	–	14	–	12
H	10	14	–	5	–
J	11	–	5	–	13
K	6	12	–	13	–

c

	A	B	C	D	E	F
A	–	8	–	–	7	5
B	8	–	3	–	–	–
C	–	3	–	2	–	6
D	–	–	2	–	9	–
E	7	–	–	9	–	–
F	5	–	6	–	–	–

3

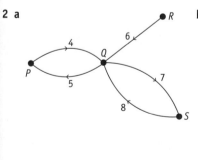

1 a

		To:		
		X	**Y**	**Z**
From:	**X**	–	10	6
	Y	9	–	7
	Z	7	6	–

b

		To:			
		A	**B**	**C**	**D**
From:	**A**	–	8	–	–
	B	–	–	7	5
	C	–	9	–	6
	D	–	–	–	–

c

		To:					
		P	**Q**	**R**	**S**	**T**	**U**
From:	**P**	–	7	–	–	–	–
	Q	–	–	11	13	–	8
	R	–	–	–	10	–	–
	S	–	–	–	–	8	–
	T	–	–	–	7	–	6
	U	–	9	–	–	–	–

2 a

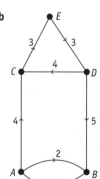

b

c

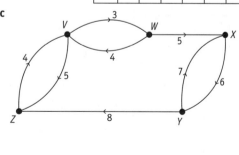

Answers

3

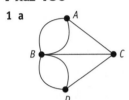 *(large graph with vertices A, B, C, D, E, F, G and weighted edges 12, 15, 5, 4, 3, 6, 7, 5, 8, 7, 6, 6, 8)*

Page 130

1 a **b** 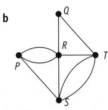 **2 a** 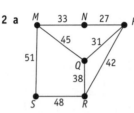 **P b**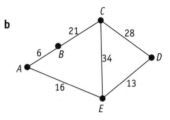

3 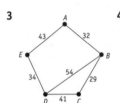 **4 a** 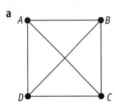 **b** 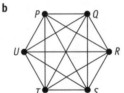 **5**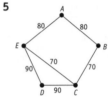

PAGE 131 **1 a** R (or S) **b** D and C (or C and D) **2 a** ABE, ABCE, ADCE **b** AE, ABE, ABCE **c** ABCE, ADCE **d** ABJE, AHJDE
3 a 2 **b** 6 **4 a** 6 **b** 4 **c** 4 **d** 4

PAGE 132 **1 a** JKPMN, 26 m **b** ABGDE, 55 m **c** QVUT, 44 m **d** ABCD, 31 m **e** MNPQR, 45 m **f** TZWX, 58 m **2 a** 39 min (ABCD)
b 41 min (PUTS) **c** 37 min (WXY) **d** 2 h 3 min (MNPQR)

PAGE 133 **1 a**  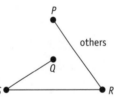 **b**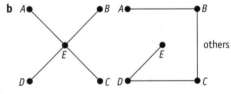

2 a 11 **b** 10 **c** 10 **3 a** 40 **b** 40 **c** 36 **4 a** 99 **b** 89

PAGE 134 **1 a**

Edge	Weight
PT	1
QS	2
QT	4
QR	4

b 11 **c**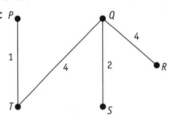

2 a

Action	Weight	Vertex visited
Start at G	–	G
Use GA	4	A
Use AF	2	F
Use AB	3	B
Use BC	4	C
Use CD	7	D
Use DE	10	E

b 30 **c**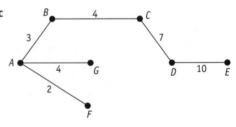

Answers

3 a 29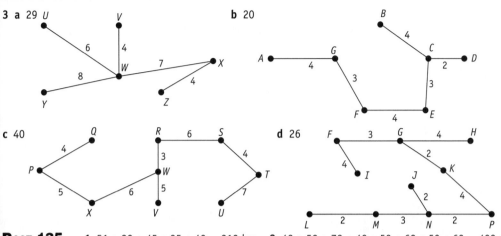

b 20

c 40

d 26

PAGE 135 **1** 51 + 39 + 45 + 35 + 40 = 210 km   **2** 40 + 50 + 70 + 40 + 50 + 60 + 50 + 60 = 420 m
3 a 9 + 13 + 18 + 16 + 12 + 21 + 15 + 18 + 20 = 142 m **b** $85 × 142 = $12 070   **4 a** 16 + 16 + 18 + 21 + 23 + 28 = 122 metres.
Hence the cost is 122 × $45 + 7 × $580 = $9550. **b** Delete 16 and 18 and include 23. Hence, 16 + 23 + 28 + 23 + 21 = 111 metres. The
cost is 111 × $45 + 6 × $580 = $8475, a saving of $1075.

PAGES 136–140   **1** B   **2** D   **3** D   **4** A   **5** D

6 a 8 **b** 4 **c** A, C, D, F

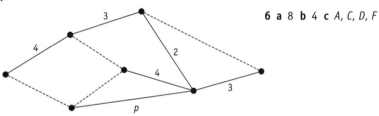

7 a

b i 13 min **ii** 14 min   **8 a** *DABCDB*, others **b** *CBAGFCDEF*, others
c *HEDCEGFBABC*, others
9 a

, others

b 24 km   **10 a** 35

b 40

c 68

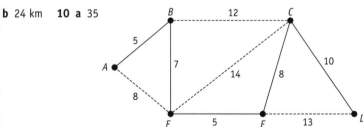

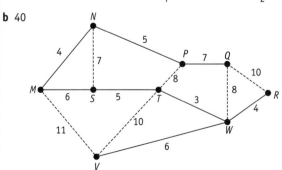

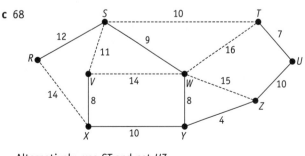

Alternatively, use *ST* and not *UZ*.

Answers

11 a $250 **b** Needs to start and finish at a vertex of odd degree. This means start/finish at D and F.
c $1000

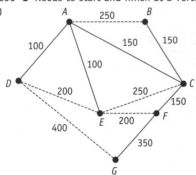

d The price would now be $1050, an increase of $50.

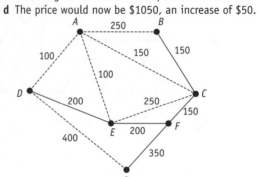

12 a 110 m **b** minimum spanning tree **c** $525

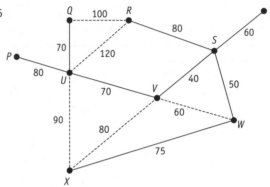

13 a

b 33 km

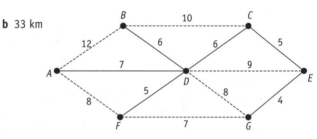

Chapter 11—Networks: Critical path analysis

1 a **b** **c**

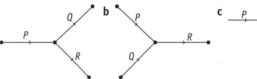

2

Activities	Time	Prerequisites
A	4	None
B	7	A
C	6	B
D	4	C
E	2	D, F
F	12	G
G	15	A

3

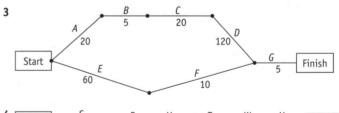

4

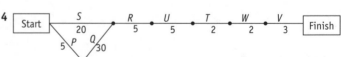

Answers

PAGE 142 **1 a** *ABCDEF*, 22 units **b** *PQRSWV*, 23 units **c** *BJFEG*, 26 units **d** *HCDEF*, 19 units **e** *SYXV*, 22 units **f** *LKHGF*, 29 units

PAGE 143 **1 a** 21

b 22

2 a i 26 min
ii

iii A 10:06 am **B** 10:18 am **C** 10:22 am **b i** 29 days **ii**
iii A 11 March **B** 14 March **C** 21 March (Note: *A*: 2–5 March;
F: 6–11 March; *H*: 12–14 March; *C*: 15–18 March;
K: 19–21 March; *Q*: 22–27 March; *E*: 28–30 March)

PAGE 144 **1 a**

b

2 a i 26 days
ii

iii A 7 August **B** 18 August **C** 23 August **b i** 29 minutes **ii**
iii A 2:10 pm **B** 2:17 pm **C** 2:20 pm

PAGE 145 **1 a**

b *GLNJD* **c i** 9:30 **ii A** 9:03 **B** 9:10 **iii A** 9:15 **B** 9:11 **d i** As 10 − 3 − 4 = 3, float time is 3 min. **ii** As 23 − 3 − 5 = 15, float time is 15 min. **e i** 9:04 and 9:08 **ii** 9:05 and 9:15
2 a

Answers

b *WABZV* **c i** 9 am Tues **ii A** 4 pm Mon **B** 6 pm Mon **iii A** 11 am Mon **B** 10 pm Mon **d i** As 8 − 4 − 2 = 2, float time is 2 hours.
ii As 20 − 2 − 8 = 10, float time is 10 hours. **e i** 10 am and midday Mon **ii** 8 pm and 10 pm Mon

PAGE 146   **1 a** cut 1: 9, cut 2: 8, cut 3: 13, cut 4: 12   **b** cut 1: 31, cut 2: 34, cut 3: 33, cut 4: 24
c cut 1: 26, cut 2: 12, cut 3: 18, cut 4: 16

2 a 80

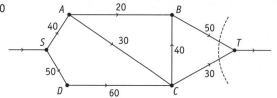

b 26

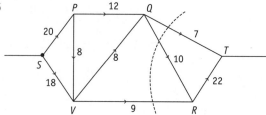

c 13

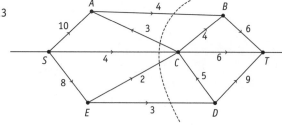

3 a 360

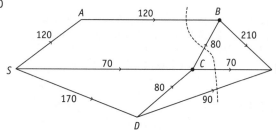

b i 120 **ii** 150

PAGES 147–152   **1** C (6 + 5 + 7 + 4)   **2** B   **3** A   **4** D   **5** C   **6 a i** 3 vehicles/minute **ii** 7 vehicles/minute
iii 2 vehicles/minute **b**   Maximum flow is 12 vehicles/minute.   **7 a** Cut 1 does not
separate source and sink.   **b** Cut 2 = 10 + 18 + 4 = 32. We ignore the 4 as it is not towards
the sink.

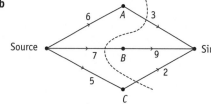

c

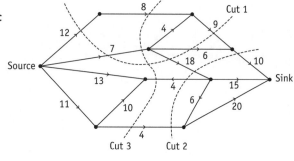

The maximum flow is 15.   **8 a** As 19 + *x* = 31, then $x = 12$
b As 15 + *y* = 23, then $y = 8$
c Cut 3 is the minimum cut so the maximum flow is 21.

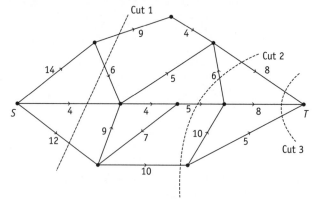

9 a 34 cars/minute
b 26 cars/minute

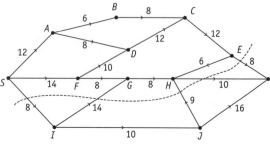

c The maximum flow is now 34 cars/minute
which is an increase of 8 cars/minute.

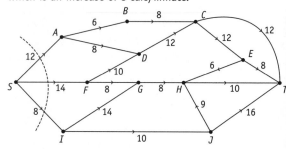

Answers

10 a i 10 **ii** 14 **b**

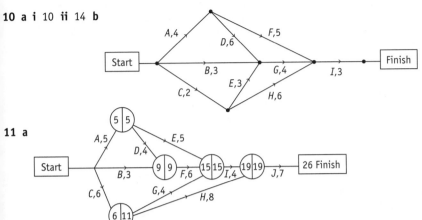

c *A, B, C, D, E* **d** 17 weeks **e** *ADGI*

11 a

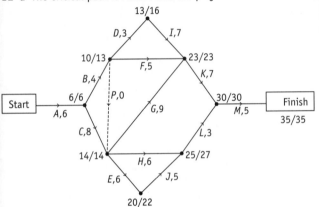

b *ADFIJ* **c i** The minimum time for the critical path is 26 minutes, so the earliest the project can conclude is 10:56 am

ii The LST for activity G is 11 minutes after the start, so it can start as late as 10:41 am.

12 a The critical path is *ACGKM* and the project will take a minimum of 35 weeks.

```
                13/16
          D,3          I,7
    10/13        F,5       23/23
      B,4                  K,7
    6/6   P,0      G,9        30/30    Finish
Start   A,6                   M,5      35/35
      C,8                  L,3
    14/14       H,6     25/27
      E,6          J,5
                20/22
```

b As 23 − 7 − 13 = 3, float time is 3 weeks.

c See dotted line on diagram

d Path *ACEJLM* takes 33 days. This means to reduce G by 2 days at a cost of $2400.

CHAPTER 12—Sample HSC Examinations

PAGES 153–164 **1** A **2** C **3** D **4** A **5** C **6** A **7** C ($1.5 = \frac{x-64}{8}$, therefore $x = 8 \times 1.5 + 64$, $x = 76$)

8 B (earnings = 100 + 0.05 × 10000 + 0.07 × 2500, earnings = $775)

9 C (variable cost = (450 − 300) ÷ 30, variable cost = $5 per person. Total cost = 300 + 5 × 40, total cost = $500)

10 A (Amount owing = 1800 + 1800 × 0.2342 × $\frac{23}{365}$, amount owing = $1826.56) **11** C (Interest = 20000 × 0.08 × 5 = 8000. Monthly

repayment = (20000 + 8000) ÷ 60 = 466.66 which is close to 470) **12** A **13** A (Gradient = $\frac{40}{800}$ = 20 and vertical intercept is 200)

14 C ($\frac{1.55}{22.7}$ × 100% = 6.8% which is the highest) **15** D (4 + 3 + 2 + 4 + 3 + p = 20. Hence, p = 4)

16 a $\frac{x}{6.4} = \frac{15.3}{9}$. x = 10.88. The width is 10.88 m. **b** Vol = 10.88 × 2.1 × 60 × 1.6 = 2193.408 kL **17 a** $\angle ACB$ = 300° − 270° = 30°

b $\frac{d}{250}$ = tan 30°. d = 144 km **c** By Pythag. AC = 288.68 km. Time = 0.722 h = 43 minutes. Hence 9:43 am **18 a** x = 9 **b** x = 61

19 a 70° **b** 3361 m² **c** 100 m **20 a** FV = 25000$\left(1 + \frac{6\%}{4}\right)^{5 \times 4}$, FV = $33671 (to the nearest dollar) **b** FV = 3000 × 12.0061,

FV = $36018 (to the nearest dollar) **c** 36018 = PV(1.015)²⁰, PV = $26743 (to the nearest dollar) Therefore he would need to have invested 26743 − 25000 = $1743 more to have the same amount as Sally at the end of 5 years.

21 a 213 **b** While they may not use much water, others do. This table is an average taken from many water users.

c 18 × 365 = 6570 L **d** 213 × 365 = 77745 L = 77.745 kL **e** $\frac{21.1}{100}$ × 213 = 45 L, so it is washing clothes. **f** $\frac{29}{213} \times \frac{100}{1}$ = 13.6%

g i Saving $\frac{20}{100}$ × 35 = 7 L/day. **ii** 7 × 365 = 2555 L **22** 320 m **23 a** Maintenance = $20/month.

Answers

Electricity cost $= 0.6 \times \$150 = \$90$/month. As $20 + 90 = 110$, then $C_2 = 6000 + 110n$ **b** $150n = 6000 + 110n$. $n = 150$.
It will take 12 years, 6 months **24 a** approximately 43 cm **b** No, it would have a capacity of more than 600 litres. By extending the graph we can see that it will reach 600 litres before it reaches 120 cm. **c** 792 litres **25 a** $\$80\,000 \times (1 - 0.12)^{10} = \$22\,280$
b $80\,000 - 10 \times 6000 = 20\,000$. The salvage value using declining-balance formula is $\$2280$ higher.

26 Time $= 8.5$ hours plus $2 = 10.5$ hours. Speed $= \dfrac{8160}{10.5} = 777$ km/h **27 a** As $r = -0.9106$, there is a strong, negative association.

b $y = 39.19 - 0.22x$ **c** $y = 39.19 - 0.22(70) = 23.79$. He has 23.79 kg in muscle mass.
28 a $40\,000 \times 30.6731 = \$1\,226\,924$ **b i** A: $\$150\,000 \div 139.5808 = \$1075$, B: $\$150\,000 \div 35.9214 = \$4176$
ii A: $\$1075 \times 240 - \$150\,000 = \$108\,000$, B: $\$4176 \times 64 - \$150\,000 = \$117\,264$. Preston pays $\$9264$ more with Loan B.

29 a $220 - 165 = 55$ **b** $208 - 0.7a = 165$. Hence $0.7a = 443$ and $a = 61$ **30** $29 = \dfrac{W}{(1.8)^2}$. $\therefore W = 29 \times (1.8)^2 = 93.96$ kg

31

Activity	Immediate Prerequisite(s)	Duration in days
A	None	4
B	None	3
C	A	5
D	A	6
E	B, D	8
F	B, D	3
G	F	4
H	C, E, G	6
I	F	2
J	H, I	4

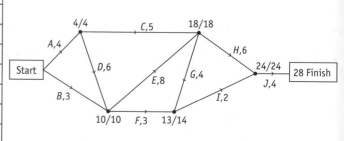

32 a $\dfrac{5}{2}(2.4 + 2(2) + 1.6) = 20$ m² **b** Pool capacity $= 20 \times 5 = 100$ kL. $0.1 \times 100 \times 2.30 = \$23$

c 10 kL $= 10\,000$ L. $10\,000 \div 100 = 100$ minutes **d** $3 + 2.5 = 5.5$ hours/day. Cost $= 5.5 \times 2.14 \times 365 \times \$0.276 = \$1185.71$ **33 a** -0.5
b $-1 < z < 2$: $34\% + 47.5\% = 81.5\%$ **c** $z < 1$: $50\% + 34\% = 84\%$. $0.84 \times 200 = 168$ **34 a** 160, by using minimum cut through
BT, BD, CD, EF **b** 210, by using minimum cut through BT, DT, GT **c** Maximum flow reduces to 180 vehicles per minute.

PAGES 165–175 **1** D **2** A **3** C **4** C **5** D (This is an exponential graph which passes through $(1, 3)$, thus D is the only possible equation.) **6** D (75 km $= 7\,500\,000$ cm. $7\,500\,000 \div 250\,000 = 30$) **7** D (Solve simultaneously, or substitute points into both equations.)

8 A **9** C ($12\,000 \times 1.02^{12}$) **10** A (Dividend/share $= \$0.40$. Dividend yield $= \dfrac{0.40}{12.50} \times 100\% = 3.2\%$) **11** D ($k = \dfrac{312.5}{(2.5)^3} = 20$)

12 B ($1\dfrac{1}{3} \times 0.84 \times 7 = 7.84$) **13** A ($0.000\,42 \times 13 \times \$1856 = \$10.13$) **14** C **15** C ($0.5 \times 8 \times 12 \times 12 \tan 34°$) **16** 12 cans

17 a $115°$ **b** $30°$ **c** 105 km **d** $060°$ **18 a** 395 km **b** 276.5 km **19 a** Candle burning time **b** 0 **c** With no length of candle, there

will not be any burning time. **d** gradient $(m) = \dfrac{(26 - 0)}{(3.5 - 0)} = 7.4$ **e** Burning time (minutes) $= 7.4 \times$ length of candle (cm).

(Note $b = y$-intercept $= 0$) **20** $200 \times 7 + 180 \times 8 = 2840$ watts, $2840 \div 1000 = 2.84$ kW Therefore, the cost is $2.84 \times \$0.48 = \$1.36$
21 a Lower quartile $= 61$ upper quartile $= 75$ **b** $1.5 \times IQR = 1.5 \times 14 = 21$. Upper 'fence' $= 75 + 21 = 96$. So 97 is an outlier.

22 $FV = 5000\left(1 + \dfrac{6.5\%}{12}\right)^{25 \times 12}$, $FV = 25\,280.989\,22\ldots$, $FV = \$25\,281$ **23** $\$40\,000$ vehicle: $\$1050 + 0.11 \times 5000 = \$1600$;

$\$20\,000$ vehicle: $0.03 \times 20\,000 = \$600$. Difference $= \$1600 - \$600 = \$1000$

24 a If the length is x m, the breadth is $(8 - x)$ m. The area is $x(8 - x)$ m². **b** $x = 4$ **c** 16 m² **d** Square **e** $M = \dfrac{1}{4}l^2$ or $M = \left(\dfrac{l}{2}\right)^2$

25 a

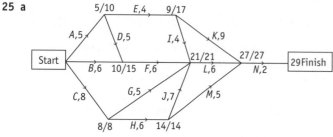

$CHJLN$ **b** 30 July **c** As $21 - 6 - 10 = 5$, float time is 5 days.
26 $4\pi \times 10^2 - 4\pi \times 3.5^2 = 1102.6990\ldots = 1100$ cm²(to 2sf)
27 a The data for Class 1 is symmetrical **b** 25% **c** Both classes
have the same median (35), while the data for class 2 is more
spread out at both ends. **28** Angle $BCD = 70°$ – angle ACD.

If angle $ACD = \sin^{-1}\dfrac{1.5\sin 20}{3}$, then the new angle of elevation is

60° to the nearest degree. **29 a** $600 \times 12.5779 = \$7546.74$
b $1200 \times 6.1051 = \$7326.12$

Answers

c Michelle: $10\,000 \div 12.5779 = 795.05$, $795.05 - 600 = 195.05$ Michelle needs to save $195 more per 6 months.
Holly: $10\,000 \div 6.1051 = 1637.97$, $1637.97 - 1200 = 437.97$ Holly needs to save $438 more per year.
30 a $AC^2 \times 12^2 + 11.32^2 - 2 \times 12 \times 11.32 \times \cos(118°) = 399.69$; $AC = 19.99$; $AD = AC = 19.99 \times \cos(45°) = 14.14$.
Perimeter $= 52$ cm. **31 a** $(41 \times \$0.039 + 24 \times \$0.022 + \$0.5825) \times 7 = \$18.97$
b $(41 \times \$0.039 + 49 \times \$0.022 + 60 \times \$0.0217 + \$0.5825) \times 365 \div 4 = \$416.24$ **32 a** $P = 30\,000(1.035)^0 = 30\,000$
b

t	0	5	10	15	20	25
P	30 000	35 631	42 318	50 260	59 694	70 897

c

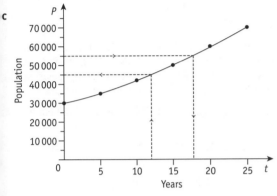

d 45 000 **e** 17.5 years **f** $t = 32$, $P = 30\,000(1.035)^{32} = 90\,200$

33 1 cm $= 20$ m. $A = \dfrac{1}{2} \times 30 \times (40 + 80) + \dfrac{1}{2} \times 80 \times 30 = 3000$ m². Volume $= 3000 \times 0.02 = 60$ m³. Water $= 60$ kL
34

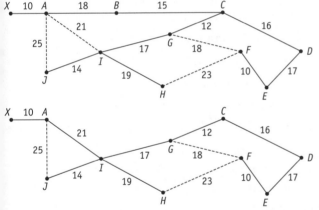

Initial length $= 148$ m. New length $= 136$ m. Savings $= \$123.40 \times 12 = \$1480.80$ **35 a** The initial radius of the cone is 1 m. Because of
similarity, the radius of the shaded circle is $\dfrac{1}{4}$ m. $A = \pi \times \left(\dfrac{1}{4}\right)^2 = \dfrac{\pi}{16}$ m². **b** $V = \dfrac{1}{3} \times \pi \times 1^2 \times 4 - \dfrac{1}{3} \times \pi \times \left(\dfrac{3}{4}\right)^2 \times 1 = 4.12$ m³

36 a $\$3400 - \$0.20 \times 6 \times 365 \times 3 = \$2086$ **b** $4600 \times 0.77^3 = \$2100.05$. Yes, Jimmy is correct. The second bike is worth $14.05 more.
PAGES 176–188 **1** C **2** B **3** D ($IQR = 6$. 30 is more than $20 + 1.5 \times 6$) **4** A (16% of students scored higher than $z = 1$)
5 B ($200 = k(5^2)$. $k = 8$) **6** C **7** C **8** A (5.5% p.a. $= 0.4583\dots$% per month) **9** A ($32\,890 \times 0.82^5$)

10 D ($380 \div 100 \times 7.9 \times 1.499 = 44.999$) **11** D ($8 + 13 + 14 + 11 + 9 + 12 + 22 + 18$) **12** C **13** D ($\dfrac{68}{80} \times 100\% = 85\%$) **14** A

15 C ($k = 0.4$. $T = 0.4(30)^2$) **16 a** $3.2n = 1.6n + 24$, $n = 15$ **b** Loss $= 24 + 1.6(12) - 3.2(12) = 4.8$. Loss of $4.80
c $C = 36 + 2n$ and $R = 5n$. Profit $= 5(24) - (36 + 2(24)) = 36$. Rose makes $36 profit **17** Dividend/share $= \$91.20 \div 400 = \$0.228$.

Answers

Hence, $\dfrac{0.228}{3.8} \times 100\% = 6\%$ **18** $1940 + $1940 \times 0.000\,565\,753 \times 36 = 1979.51 **19 a** $54° + 36° = 90°$

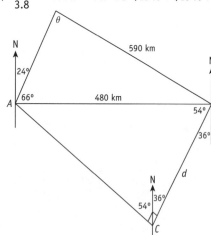

b $\dfrac{d}{480} = \cos 54°$. $d = 282.1369$. Time $= \dfrac{282.1369}{340} = 0.829\,81 = 50$ minutes

c $\dfrac{\sin\theta}{480} = \dfrac{\sin 66°}{590}$. $\theta = 48°$. Bearing is $180° - (48° - 24°) = 156°$.

20 a $327 \times $7.4581 = 2438.80 **b** $2438.80 \times 240 - $327\,000 = $258\,312$

21 a $\dfrac{1}{2} \times 8 \times 8 \times \sin 100° = 31.51$ cm² **b** $\dfrac{100}{360} \times \pi \times 8^2 - 31.51 = 24.3$ cm²

22 $\dfrac{1200}{360} \times 15 = 50$ drops/minute **23 a** $y = 6.7x + 74.7$

b As $y = 6.7(4) + 74.7 = 101.5$, the boy is 101.5 cm. **c** As $152 = 6.7x + 74.7$, $x = 11.54$. As $160 = 6.7x + 74.7$, $x = 12.73$. As $12.73 - 11.54 = 1.19$, it will take 1.19 years, which is 14 months, to nearest whole.   **24** Let x = total population of buffalo. From first catching = 16 out of x. From second catching = 4 out of 30 $\therefore \dfrac{16}{x} = \dfrac{4}{30}$. $4x = 480$ (by cross-multiplying), $x = 120$. There are about 120 buffalo on the property.

25 z-score for $3 = -1$, z-score for $4 = 1.5$ $P(-1 \le z \le 1.5) = 0.9332 - (1 - 0.8413) = 0.7745$. As $0.7745 \times 4000 = 3098$, the number of customers was about 3098.

26 16 units = 800 m means 1 unit = 50 m. $A \approx 800 \times 800 - \dfrac{400}{2}[300 + 2 \times 100 + 200 + 500 + 2 \times 200 + 350] = 250\,000$ m².

Volume $= 250\,000 \times 2.8 = 700\,000$ m³. There is approximately 700 ML in dam.   **27 a** $1.75 \times 1200 \div 1000 \times $0.151\,91 \times 2 = 0.64
b Difference $= 4.2 \times 2 \times $0.225\,94 \times 52 \times 5 = 493.45 **28 a** 2 m **b** 32 trees at High School, 48 trees at Primary School
c HS is positively skewed, PS is negatively skewed; median of HS (14) is higher than median of PS (12); IQR of HS (10) is more than the IQR of PS (9) **29** Volume $= 16 \times 12 \times 0.075 = 14.4$ m³. Now, as $14.4 = \pi \times 2.3^2 \times h$, $h = 0.866\,47$, which is 87 cm.
30 $0.095 \times $103\,200 - $2800 = 7004 to be invested. Balance $= $7004 \times 6.8019 = $47\,640.51$ **31** Let C = cost per passenger,
n = number of passengers, $C = \dfrac{k}{n}$. As $16 = \dfrac{k}{24}$, then $k = 384$. As $C = \dfrac{384}{32}$, then $C = 12$. The cost is $12 per passenger.

32 a Total amount $= $3525 + 36 \times $655.60 = $27\,126.60$. **b** Deposit $= 3525, balance $= $19\,975$.

Total interest $= 36 \times $655.60 - $19\,975 = 3626.60. Annual interest rate $= \dfrac{3626.6}{19\,975} \times 100\% \div 3 = 6.1\%$ p.a.

33 a

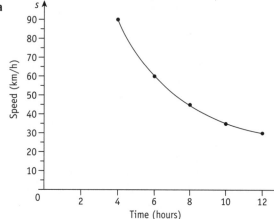

b $k = 360$ **c** As $13 - 5 - 6 = 2$, float time is 2 hours.

d 15 m/s = 54 km/h. $54 = \dfrac{360}{t}$, means $t = 6.6666...$ which is 6 h 40 min

34 a $1.5 \times 18.43 \times 68 = 1880$ kJ **b** $870 \times 4.184 = 3640.08$ kJ. Energy from walking $= 83 \times 9.22 = 765.26$ kJ.

Number of 30-minute periods $= \dfrac{3640.08}{765.26} = 4.756\,66$.

Total time $= 2.378$ hours.
Distance $= 6 \times 2.378 = 14$ km (nearest whole)

35 a

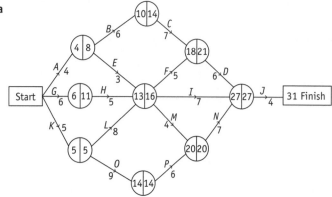

b Tuesday 7 pm **c** 5 hours **36 a** $\dfrac{20}{h} = \tan 28°$, $h = 37.6$

b $V = \dfrac{1}{2} \times \dfrac{4}{3} \times \pi \times 20^3 + \dfrac{1}{3} \times \pi \times 20^2 \times 37.6 = 32\,500$ cm³

Notes

Notes